CHOOSING SUCCESS:
Transactional Analysis on the Job

D1277729

Dorothy Jongeward, Ph.D.

President
Transactional Analysis Management Institute

Philip C. Seyer, M.A.

Instructional Technologist
University of California Extension

John Wiley & Sons, Inc.
New York • Chichester • Brisbane • Toronto

Editors: Judy Wilson and Irene Brownstone
Production Manager: Ken Burke
Copyeditor: Judith Fillmore
Cartoonist: Martha Weston
Line Illustrator: Brenda Tighe
Makeup: Meredythe

Library of Congress Cataloging in Publication Data

Jongeward, Dorothy.
    Choosing success.

    Bibliography: p.
    1. Transactional analysis.   2. Psychology,
Industrial.   I. Seyer, Philip C., joint author.
II. Title.
HF5548.8.J565   650′.13′019   78-16717
ISBN 0-471-02884-3

Printed in the United States of America

78 79 10 9 8 7 6 5 4 3 2

Preface

Choosing Success is a personal and practical book about people—you and the other people in your life, especially those you work with. It stresses the possibilities of personal growth, improved relationships, and greater effectiveness through using Transactional Analysis (TA).

TA gives people a ready handle on what's happening in their lives and offers a framework for making basic changes and choices—a framework so simple that people can easily apply it. That's what Dr. Eric Berne, founder of TA, wanted—to cut through stilted psychiatric jargon and to give the average person the dignity and personal power of self-knowledge and self-determination.

Human beings count. What we produce is often not only essential to other people but it is also important to our own sense of well-being. We each have unique qualities that we can express through our work. But sometimes we unwittingly choose paths and people who lead us away from excitement and challenge toward disappointment and failure. TA gives us a kind of knowledge and awareness that points the way for choosing more often the paths and people who enrich our lives and encourage a more successful expression of ourselves.

How does TA work on the job? Here's what one man, who has training responsibilities in a utility company, said in a personal communication:

> Our field people make collection calls on past due customers. Experience showed us that they were not prepared to cope with many of the contacts they face with angry or scared customers. In fact, collectors often received verbal and physical abuse—sometimes serious.
>
> With only a minimum presentation of Transactional Analysis, these people could quickly see its application and usefulness in improving their collection contacts.
>
> As a direct result of these meetings there is no doubt that our collection contacts improved vastly. And we've not had a really bad situation since.
>
> Our experience has left me with three convictions about TA: (1) the techniques of TA can be readily understood, (2) they can be applied, (3) they work!

Choosing Success draws not only on TA but also on many other important new techniques for self-management and troubleshooting. Everyone has problems working day in and day out with other people—subordinates, supervisors, bosses, clients, customers, partners, colleagues. That's why we've personalized this book. Throughout you will learn how to apply new ideas and techniques by working with many case situations and specific problems. Then, through specially designed exercises, you'll apply TA and other techniques to your own life situations. On the job and off, you'll be able to draw up your own personal plan for *Choosing Success*.

ACKNOWLEDGMENTS

Our thanks go to:

- Ethel Brubaker, Bess Craft, James Evans, Dane Pascoe, Peter Pipe, Sharon Rigdon, and Sivasailam Thiagarajan for reading the first draft of this book and giving us helpful suggestions;
- Dona Bishop for helping to arrange for a tryout of the first draft with a group of TA students;
- Jean Fisher for her superb stenographic help;
- Louise Seyer for her vitally supportive efforts in typing, getting permissions, proofreading, and preparing the index;
- Irene Brownstone for brilliant editorial help;
- Ken Burke for coordinating the final book production;
- Judith Fillmore for meticulous copyediting;
- Meredythe Miller for speedy and accurate typography;
- Martha Weston for her entertaining and instructive cartoons;
- Barbara Gendler Soll for designing the book cover;
- Judy Wilson for coordinating all of the above.

We would like to give a special thanks to Richard Underhill, University of Richmond, for his thoughtful comments and suggestions, and to the many others whose encouragement, support, and caring helped to bring this book to life.

August, 1978   *Dorothy Jongeward*
                                                                 Philip C. Seyer

Contents

Part **I**

YOU AND TA
ON THE JOB

1

Success Is for You

One poet says this about success:

> To laugh often and much;
> To win the respect of intelligent people and the affection of children;
> To earn the appreciation of honest critics and endure the betrayal of false friends;
> To appreciate beauty;
> To find the best in others;
> To leave the world a bit better, whether by a healthy child, a garden patch, or a redeemed social condition;
> To know even one life has breathed easier because you lived.
> THIS is to have succeeded.[1]*

The American Heritage Dictionary tells us that success means "the achievement of something desired, planned, or attempted."[2]

Success may hold a different meaning for each of us. Yet most of us know we want to succeed in some way. We want to tap our potential and be more fully ourselves. We push to create, to grow, to somehow express our own astounding uniqueness.

Work—whether it is serving food, building bridges, managing a zoo, caring for a child, or running a corporation—gives us one avenue for such expression. Through work we can express our intellect, our physical talents, our skills. We can create. Yet many of us do not experience the kind of success we want and deserve on the job. There are many reasons for this. We want to focus on a very important one—personality—and see how it affects our personal achievements and relationships.

Sometimes, usually without realizing it, we choose failure over success. Unaware, we fulfill narrow, distorted self-imagery and restrict our possibilities. We learn to believe things about ourselves that hold us back. For example, if someone has decided to believe anything like:

> "I can't possibly do that,"
> "I'll never be wealthy,"
> "I always make mistakes and botch things up,"
> "I just don't have any special talents,"
> "I'll never be as good as Alvin,"
> "I don't deserve to make it,"

that's exactly what will happen!

---

*Numbered source notes appear at the end of the chapter.

Indeed we tend to stand in our own way. Without knowing it we often create our own tunnel vision and block our own paths. Because we put our energies into keeping things as they are, we stop growing and fail to achieve all that we can.

In subtle ways we make choices that eventually decide our destiny. We choose certain people to be close to and those we want to be like. We decide where to live and how to educate ourselves. The cast of characters, scenery, settings, dialogue, and plot begins to emerge and we eventually act out many scenes of our personal drama through our work. Our choices can determine whether our work brings us success or failure, but we often make these choices without even being aware of them.

LEVELS OF AWARENESS

We all have at least four levels of awareness about our actions, feelings, and motivations. Each level can be defined by *who knows what is happening* when we transact with each other.

Joseph Luft and Harrington Ingham have developed a diagram that gives us an interesting way to look at what we're conscious of in our social exchanges and what we're not. Their Johari window diagram (named by combining the first few letters of their first names), looks like this:[3]

	Information known to self	Information not known to self
Information known to others	1 Open	2 Blind
Information not known to others	3 Hidden	4 Unknown

These four quadrants show how an act, feeling, or motive can be seen according to who in a relationship knows about it.

— The *open quadrant* refers to things about yourself such as behaviors, feelings, and motivations that *you know* about and are *willing to share* with others. (It's public. You both know what's happening.)
— The *blind quadrant* refers to things about yourself known to *others* but *not to you.* (Other people know what's happening but you don't.)
— The *hidden quadrant* refers to things about yourself known to *you,* but *not others.* (It's private. Only you know what's happening.)
— The *unknown quadrant* refers to things about yourself that *no one,* not even you, *knows about.* (No one knows what's happening.)

These quadrants shift between us as we interrelate. Our energy shifts too. It takes energy to hide, deny, or be blind to part of ourselves. Let's look at these quadrants one by one.

The Blind Self

Subtle bars to our personal effectiveness are often in the blind quadrant. We may speak in a certain way—with a tone of voice, a look on our face, a gesture—that we're blind to, but other people are acutely aware of. In fact, our manner can affect how they perceive us and, in turn, how they believe they can interact with us.

For example, Gloria Waters' face seemed almost fixed in a stern frown much like her mother's. Her jaw was set, her brows knit, and her eyes narrowed. She appeared disapproving no matter what she was saying. As a result, she unwittingly intimidated the six people who worked under her. Even when she praised them, they read disapproval into it.

Often such blind behaviors are absorbed and copied from significant people in our lives when we were small children. Because we copy these behaviors unconsciously early in life, we don't see them later: they make up our Blind Self. You'll be learning more about the Blind Self when you study the Parent ego state.

The Hidden Self

The Hidden Self, unlike the Blind Self, is within our "field of vision" but we choose not to share it. In response to our early childhood experiences, many of us learned to hoard our feelings, ideas, and fantasies. Our Hidden Selves then wear masks. We put on a front and others don't know how we feel.

For example, Gregg Sellers worked for Gloria. Because he felt she never really approved of either him or his work, he sulked and smoldered, keeping his anger inside. Although he liked his job with the magazine, he began to think about leaving, yet he didn't show this on the surface. On the contrary, he acted cheerful and politely friendly even though much of his energy went into rehearsing in his head what he'd really like to say to Gloria.

There certainly are things that all of us choose wisely to keep to ourselves. Yet sometimes risking self-disclosure is the most effective way to solve problems between people. But this is easier said than done! In this book you will learn to broaden your understanding of the feeling side of your personality. You may decide there are times—and good reasons—to share these feelings and risk self-disclosure.

The Unknown Self

The Unknown Self seems more mysterious than either the Hidden Self or the Blind Self. Many times our motivations go very deep and *no one*, including ourselves, knows what's happening. We often experience these parts of ourselves disguised in dreams or in deep-rooted fears or compulsions. These acts, feelings, and motives remain unclear and vague to us until we allow them to surface.

Gloria, for example, had a recurring dream. She saw a long bridle path winding endlessly through a green meadow. To unlock the part of herself that she experienced in her dream, she imagined she was the path and began a dialogue. "I'm a path. I'm stretched out through a green meadow . . . ." After awhile her voice grew louder and she finally shouted, "People walk all over me and I just lie here!" Gloria discovered the way she really felt about how she was handling her job. No one would have guessed it. Not even she.

As you become more aware of your Blind Self and more skilled at sharing parts of your Hidden Self, more of your Unknown Self will emerge into your awareness. In fact, as you grow, these quadrants constantly shift, opening up more of who you are to yourself and to others.

The Open Self

Sometimes in a relationship we are straightforward, open, and sharing. It's clear to both of us what we're doing, how we're feeling, and what our motivations are. Our Open Selves are aware and willing to share.

For example, a co-worker mentioned to Gregg, "Have you noticed that Gloria seems to look cross no matter what she's saying? The other day she told me she'd recommended me for the Editor's Award and she had a trace of a smile on her face I hadn't seen before. I told her how great she looked and talked about the fact that I 'read' her as unhappy about my work lots of the time because of the look on her face. She was really surprised. And we talked about it for quite awhile." What had been blind to Gloria and hidden by her subordinates was now open between them.

Think of the Johari window as a pie equaling 100% with each section cut in quarters, like this:

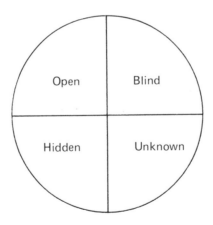

We can show one section in the window as larger or smaller than another simply by drawing the sections in different sizes. For example, if you have a small Open Self and relatively large Blind, Hidden, and Unknown Selves, you might draw *your* Johari window like this:

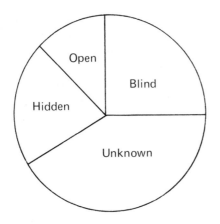

(You might draw the Johari window like this if you rarely share your thoughts and feelings and don't get much feedback from others.)

On the other hand, if you have a small Open Self and a small Hidden Self, but rather large Blind and Unknown Selves, you might diagram your levels of awareness like this:

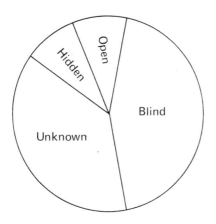

(You might draw the Johari window like this if you tell people what you think and how you feel but don't get many compliments or criticism from others.)

Take a moment and draw a circular Johari window that shows the relative size of your levels of awareness as you perceive them *now*. (Show your Blind, Unknown, Hidden, and Open Selves.)

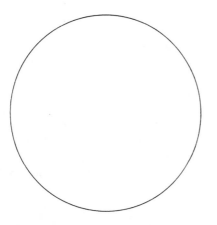

(Date) _____

As a rule of thumb, the smaller the area of our Open Self, the poorer we communicate. With a large Open area, we can often work together with remarkable ease. Ideas flow. Everyone involved usually finds it easier to apply available resources and skills to the task at hand.

You can use some of the ideas and skills offered in this book to learn new things about yourself, to strengthen and broaden your Open Self, and to develop new skills for personal achievement as well as personal and interpersonal satisfaction.

PATHWAYS TO SELF-DISCOVERY

A key to expanding the Open Self and exploring new vistas lies in discovering more about ourselves and in becoming more understanding, aware, and sensitive to others.

You can take many paths to the discovery of how and why people are who they are and do what they do. We will explore just a few. The primary tool we focus on is transactional analysis (TA), originally developed by Dr. Eric Berne[4] as a method of psychotherapy.

TA is a practical tool for getting a handle on what makes people tick. Although it has its jargon, the words are simple and anyone can learn its language and apply many of its principles almost immediately. In a way, the ideas in TA bring into sharp focus what we were vaguely aware of already. This clarity opens up new insights and options. As we apply TA to our jobs, our understandings deepen with a continuing unfolding of its possible uses.

One of the strengths of this nonclinical use of TA is that it applies to everyday problems of living and working. (It's not just for disturbed or emotionally upset people.) And almost anyone can use it. Because of this, TA offers practical ways to deal with people problems on the job. Most of us neglect our "people skills." We get training in the business and technological skills we need, but we get little training in how to deal with people—including ourselves. As one engineer put it, "I thought I had all the skills I needed to do my job. Now all I do is engineer people and with only half the training!" TA helps fill this gap.

In addition to TA, we also draw from our own experiences and the ideas of such authors as B. F. Skinner (behavioral reinforcement), David Premack (the Premack principle—high-probability behaviors can act as reinforcers), and Joseph Wolpe (techniques for thought stopping).

We've divided this book into three major parts. Part I, "You and TA on the Job," will teach you the basics of transactional analysis, particularly the ideas of ego states, strokes, psychological games people play, and psychological stamp collecting. You will see how these concepts function on the job. You'll also learn how to be a better motivator, how to stop games, and how to fill your time more productively.

Part II, "The Self-Care Program," presents a series of self-management techniques you can apply for increased success on the job and in your personal life. We have found that people often try out their new skills and insights at home first. This is fine. Whenever you are able to apply a TA principle successfully, you are better able to apply it elsewhere. You will learn to:

 — develop a commitment to specific measurable goals,
 — increase your awareness of your environment,
 — rearrange your environment so it promotes success, and
 — evaluate your efforts and revise them when necessary.

Part III, "Putting It All Together," combines self-management techniques with TA concepts. You will learn some of the "do's" and "don't's" about productive transactions; some special techniques will help you focus more on the "do's." You will also learn how to develop more autonomy and finally to transact more authentically.

Success as used here means getting in touch with yourself, being yourself as fully as possible, and expressing your uniqueness in positive ways through your work. It means getting along better with more people—clarifying what you want, going after it, and getting it without hurting anyone. With this book, you will be able to master key TA ideas, to take responsibility for your own life by using self-management techniques, and as a result to choose even more often the pathway to success. We hope you'll enjoy and profit from your journey.

SOURCE NOTES

[1] This poem appeared anonymously. It seems to be an adaptation of the poem "Success" by Bessie Anderson Stanley.

[2] *The American Heritage Dictionary* (New York: American Heritage, 1973).

[3] Adapted from Joseph Luft, *Of Human Interaction,* by permission of Mayfield Publishing Company (formerly National Press Books), copyright © 1969 by The National Press. Also see John Stewart and Gary D'Angelo, *Together* (Reading, Mass.: Addison-Wesley, 1975), p. 159.

[4] For information about other books and materials on TA as well as about training or professional memberships, write to: International Transactional Analysis Association, 1772 Vallejo Street, San Francisco, CA 94123. This association also has a *Directory of Affiliates* and a *Geographical List of Members.*

2
TA in a Nutshell

This chapter introduces you to the main ideas of transactional analysis. In later chapters we'll explore how to use TA to enhance your life on the job.

OBJECTIVES

When you finish this chapter, you'll be able to:

- identify your probable ego state in a given situation;
- tell whether a transaction is open, blocked, or ulterior and draw a diagram to illustrate the transaction;
- distinguish between warm fuzzies and cold pricklies;
- predict what will happen to the job performance of a person who gets a heavy diet of cold pricklies and few, if any, warm fuzzies;
- characterize a psychological game;
- identify the ulterior transaction and the payoff when given the dialogue of a psychological game;
- identify a psychological position when given a capsule description of a personality.

If you're familiar with TA and feel you have mastered the objectives listed above, you may wish to skip ahead to Chapter 3.

TA consists of several different ways of analyzing people and their interactions. In this chapter we will look at:

- — structural analysis: how to analyze the personality;
- — transactional analysis: how people transact;
- — stroke analysis: how people touch and recognize each other;
- — game analysis: ulterior transactions;
- — script analysis: life plans.

STRUCTURAL ANALYSIS

According to TA theory, everyone's personality has three parts, called *ego states.* These ego states are named *Parent, Adult,* and *Child.* When we capitalize these words, we're talking about ego states rather than real parents, adults, or children. Structural analysis involves analyzing the personality to discover the nature of our ego states. You can use structural analysis to better understand who you are and how you got that way. It will help you learn about the various sources of thoughts, feelings, and opinions in your personality. Knowing your personality better can add to your effectiveness on the job.

The Parent Ego State

Everyone develops a Parent ego state when as children they absorb certain attitudes and ways of behaving from parental figures. *When you feel, think, or act as you saw your parents (or other authority figures) act when you were little, you are in your Parent ego state.* While in your Parent, you may act in either a controlling, sometimes critical way or in a nurturing, sometimes loving way. Here are some examples of statements you are likely to make while in your Parent:

— Controlling Parent: "Nobody can leave until this report is finished."
— Nurturing Parent: "I'm sorry you're not feeling well today. Would you like to go over to the nurse's office and get some help? I'll take care of your station."

While in our Parent we respond *automatically* almost as if a tape recording were playing in our heads and directing our words and actions. For this reason, we often use the phrase "Parent tapes" to refer to:

— dialogue from Parent figures stored in our heads, and
— *automatic* responses we make while in our Parent ego state.

The Adult Ego State

Although we respond automatically when in our Parent, we respond *analytically* when in our Adult. Whenever you are gathering information, reasoning things out, estimating probabilities, and so on, you are in your Adult ego state. While in this ego state you are cool and collected: you make decisions unemotionally. You just want the facts. The Adult ego state has nothing to do with age. Little children have Adult ego states too! For example, when four-year-old Kristi says, "I bet Jeff is home—I see his car," she is using her budding Adult, since she is calmly estimating probabilities on the basis of facts.

The Child Ego State

Yes, even though you're an adult, you have a Child inside you. While in your Child ego state, you feel and act like the little person you once were. Your Child has all of the feelings and impulses of a newborn. It also includes your mental recordings of your:

— early experiences,
— reactions to these experiences, and
— learned view of yourself and other people.

Responses that come from a Child ego state are usually emotionally charged. Here are some examples:

"Oooo! That's a neat report!"

"Nobody cares about me. Just look at what I have to go through with these customers."

"Why are you always picking on me?"

"Hmm! Feel that warm sun. What a day!"

"Wow, that's the biggest sale of the whole darn year!"

APPLICATION ———————————————————————————

1 Here's some practice in structural analysis. In these situations, indicate whether the supervisors seem to be in their Parent, Adult, or Child ego states.

   (a) Subordinate: "How do you like the new filing system I just set up?"
      Supervisor: "You spend too much time deciding how to do things. If you have something to do, you should just do it and be done with it."

      ___Parent ___Adult ___Child

   (b) Subordinate: "How do you like my new filing system?"
      Supervisor: "Wow! What organization! I really like it. I wish I'd had a system like that when I had your job five years ago."

      ___Parent ___Adult ___Child

   (c) Subordinate: "How do you like my new filing system?"
      Subordinate: "Poor baby! You must have worked all day to set up that system. Can I help you catch up on your other work?"

      ___Parent ___Adult ___Child

(Throughout this book, compare your answers with those below the line of wavy dashes.)

~ • ~ • ~ • ~ • ~ • ~ • ~ • ~ • ~ • ~ • ~ • ~ • ~ • ~ • ~ • ~ • ~ • ~

   (a) Parent. (The word "should" is often a tipoff that a person is probably in a Parent ego state.)
   (b) Child. (Eager, enthusiastic responses usually come from the Child.)
   (c) Parent. (Sympathetic responses like this usually come from the Parent.)

Remember that when identifying someone's probable ego state, you can only make an educated guess on the basis of a bit of conversation. After all, you'd have to know everyone and their parents to be totally right.

As you'll soon see, it's also possible for people to sound as if they're in one ego state when they're actually in another.

~ • ~ • ~ • ~ • ~ • ~ • ~ • ~ • ~ • ~ • ~ • ~ • ~ • ~ • ~ • ~ • ~ • ~

2 Imagine that a co-worker unexpectedly pats you on the back. What ego state is shown by each of the responses below?

   (a) You think, "I would like to know what made him do that."

      ___Parent ___Adult ___Child

(b) You respond silently, "Hmm, that feels good."

___Parent ___Adult ___Child

(c) Suddenly you hear a mental voice saying, "Never let anyone touch you. Familiarity breeds contempt."

___Parent ___Adult ___Child

~ • ~ • ~ • ~ • ~ • ~ • ~ • ~ • ~ • ~ • ~ • ~ • ~ • ~ • ~ • ~ • ~

(a) Adult. (When you ask a straightforward question, you are probably in your Adult ego state.)
(b) Child. (When you are experiencing strong feelings, you are in your Child.)
(c) Parent. (When you focus on advice that includes such words as *always* or *never,* you're probably in your Parent ego state.)

~ • ~ • ~ • ~ • ~ • ~ • ~ • ~ • ~ • ~ • ~ • ~ • ~ • ~ • ~ • ~ • ~

3 Betty, one of your co-workers, shows up at work an hour late. What ego state is shown by each of the responses below?

(a) "It's not fair that she always gets away with that. That makes me mad. Grrr!"

___Parent ___Adult ___Child

(b) "Poor Betty. She must have had a hard night."

___Parent ___Adult ___Child

(c) "I wonder what the boss is going to say to Betty."

___Parent ___Adult ___Child

~ • ~ • ~ • ~ • ~ • ~ • ~ • ~ • ~ • ~ • ~ • ~ • ~ • ~ • ~ • ~ • ~

(a) Child. ("Mad" and "grrr" are the clues.)
(b) Parent. (Sympathy is often Parent. So is "excusing" bad behavior because of tiredness.)
(c) Adult. (When you consider the facts and ask careful questions, you are in your Adult.)

ANALYZING TRANSACTIONS

Now that you're familiar with ego states, you're ready to learn to analyze transactions. Whenever people communicate, a transaction takes place between their ego states. The transaction may be classified as:

— open (continuous and ongoing),
— blocked (closed off or diverted), or
— ulterior (hidden or disguised).

In this next section, you will learn how to identify clear-cut examples of these transactions and draw diagrams illustrating them. Doing this will help you understand better what parts of your personality talk to other people and with what results. You may even learn why you are not getting along with someone on the job.

Open Transactions

When you send a direct message to someone and get an expected response, an open transaction has taken place.

Example

A boss expresses regret at losing an important account and is reassured by her assistant.

> Ms. Scott (boss): "I'm so upset. I just feel sick about losing that Alax account."
>
> Jane (assistant): "Don't fret about it, Ms. Scott. You did the best you could. Mr. Alax is just impossible to deal with."

Here's how we would diagram this open transaction:

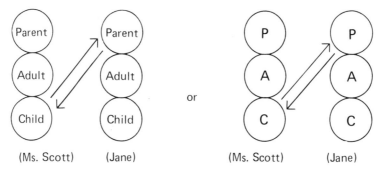

(Ms. Scott)   (Jane)   or   (Ms. Scott)   (Jane)

Note that Ms. Scott is using her Child and is sending a plea for help to Jane's Parent. Jane responds appropriately from her Parent and returns a reassuring message to Ms. Scott's Child.

In this example you saw an open transaction between a Child and a Parent, but open transactions can take place between any two ego states.

Open Transaction

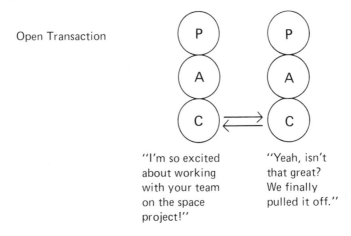

"I'm so excited about working with your team on the space project!"

"Yeah, isn't that great? We finally pulled it off."

Open Transaction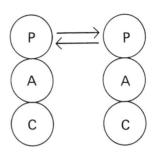

"Salesmen today
are so sloppy
with their work."

"Yes, and look
at how sloppy
they dress, too.
They don't seem
to care about
the impression
they make any-
more."

APPLICATION ——————————————

1 You can often understand a transaction better by drawing ego-state diagrams, complete with arrows. In the following open transaction we have omitted the arrows from the diagram. Try putting them in.

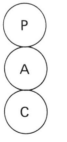 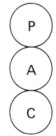

Ray:
"Is there a
sprinkler
system back-
up to protect
the computer
room?"

Jerry:
"I'm not sure.
I'll check into
it and get back
to you this
afternoon."

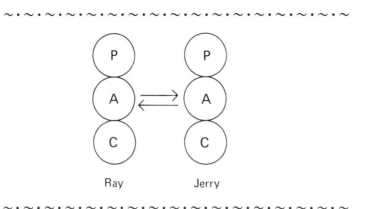

Ray   Jerry

2 When people are upset, often they are looking for someone who will take care of them for a moment or two. In this next diagram, George is looking for support, which he gets from Mark who responds to him warmly. Show your understanding of the transaction by putting in the missing arrows.

Open Transaction

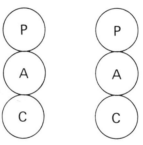

George:
"I feel like
tearing up
my proposal
after getting
this rotten
memo."

Mark:
"You look like
you're ready to
climb the walls!
It really must
be tough to work
on that proposal
when you're angry."

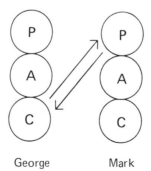

George   Mark

3 In open transactions a message sent by the first person is usually received by:

___ (a) The second person's Adult.

___ (b) The second person's Child.

___ (c) The ego state to which the message was sent.

4 In open transactions, the expected ego state in the second person usually replies to:

___ (a) The first person's Adult.

___ (b) The ego state that started the transaction.

___ (c) The ego state that the second person is most interested in speaking to.

~ • ~ • ~ • ~ • ~ • ~ • ~ • ~ • ~ • ~ • ~ • ~ • ~ • ~ • ~

3 (c) In open transactions a message sent by the first person is usually received by *the ego state to which the message was sent.*

4 (b) In open transactions the expected ego state in the second person usually replies to *the ego state that started the transaction.*

Blocked Transactions

Transactions are *not* always open and ongoing. In fact, sometimes the transaction is blocked. The flow stops and communication is closed off or diverted in another direction. Have you ever asked someone a question and gotten a totally unexpected response? If so, you may have gotten angry or confused or even walked away. TA can shed some light on what is happening and give you some new choices on how to respond in such situations. Here's how a blocked transaction might look:

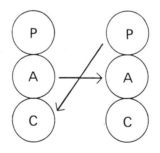

Tom:
"Where is
the file on
the Armstrong
account?"

Gretchen:
"Right where
you left it."

In this blocked transaction notice that Tom is using his Adult and is asking Gretchen a straightforward question, directing it to *her* Adult. But Gretchen responds from her Parent, returning a message to Tom's Child. Their lines of communication are blocked.

APPLICATION ───

1   In a blocked transaction the first person sends a message to a specific ego state

in another person. The message activates the _____
(*expected or unexpected?*) ego state.

～ ． ～ ． ～ ． ～ ． ～ ． ～ ． ～ ． ～ ． ～ ． ～ ． ～ ． ～ ． ～ ． ～

unexpected

～ ． ～ ． ～ ． ～ ． ～ ． ～ ． ～ ． ～ ． ～ ． ～ ． ～ ． ～ ． ～ ． ～

2   The transaction is blocked and the first person often gets angry or confused in

response to the _____ (*expected or unexpected?*)
answer.

～ ． ～ ． ～ ． ～ ． ～ ． ～ ． ～ ． ～ ． ～ ． ～ ． ～ ． ～ ． ～ ． ～

unexpected

～ ． ～ ． ～ ． ～ ． ～ ． ～ ． ～ ． ～ ． ～ ． ～ ． ～ ． ～ ． ～ ． ～

3   When communicating with another person it's helpful to recognize when a transaction is blocked. Here's some practice that will help you do this. Indicate
whether each of these transactions is blocked or open. Then complete the
diagram of the transactions to be sure you understand what is going on between
their ego states.

(a) Nannette: "I have a sales report I have to finish by tomorrow morning."
Linda: "Why are you always procrastinating?"

Transaction: ____ Blocked   ____ Open

Diagram of the transaction (add arrows):

P   P

A   A

C   C

Nannette   Linda

(b) Peter frowns, puts his hands on his hips and says, "I can never tell what is
going to happen next in this department."

Alan nods, throws up his hands in disgust, and says, "There's just no communication around here, is there?"

Transaction: ____ Blocked   ____ Open

Diagram of the transaction (add arrows):

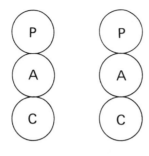

Peter   Alan

~ . ~ . ~ . ~ . ~ . ~ . ~ . ~ . ~ . ~ . ~ . ~ . ~ . ~ . ~ . ~ . ~ . ~

(a) Blocked

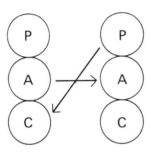

Nannette   Linda

(b) Open

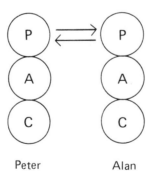

Peter   Alan

The response by Alan is an expected one, so this transaction is open.

~ . ~ . ~ . ~ . ~ . ~ . ~ . ~ . ~ . ~ . ~ . ~ . ~ . ~ . ~ . ~ . ~ . ~

4 Here is some more practice. Analyze each transaction, indicate whether it is blocked or open, and then diagram it.

(a) Sylvia: "Do you think we'll be able to finish by this evening?"
    Darlene: "Gee, couldn't we stop now? Please?"

    Transaction: ___Blocked ___Open

Diagram the transaction between Sylvia and Darlene:

(b) Kirk: "This mail won't go out until Monday."
John: "So what! Nobody seems to care!"

Transaction: ___ Blocked   ___Open

Diagram the transaction:

~ • ~ • ~ • ~ • ~ • ~ • ~ • ~ • ~ • ~ • ~ • ~ • ~ • ~ • ~ • ~ • ~

(a) Blocked

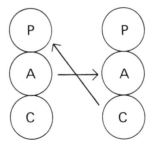

Sylvia   Darlene

Sylvia is asking a question, matter-of-factly expecting a reply from
Darlene's Adult. But Darlene responds with her Child in an effort
to appeal to Sylvia's Nurturing Parent.

(b) Blocked

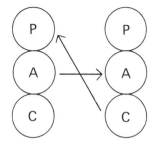

Kirk   John

Kirk is coming on straight, giving information to John. Somehow the statement seems to stir up the feelings in John's Child. John's reply may be a plea for help or perhaps for a little sympathy from Kirk. (John may actually be answering in this way for reasons outside the immediate situation. The important thing to see here is that John is responding from his Child while Kirk was speaking to his Adult.)

Blocked transactions can occur quite frequently on the job. They can get in your way, lead to hurt feelings and misunderstandings, and cut down productivity. To avoid blocked transactions, you must first be able to identify them, as you have just learned to do. Later, in Chapter 15, you'll learn more about how to keep transactions open and to deal with blocked transactions if they should occur.

Ulterior Transactions

Ulterior transactions, like blocked transactions, are generally undesirable. An ulterior transaction happens when a person appears to be sending one kind of message but is secretly sending another. The real message is disguised.

APPLICATION

1 Which of these transactions is most likely to be ulterior?

___(a) Maria says to her boss, "Mr. Brown, I'm so exhausted, I think I'm going to collapse with all this work."

___(b) "Mr. Brown, would you consider assigning another clerk to my section? I'm really swamped with work."

~ • ~ • ~ • ~ • ~ • ~ • ~ • ~ • ~ • ~ • ~ • ~ • ~ • ~ • ~ • ~ • ~ • ~

Example (a) is more likely to be an ulterior transaction. Here's how we would diagram it (the dotted arrow shows the ulterior message):

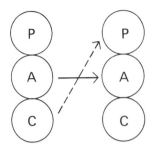

Maria   Mr. Brown

Marja is not talking straight about her needs, but is sending her message in a disguised way. She appears to be giving Mr. Brown factual information in an Adult-to-Adult transaction. Actually, however, she is probably resentful, feeling overworked. Perhaps she would like to ask Mr. Brown directly for help, but can't bring herself to do that. "I think I'm going to collapse" may be a plea for help from Maria's Child to Mr. Brown's Parent or a try at a con job.

~ . ~ . ~ . ~ . ~ . ~ . ~ . ~ . ~ . ~ . ~ . ~ . ~ . ~ . ~ . ~ . ~

2 Which of these seems to be an ulterior transaction?

Transaction A

Transaction B

Tom: "Well, John, I'm glad you got here."

___ (a)   Transaction A

___ (b)   Transaction B

___ (c)   Both

___ (d)   Neither

~ . ~ . ~ . ~ . ~ . ~ . ~ . ~ . ~ . ~ . ~ . ~ . ~ . ~ . ~ . ~ . ~

Answer (c) is correct. Both transactions seem to be ulterior. Here's how we would diagram the second one:

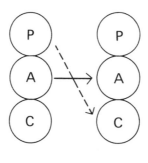

Tom   John

The words themselves seem to be coming from Tom's Adult. But Tom is definitely coming on Parent with his body language (his frown, cocked head, protruding lip, and pointed index finger).

So far we've been discussing short, spoken transactions as if they were always neat and complete in themselves. But transactions take place in a larger setting. To be accurate in analyzing a transaction, we need to consider such things as:

— the physical setting,
— what has just happened,
— body language, and
— the tone of voice.

APPLICATION ────────────────────────────────

1   Now finish this diagram of the transaction between Ron and Marsha. Put in a *dotted* arrow coming from Ron and heading to one of Marsha's ego states. (Take a good look at the setting and at Ron and Marsha's body language in the cartoon. Imagine what has just happened and how their voices sound.)

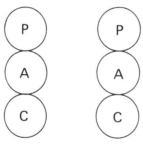

Marsha:
"Nice night
isn't it?"

Ron:
"Yes, but
I feel a bit
chilly, how
about you?"

~·~·~·~·~·~·~·~·~·~·~·~·~·~·~·~·~·~

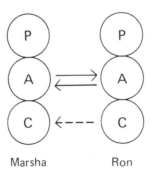

Marsha   Ron

Outwardly Ron is merely talking about the weather (from his Adult). His Child might really be sending a message to Marsha's Child that says, "Let's get closer."

~·~·~·~·~·~·~·~·~·~·~·~·~·~·~·~·~·~

2 Here's one more exercise in spotting and analyzing ulterior transactions. (We've left out the arrows.)

Transaction A

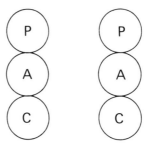

Arleen (salesperson):   Patty
"Of course this dress
is just right for you.
You look ten years
younger. But perhaps
it's a bit too daring."

Transaction B

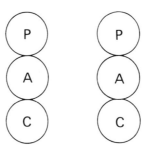

Arleen: Patty
"What kind of
dress are you
looking for?"

(a) Which is probably the ulterior transaction—A or B?
(b) Put in the missing arrows coming from Arleen to Patty to complete the
     ulterior transaction. Use a solid arrow to show the outward transaction and
     a dotted arrow to show the ulterior one. (Since Patty is silent, we need no
     return arrows at this point.)

~•~•~•~•~•~•~•~•~•~•~•~•~•~•~•~•~•~•~•~

Example A is more likely to be an ulterior transaction. Here's our
diagram:

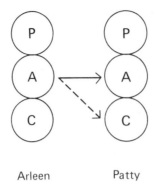

Arleen   Patty

According to this analysis, Arleen (the salesperson) is transacting from
her Adult. On the surface she seems to be sending a message to Patty's
Adult. But Arleen may be trying to trick Patty's Child into giving an
"I'll show you" response. If the trick works, Patty will end up proving
to Arleen that the dress *is* right for her.

Strokes

You've seen that transactions can be open, blocked, or ulterior. It's also important to recognize that *whenever* two people are transacting, they are
exchanging "strokes." What are strokes? To help you understand that term,
let's look at an important discovery made by Rene Spitz.[1] Spitz found that
keeping infants fed and in a clean environment was not enough. Such infants
became weak and almost seemed to shrivel up if they were not cuddled and
stroked. Infants who are touched very little may become physically and mentally retarded; those not touched at all seem to "give up" and die. Before
Spitz discovered this, doctors often puzzled at the high death rate in orphan-
age nurseries. Today in such nurseries "grandmothers" and "grandfathers"
volunteer to come in and just cuddle infants.

In TA language, the term "stroke" refers to the giving of some kind of
recognition to a person. This may or may *not* involve physical touching. As
we grow from infancy into childhood and then adulthood, we do not entirely
lose our need for stroking. Part of our original need for physical stroking
seems to be satisfied with *symbolic stroking*. We no longer need constant cud-
dling, but we still need attention. When we receive a stroke, we may choose
to feel either good or bad. If we choose to feel good, we might think of the
stroke as a "warm fuzzy" (or positive stroke). On the flip side, if we choose
to feel bad, we can think of it as a "cold prickly" (or negative stroke).[2]

Since we have a basic need for strokes, we will work hard to get them.
For example, ignored children will engage in all sorts of creative acts to get
stroked. Often such children quickly learn that they *can* get strokes by:

— talking in a loud, whiny, high-pitched voice,
— spilling milk on a clean tablecloth, and
— injuring themselves.

A child who carries out one of these actions is likely to get a cold prickly (negative stroke). But it seems to make no difference to a stroke-deprived child. To such a child, any kind of stroke is better than none at all: a cold prickly is better than nothing! The same is true for adults who work in a stroke-deprived environment.

Example

Lennie, a shipping clerk in a small mail-order firm, worked alone. Yet he got a lot of strokes from Kevin, his supervisor. Kevin often stopped by Lennie's work station just to chat. These strokes were not usually given for any particular job performance since Lennie's job was rather routine and didn't require any special skills. However, Kevin did compliment Lennie for his consistent performance.

Then one day Kevin was promoted. Lennie's new supervisor, Laura, had a different approach. She didn't stop to chat with her subordinates and spoke to them only when she was dissatisfied with their work.

APPLICATION

What do you think happened to Lennie's performance on the job?

___ (a) It improved.

___ (b) It got worse.

___ (c) It stayed the same.

~ . ~ . ~ . ~ . ~ . ~ . ~ . ~ . ~ . ~ . ~ . ~ . ~ . ~ . ~

(b) Lennie's performance got worse. With Laura as a supervisor, Lennie was working in a stroke-deprived environment. About the only time he got strokes was when he made an error of some kind. So Lennie unwittingly made errors to provoke a response from Laura. Lennie was hungry for strokes and, since he didn't know how to get warm fuzzies from Laura, he went after cold pricklies.

When employees don't get enough strokes on the job, they'll use a variety of techniques, some harmful, to make up their stroke deficit. For example, to "fill up their stroke bucket," people may play *psychological games.*

PSYCHOLOGICAL GAME ANALYSIS

A psychological game is a set of transactions with these characteristics:

  — The transactions tend to be repeated.
  — They make sense on a superficial or social level.
  — One or more of the transactions is ulterior.

— The set of transactions ends with a predictable payoff—a negative feeling. Payoffs usually reinforce a decision made in childhood about oneself or about others. They reflect feelings of not-OKness, as we shall see.

Example

Here's an example of a game called *Yes, But:*

Erika: "I need your help again, Mary. I just don't seem to be getting anyplace. I've had this same job for ten years now."
Mary: "Why don't you ask for a promotion?"
Erika: "Yes, I've thought of doing that, but there are too many people ahead of me who deserve promotions more than I."
Mary: "Why don't you have your job reevaluated or reclassified?"
Erika: "Yes, that's possible, but that would be too hard to do."
Mary: "I know! You could have a resume printed and send it to . . ."
Erika: "Yes, but most people get jobs through personal contacts."
Mary: (Silent)

Notice how each of the characteristics of a psychological game is present in this example.

— *Repeated transactions:* Mary and Erika have played this game before. Note Erika's opening line, "I need your help *again*, Mary."
— *Transactions make sense:* Outwardly it seems that Erika is honestly asking Mary for help. Mary's suggestions are reasonable and Erika's replies also seem to make sense.
— *Ulterior transactions:* Notice that Erika consistently rejects all of Mary's advice. On the social level, Erika is giving reasons why Mary's advice won't work. But she is also simultaneously sending an ulterior message that says, "Nobody's going to tell me what to do." Erika may still be rebelling against the advice her parent figures gave her when she was young. She operates from a belief that authority figures are not-OK.
— *Predictable payoff:* According to TA theory, the game of *Yes, But* is often played by people whose parents either dominated them or didn't give them reasonable answers. So they tend to take a stand against parental figures. They play *Yes, But* to prove to themselves that nobody can tell them anything they don't already know. The feeling of power they get becomes a payoff for playing the game, which they seek over and over again. They prove once more that "Parents can't tell me anything."

APPLICATION ──

1 Here are two diagrams. Which one do you think more accurately shows the ulterior transactions in *Yes, But*—A or B?

Transaction A

Transaction B

Erika   Mary   Erika   Mary

~·~·~·~·~·~·~·~·~·~·~·~·~·~·~·~·~·~·~·~

B shows the ulterior transaction. On the social level it's Adult to Adult; psychologically, Erika's Child is trying to appeal to ("hook") Mary's Parent.

~·~·~·~·~·~·~·~·~·~·~·~·~·~·~·~·~·~·~·~

2 Here's another psychological game. Read over the transactions first and then we'll analyze them.

    Joe: "You know, Andrea doesn't think much of your work."
    Diane: "Oh?"
    Joe: "Yeah, she told me last week. You're not one of her favorite people. She said she thinks your advertising campaign stinks. Do you think she should get away with making remarks like that?"
    Diane: "Well, who does she think she is, anyway!"

    Diane (later that day): "Well, I really told *her* off!"
    Joe: "Wow! What'd you say?"

Let's analyze this game. The transactions are ongoing and they make sense on a social level. On the social level Joe is just giving Diane information, but on the psychological level, what do you think Joe is saying?

___ (a) I'm willing to stick up for you.

___ (b) Let's you and her fight.

___ (c) Some people don't deserve respect.

~·~·~·~·~·~·~·~·~·~·~·~·~·~·~·~·~·~·~·~

(b) Let's you and her fight.

~·~·~·~·~·~·~·~·~·~·~·~·~·~·~·~·~·~·~·~

3 In playing this game (*Let's You and Him/Her Fight*), Joe is trying to maintain the psychological position "people are fools," and the situation certainly does make them look that way.

What do you think the payoff of the game is?

~ . ~ . ~ . ~ . ~ . ~ . ~ . ~ . ~ . ~ . ~ . ~ . ~ . ~ . ~ . ~ . ~

The payoff for Joe comes when he hears how Diane and Andrea made fools of themselves. Perhaps he delights in seeing them argue as his folks did. (We'll talk more about various kinds of games throughout this book, especially in Chapter 6.)

PSYCHOLOGICAL POSITIONS

People take basic psychological positions about themselves and others. These positions are tied into their identity, sense of worth, and perceptions of other people. The four basic positions are these:

— I'm not-OK, you're OK.
— I'm OK, you're not-OK.
— I'm not-OK, you're not-OK (neither of us is OK).
— I'm OK, you're OK (we're both OK!).

We'll discuss each of these positions separately. Then we'll explore how these psychological positions might affect the behavior of people in leadership roles.

I'm Not-OK, You're OK

Many people develop a not-OK position because their parents unwittingly put them down with subtle cold pricklies like these:

"Those nasty shoestrings. Let me tie them for you."
"Don't worry about that if you can't do it."
"You know we'll always wait for you."
"Let your brother make your sandwich."
"Don't worry about your grades. We don't expect you to do as well as your sister. After all, she's an exceptional child."

Note how these statements put down children in a very subtle way. Because they are subtle, children are likely to accept their parents as OK, especially since their parents seem to be so skilled at everything. After all, they *can:*

— tie their shoes in a flash;
— walk agilely across the room without tripping on their feet; and
— dress themselves with ease.

Grownups who assumed the I'm not-OK, you're OK position as children feel inadequate and often compare themselves unfavorably to others. They tend to seek approval from others unnecessarily and admire them from an envious position. Just the opposite of this position is the I'm OK, you're not-OK position, which we'll discuss next.

I'm OK, You're Not-OK

Some children develop an I'm OK, you're not-OK position when their parents treat them as if they're always right. Such parents are continually blaming themselves, putting themselves down. For example, Julie often heard her mother say things like, "Oh, how stupid of me. Look what I've done. I bought you the wrong size sweater again," or "I'm just terrible. I shouldn't have put that milk on your tray." Children of these parents understandably often develop a false sense of power and superiority over their parents and other people. When people assume the I'm OK, you're not-OK position, they usually don't accept responsibility for their problems, and may not even realize they have any problems. They project blame on others.

In extreme cases they tend to act in a paranoid way. They think they are right and other people—being not-OK—are out to get them. Sometimes people who take this position end up as criminals. They think, "If I'm OK and others aren't, then I have the right to do as I want. I can steal from them or hurt them." Such a person might embezzle from the company for twenty years and feel no guilt or remorse.

Some people cover a not-OK position by acting super-OK. Underneath the false surface of I'm OK is a very deep I'm not-OK. Their real position, then, is I'm not-OK, you're not-OK, which we discuss next.

I'm Not-OK, You're Not-OK

Often children develop an I'm not-OK, you're not-OK position if their parents ignore them, show them little respect, put them down, and give them rude cold pricklies like:

"Can't you do anything else but whine?"
"Hurry up, you're always too slow!"
"You're a mess again as usual!"
"You'll never learn, will you?"

It's not hard to see why many of these children assume an I'm not-OK position. In fact, most of us base our first self-concept on someone else's evaluation of us. The you're not-OK side develops when these children decide that their parents are being unfair and sometimes even cruel.

Cruel treatment of children in America is not unusual. Every year child abuse and neglect is reported approximately 300,000 times.[3] As these children suffer in pain from such abuse, they begin to think, "I must be terrible. I must be rotten, the way they treat me all the time." (Note that not all battered children develop an I'm not-OK, you're not-OK position. People react differently. Some battered children may hold a you're OK position for quite some time until they discover—perhaps through what nurses or doctors say—that their parents are not-OK for beating them. Their position may then switch to I'm not-OK, you're not-OK, and perhaps later to I really am OK— "They're the ones who are to blame!")

When people assume an I'm not-OK, you're not-OK position, they often lose interest in life and in extreme cases commit suicide or homicide. The I'm not-OK, you're not-OK position is probably the least desirable one because it involves bad feelings on both sides of the fence: toward oneself and toward others. In sharp contrast to this is the I'm OK, you're OK position.

I'm OK, You're OK

This is a healthy, constructive position in which people feel good about themselves and others. People with this position are happy, productive, energetic, and at peace with themselves and the rest of the world. We're not talking here about an unrealistic, sugarcoated, everybody's perfect position, but about a genuine acceptance of the significance of people.

Although many people in our complex culture assume a not-OK position, in some cultures, the I'm OK, you're OK position seems to be more of a way of life. For example, in the village of Vilcabamba, Ecuador, crime and mental and physical illnesses are remarkably absent. If you met 100 people in this village, you'd probably meet one who was 100 years of age or older. (In the United States, only one person out of 33,000 is that old.)[4] Part of their success at living together seems due to the respect and care they show for each other. They give one another little stress. Speaking of their ability to deal with stress, Grace Halsell says:

> . . . The Vilcabamba natives lead lives that are open, receptive, *vulnerable*. If they have built armor against hurt, it is nowhere displayed. Like innocent animals of the field, they seek no shelter from the thrusts and cuts of everyday living. They seem to recognize a maxim of their spiritual guides that "Only the gods go woundless on their way." . . . I never before experienced people who had so little and gave so much. Without any material possessions, they somehow assert their personalities, their individuality, their right to be giving.[5]

Another group of people who seem to assume the I'm OK, you're OK position frequently are the Senoi who live in the jungles of central Malaysia. Patricia Garfield describes their I'm OK, you're OK position this way:

> Perhaps the most striking characteristic of the Senoi is their extraordinary psychological adjustment. Neuroses and psychoses as we know them are reported to be nonexistent among the Senoi. Western therapists find this statement hard to believe, yet it is documented by researchers who spent considerable time directly observing the Senoi. The Senoi show remarkable emotional maturity. Desire for possession of things and people seems extraordinarily slight, perhaps as a result of their advanced psychological development.[6]

Most of us do not consistently act from a single life position. Instead, our feelings of OKness tend to change from situation to situation. Phil, for example, experiences a greater sense of OKness when he is playing softball than when he is reading an editor's comments on his writing. (Furthermore, he feels more OK when he is pitching than when he is playing first base.) Some of us feel more OK on the job than we do at home. For example, many men feel competent and skillful in their work life, but feel less OK as fathers and husbands. In contrast, traditionally many women feel competent at home as mothers and wives, but less competent dealing with company politics. A major goal of TA (and this book) is to help people increase the number of situations in which they feel OK about themselves and other people.

APPLICATION

Now check your understanding of the basic psychological positions by identifying the position each of these people is most likely acting out.

1 Joe seems to seesaw back and forth when it comes to handling subordinates. He often disciplines subordinates cruelly and then later feels bad about it. He scolds himself with, "How could I have been so cruel?" and then feels depressed. He tends to give and get a lot of bad feelings. Which position is Joe acting out?

___ (a) I'm OK, you're OK.

___ (b) I'm OK, you're not-OK.

___ (c) I'm not-OK, you're OK.

___ (d) I'm not-OK, you're not-OK.

2 Sandy trusts herself and others. She communicates openly. She frequently pats herself on the back when she's done something right. Her subordinates do the same when things go well and are often seen laughing and joking. When conflict arises, she avoids becoming defensive. Instead, she listens to options, seeks clarification and mutual resolution, and then takes necessary action. Which position is Sandy acting out?

___ (a) I'm OK, you're OK.

___ (b) I'm OK, you're not-OK.

___ (c) I'm not-OK, you're OK.

___ (d) I'm not-OK, you're not-OK.

3 Tom holds the attitude that he is always right. Even when he procrastinates, he blames others. He's stingy with warm fuzzies, habitually pointing out flaws and giving cold pricklies. He often gives unclear directions with the hidden motive of pouncing on subordinates when they don't perform as desired. Which position is Tom acting out?

___ (a) I'm OK, you're OK.

___ (b) I'm OK, you're not-OK.

___ (c) I'm not-OK, you're OK.

___ (d) I'm not-OK, you're not-OK.

4 Gretchen often says things like, "I wish I could manage my people the way you do." When others compliment her she often answers, "Oh, it was nothing, really." She provokes others to give her cold pricklies by messing up projects through poor delegation, poor timing of decisions, and stupid mistakes. She often looks to others for help in stressful situations rather than thinking things through herself. Which position is Gretchen acting out?

___ (a) I'm OK, you're OK.

___ (b) I'm OK, you're not-OK.

___(c) I'm not-OK, you're OK.

___(d) I'm not-OK, you're not-OK.

5 Bill frequently is overly helpful when subordinates are having difficulties. He often says things like, "I guess you don't have the knack for that. Here, let me do it for you." Which position is Bill acting out?

___(a) I'm OK, you're OK.

___(b) I'm OK, you're not-OK.

___(c) I'm not-OK, you're OK.

___(d) I'm not-OK, you're not-OK.

~•~•~•~•~•~•~•~•~•~•~•~•~•~•~•~•~

1 Joe is acting out the I'm not-OK, you're not-OK position. The way he *cruelly* disciplines subordinates shows that he is taking a you're not-OK position. The way he scolds himself shows that he also feels not-OK about himself.

2 Sandy is acting out the I'm OK, you're OK position. She really sounds like a winner, doesn't she? (If any of you know where she is working now, please let us know.)

3 Tom is acting out the I'm OK, you're not-OK position. He feels superior to others. He reveals his you're not-OK side by blaming and pouncing on others.

4 Gretchen is acting out the I'm not-OK, you're OK position. She reveals her I'm not-OK aspect by the way she puts herself down when others stroke her. Her lack of self-reliance also shows her I'm not-OK position. She reveals the you're OK side of her position by the fact that she looks to others for solutions to her problems and compares herself unfavorably with them.

5 Bill is acting out an I'm OK, you're not-OK position. He shows this by his overprotective attitude. Since others are not-OK, he doesn't expect them to do their jobs properly. Since he *is* OK, he takes their jobs over for them.

As we've pointed out, the psychological positions that people act out tend to vary according to the situation. The psychological positions that we learn to take and the games that we learn to play are part of what we call a "script."

SCRIPT ANALYSIS

In everyday language, a script is the text of a play, motion picture, or radio or TV program. In TA, a person's life is compared to a play and the script is the text of that play. A person's psychological script is a life plan—a drama he or she writes and then feels compelled to live out. These plans may be positive, negative, or circular—endless repetition headed nowhere.

Everyone has a script. You developed yours based on your experiences as a child. One potent influence was your various transactions with your parents (or other authority figures). These in turn led you to make certain decisions, formulate psychological positions, play psychological games, and start the drama of your script.

APPLICATION ———————————————————

1 Since two important parts of your script are your typical psychological positions and the games you play, how might you become more aware of your script?

2 What might be the advantage of becoming more aware of your script?

~ · ~ · ~ · ~ · ~ · ~ · ~ · ~ · ~ · ~ · ~ · ~ · ~ · ~ · ~ · ~ · ~ · ~

1 A good way to become aware of your script is to identify the *psychological* positions you tend to take and the *games* you play. (We'll give you some practice in doing just that later: see Chapters 6 and 8 for more information on exploring your script.)
2 You can gain greater control of your life. You can learn to rewrite your script rather than to act it out blindly.

Example

As Edwin was growing up he was frequently put down and compared to his older brother, Sid. He constantly heard things like:

> "Well, Edwin, you only got 60% on this test, but gee, that's pretty good for you, considering your ability."
> "Edwin! You spilled the soda all over my new chair. What's wrong with you? Why are you always doing such dumb things? Don't you have a brain in your head?"
> "Edwin is not as bright as Sid, you know, so don't expect much from him."
> "What a stupid thing to do, Edwin. Sid would never have done a thing like that."

APPLICATION ———————————————————

1 What psychological position do you think Edwin usually took as a child?

2 Assuming that Edwin believed what he heard about himself, imagine him as a high-school student.

Does he like school? _____ Is he a good student? _____

3 Now imagine Edwin on the job later in life. He is talking to one of his co-workers about a report he is working on. Which one of these things would he be most likely to say?

____ (a) "I feel concerned about the progress I've made on this project."

____ (b) "I'm just a bungling idiot. I misplaced that report again! I'll never learn, will I?"

4 It is clear that Edwin was born with inferior mental capacity. True or false? ____

~•~•~•~•~•~•~•~•~•~•~•~•~•~•~•~•~

1 Edwin most likely took an I'm not-OK, you're not-OK position on many occasions as a child. He often felt not-OK about himself because of all the negative things he heard from his parents. He probably felt his parents (and others) were not-OK because of the cruel way they spoke to him.
2 Given his predominant psychological position, Edwin would probably dislike school and be a poor student. (Occasionally, however, a person like Edwin takes an "I'll show you" stance and knocks himself out trying to be perfect at everything, yet rarely satisfied with how he's doing.)
3 (b).
4 False! Edwin might have a good brain and the potential to become a brilliant executive. But he has come to believe that he *is* stupid. Consequently, Edwin may have unconsciously (and compulsively) arranged things to strengthen this script.

All of us have scripts. And like Edwin, without being aware of it, we tend to arrange our environment so that our script is perpetuated. As you'll see, however, we can become more aware of our Hidden Self and our Blind Self so that we can write a new script, choosing even more successful pathways.

SUMMARY

According to TA, everyone's personality has three ego states: Parent, Adult, and Child. While in our Parent we act as our parents did, often in either a controlling or a nurturing way. When we are cool and collected, when we are making predictions and decisions rationally, when we are deciding what will probably happen next on the basis of hard data, we're using our Adult. When we act as we did when we were children, we're using our Child. Responses that come from a Child ego state are usually charged with feeling.

Communication between different ego states is a transaction. When a direct message gets a natural, expected response, the transaction is open. When a direct message gets an unexpected response, the transaction is blocked. An ulterior transaction contains a hidden message. Transactions can carry a sense of OKness or not-OKness.

All transactions involve the exchange of strokes, either positive (warm fuzzies) or negative (cold pricklies). When you stroke people, you recognize them in some way. People need strokes to survive. If they don't get enough warm fuzzies, they'll go after cold pricklies. The kinds of strokes we learn to give or get determine in many ways how often we choose success.

People often go after cold pricklies by playing games. A psychological game is a set of transactions with these characteristics:

— The transactions tend to be repeated.
— They make sense on a superficial or social level.
— One (or more) of the transactions is ulterior.
— The set of transactions ends with a predictable payoff—a negative feeling.

Often people play games to strengthen the psychological positions they have taken about themselves and others. There are four basic psychological positions:

— I'm not-OK, you're OK (I wish I could disappear).
— I'm OK, you're not-OK (I wish you'd disappear).
— I'm not-OK, you're not-OK (let's both get lost).
— I'm OK, you're OK (together we can do it).

The games we play and the psychological positions we take are important parts of our script. In TA a script is a person's life plan. Many people compulsively organize their environment to strengthen their script. It's important to become aware of your script because then you can decide whether to keep it or change it. You can become more aware of your script by identifying your favorite psychological positions and games.

You can get in touch with your favorite games and positions by beginning to explore your ego states in more depth. That's what you'll do in Chapter 3.

SOURCE NOTES

[1] Rene Spitz, "Hospitalism, Genesis of Psychiatric Conditions in Early Childhood," *Psychoanalytic Study of the Child*, 1945:53–74.
[2] The phrases "warm fuzzy" and "cold prickly" were first introduced by Claude Steiner in a delightful story called *Warm Fuzzy Tale* (Sacramento, Calif.: Jalmar Press, 1977).
[3] From an edited speech by C. Henry Kempe, "Predicting and Preventing Child Abuse: Establishing Children's Rights by Assuring Access to Health Care Through the Health Visitors Concept," *Proceeding of the First National Conference on Child Abuse and Neglect*, January 4–7, 1976.
[4] Grace Halsell, *Los Viejos* (Emmaus, Pa.: Rodale Press, 1976), p. 14.
[5] *Ibid.*, p. 154.
[6] Patricia Garfield, *Creative Dreaming* (New York: Ballantine, 1974), p. 83.

3

Exploring Personality

☆ Have you ever thought you were communicating in one way and later learned you were perceived in a completely different way?

☆ Have you ever asked a question at a meeting and then felt about two years-old?

☆ Have you ever felt that you really wanted to cry but held it back and acted bossy or domineering on the surface?

☆ Have you ever solved a problem in the middle of the night and felt creative and excited about your idea?

☆ Have you ever scolded someone and then kicked yourself for it later?

☆ Have you ever used the same technique to get what you want from your boss that you used as a child?

☆ Do you often find yourself being defensive about your ideas or your point of view?

☆ Do you often feel you have to take care of too many people who should be taking care of themselves?

☆ Do you see yourself as being calm, cool, and collected most of your working day?

We have all experienced some of these feelings or situations. But you may not recognize that they are related to different parts of your personality. This chapter and the next offer you some personal insights into why you may think, feel, and act as you do. You'll look a little deeper into ego states and begin to analyze the structure of personality—your personality in particular. You'll begin to discover what *your* Parent, Adult, and Child are all about and how you can use them to express yourself more meaningfully and more happily through your work.

OBJECTIVES

When you finish this chapter, you'll be able to:

- identify these ego states:

    — Controlling Parent,
    — Nurturing Parent,
    — Adult,

— Natural Child,
— Adapted Child,
— Little Professor;

- identify some of the acts, feelings, and thoughts that typically characterize each of your own ego states;
- identify parts of your ego states that may be archaic and no longer useful to you.

Let's begin by exploring more fully the structural analysis of ego states.

STRUCTURAL ANALYSIS

The Parent Ego State

Sometimes parents treat their children in a loving way, speak kindly to them, offer shelter and protection, or take care of them in other ways. We call this *nurturing behavior.* If it is nourishing, it helps children grow.

At other times parents criticize, make rules, give commands, or punish their children. Since the main objective of these behaviors is to *control* the child, we call them *controlling behaviors.*

Because small children repeatedly see parents behaving in these two major ways, and they unconsciously *copy* these behaviors, their Parent ego state also develops two major aspects. In this book, we will call these two aspects the Nurturing Parent (NP) and the Controlling Parent (CP). Here's how this might be diagrammed:*

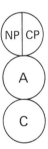

*This diagram is somewhat misleading because the Parent ego state has more in it than just controlling and nurturing aspects, as we shall see. For simplicity, however, we will often focus our attention on just the nurturing and controlling aspects of the Parent state.

Transaction A

___ NP ___ CP

Transaction B

___ NP ___ CP

Transaction C

_____ NP   _____ CP

~ • ~ • ~ • ~ • ~ • ~ • ~ • ~ • ~ • ~ • ~ • ~ • ~ • ~ • ~

A: Nurturing Parent. Notice Marge's choice of words and her body language—worried facial expression and upturned hands. They show she is concerned for Bess's welfare.

B: Controlling Parent. These things suggest that the boss is in his Controlling Parent: facial expression, gesture with index finger (this one's a sure tipoff that the Controlling Parent is in action), the words he is using, especially, "Be sure to . . ."

C: Nurturing Parent. Notice Mark's nurturing body language—arm around John and sympathetic expression. Mark's comment is likely to be coming from his Nurturing Parent. The comment seems to be designed to help John get rid of his depressed feelings.

Notice that the words, "Oh. Don't let it get you down, John," if spoken harshly, could very well come from the Controlling Parent. Since the meaning of messages can be conveyed in many different ways, you would really have to hear the words to make an adequate judgment. You would also need to see the person saying them. The body language of pointing fingers, crossed arms and legs, slumped shoulders, set jaws, sideways glances, broad smiles, and so on, often speaks louder than words.

Here the tone of Mark's voice would be a strong hint. Usually, the Controlling Parent speaks in a loud, strident voice or in a firm voice. The Nurturing Parent usually speaks slowly, softly, and smoothly. We hinted that Mark was in his Nurturing Parent by showing that he was speaking softly.

As noted in Chapter 2, when you are in your *Parent*, you respond *automatically*, almost as if a tape recording were playing in your head and directing your words and actions. All of us have *Parent tapes* that can affect our job performance. Many of these tapes are helpful. They enable us to carry out countless routine tasks automatically without the need to think them through each time. But sometimes Parent tapes can get in our way.

APPLICATION

Here are some typical Parent tapes. Put a plus (+) in the blank before each tape that you would consider generally helpful to a person on the job and a minus (–) in the blank before each tape you would consider generally self-defeating.

____ (a)   "You'll never amount to anything."

____ (b)   "Whatever that kid touches is going to turn to gold."

____ (c)   "You're just like your father. He can never stick to anything until it's finished."

____ (d)   "You've got a good head on your shoulders. Use it."

____ (e)   "You made your own bed; now sleep in it."

____ (f)   "Finish one thing before you start another."

____ (g)   "If something needs to be done, it's your responsibility to do it."

____ (h)   "You'd fall over spots on a rug."

____ (i)   "That kid could sell refrigerators to Eskimos."

~ . ~ . ~ . ~ . ~ . ~ . ~ . ~ . ~ . ~ . ~ . ~ . ~ . ~ . ~ . ~ . ~ . ~

We would say that tapes (b), (d), (f), (g), and (i) would *generally* tend to be helpful. Tapes (a), (c), and (h) would generally tend to be self-defeating. Parent tapes can have different effects with different people. For example, many people would also regard tape (e) as self-defeating, since to them it conveys the message, "No one will ever help you." But when Dorothy, for example, got this tape from her grandmother, she took it to mean, "Be responsible," so the tape had a positive influence on her.

Remember that unless we make a special effort to become aware of Parent tapes, we respond to them automatically without realizing that they are "playing in our heads." As a result, even generally helpful Parent tapes can sometimes get in our way, because our Parent ego state does *not* examine our environment to decide whether a given Parent tape is appropriate. So Parent tapes are sometimes triggered automatically in inappropriate situations.

For example, one generally helpful Parent tape is "finish one thing before you start another." But if we follow such a tape blindly, without thinking, we will not be aware of situations in which it would be self-defeating. Say we are working on a project and we get stuck. The harder we try, the more frustrated we become. In such situations, it can help to lay aside that project and come back to it later with a fresh viewpoint.

Let's look at another situation in which this tape can be self-defeating. When Gus, a repair technician for a data-processing corporation, was given a computer system to repair, he would work on it intensely without a break until it was properly repaired. Every now and then Gus would be in the middle of fixing a demonstration unit (used by the corporation's salespeople) when his supervisor would tell him of some equipment that an important customer wanted repaired as soon as possible. Gus's usual response was, "OK. I'll get to that just as soon as I finish this system I'm working on." After listening to several important customers complain about the delay in service, Gus's supervisor began to demand that he focus his attention on the more important jobs, that he set priorities and manage his time more effectively. After putting up an argument, Gus began to lay aside less important projects when important ones came in. But whenever he had to do this, he felt angry and frustrated, unaware that he was using his Parent tape in an unproductive way.

APPLICATION

The following tapes are generally helpful to people on the job, but if followed automatically, they may not be. For each tape describe a situation in which it would *not* be helpful to respond *automatically* to these tapes.

1 "If something needs to be done, it's your responsibility to do it."

2 "Whatever's worth doing is worth doing right."

~ . ~ . ~ . ~ . ~ . ~ . ~ . ~ . ~ . ~ . ~ . ~ . ~ . ~ . ~ . ~

1 Sometimes it's important to delegate to other people the authority to carry out an activity. Although it may be your responsibility that a job gets done, it's not always necessary (or appropriate) for *you* to do it.
2 The tape, "Whatever's worth doing is worth doing right," could give a person the motivation to reach a standard of excellence that brings much success. If it's followed compulsively, however, it can get in the way of simply doing *something* without worrying if it's exactly right. Sometimes it's more important to make a beginning, to rough out something, than to make it "right." If we become too concerned about doing *everything* right the first time, then we may be so

inhibited that we are unable to be productive in situations where creativity is called for. Also, if we invest energy in diligently following this tape, we may do many things right but not do the right things!

The Ego States of Your Parental Figures

As we've discussed, people's Parent ego states are made up of behaviors they have *copied* from their parents. The Parent ego state contains more than just nurturing and controlling aspects, and impressionable children tend to copy *everything* they see their parents doing. For example, while in his Child ego state, Bob's father had a habit of tossing things on the floor: apricot pits (behind the sofa!), newspapers, shoes, clothes, and so on. Since Bob watched his father do this again and again, he incorporated this behavior pattern into his Parent ego state. As a grownup in his office, he often unthinkingly tossed various objects on his desk. As a result, it was usually a big mess and he wasted a lot of time looking for important papers that were buried under the rubble.

Each of your parental figures developed three ego states. So, when your parents interacted with you:

— sometimes (while in their *Parent* ego states) they treated you the way their parents treated them.
— sometimes (while in their *Adult* ego states) they thought for themselves, sought out facts, estimated probabilities, and acted rationally.
— sometimes (while in their *Child* ego states) they acted impulsively or emotionally or did things for fun. They also may have sulked, manipulated others, or shown avoidance behaviors.

As a small child you watched your parents carry out different kinds of behaviors from their Parent, Adult, and Child ego states. So when *your* Parent ego state developed, it incorporated Parent, Adult, and Child ego states from both your mother and father (or other parental figures). Now, *you* might act in any of these ways from your Parent ego state. For example, if you have children, you may play with them the same way your folks played with you (or didn't play with you). The following exercise will help you explore the makeup of your own Parent ego state.

APPLICATION

1 Think of a parent figure who influenced you as a child. Let the diagram below represent that person's ego states. Beside the P in this diagram, write two or three adjectives that characterize this person's Parent ego state. In the same way write two or three adjectives to describe this parent figure's Adult and Child.

2 Do the same exercise with a second parent figure.

3 Now consider your *own* Parent ego state. Which of the adjectives above could be used to describe it?

Since your Parent has many ego states within it, some of your thoughts and behaviors have their roots deep in history. You may drum your fingers on the table when you're annoyed as your great-great-grandfather did. He may have copied this habit from his father, who copied it from his mother, who may have copied it from a mysterious prince or princess in an ancient land!

The Child Ego State

Just as the Parent has different aspects, so does the Child. According to TA theory, the Child develops into these three parts:

— Natural Child,
— Little Professor, and
— Adapted Child.

The Natural Child is spontaneous, energetic, feeling, curious, loving, un-inhibited. It's the part of us that feels free and loves pleasure. If you've ever had a warm or excited feeling when you were with someone, you were probably tuning in to this person's Natural Child.

When you are in your Natural Child, you transact freely and openly with others. The Natural Child is the ego state you came into the world with as a newborn baby. It's what comes naturally. The Natural Child isn't entirely without fault, however. It can be self-centered, impatient, and greedy.

In contrast, the Adapted Child acts in patterns learned from the environment. Your Adapted Child developed when you learned to *change* (adapt) your feelings and behavior in response to the world around you. *Learned* feelings of guilt, fear, anxiety, depression, and envy are characteristics of the Adapted Child. The pride you feel when somebody praises you for your good performance often comes from the Adapted Child. Similarly, the good feeling you get after you've done a job "right" (particularly if somebody notices or cares) is often a learned feeling. Your strokes tend to come from others rather than from your good feeling about the activity itself. (People who are using their unique potential like strokes of approval but also collect many good feelings from just "doing their thing." They tend to be self-starters and rely less on approval from the outside.)

It's through adaptations that we originally become socialized—able to cooperate with others and live in groups. Through socialization we learn to take turns, to share, to be friendly, to be concerned about how something feels to others. We must learn these valuable skills to get along socially. It's our Adapted Child that says "please" and "thank you" to customers.

However, the Adapted Child can become the most troublesome part of our personalities, the part that gets in our way. It's the part that may feel not-OK if we are:

— frightened when we must speak before a group;
— depressed when someone criticizes our work;
— hurt when things don't go our way at a meeting; or
— anxious when important deadlines confront us.

Behaviors associated with these feelings are also typical of the Adapted Child. As a child you probably learned to adapt in different ways. For example, sometimes you may have done what you were told; at other times you may have sulked or avoided the situation (by withdrawing or procrastinating). As a grownup, you may still occasionally react the same way to a project deadline. From their Adapted Child, people often react to external demands by:

— complying,
— sulking, or
— avoiding situations.

It is the Adapted Child that may:

— try to please everyone in its department;
— turn its back on people with problems; or
— procrastinate by putting off work until the deadline passes.

These actions can stand in the way of choosing success.

APPLICATION ——————————————————————

All of the following transactions are usually associated with the Child. In the blank under each one, write NC if the person designated by the arrow is using his or her Natural Child. Write AC if the Adapted Child is being used.

Transaction A _____

Transaction B _____

Transaction C _____

Transaction D _____

~ • ~ • ~ • ~ • ~ • ~ • ~ • ~ • ~ • ~ • ~ • ~ • ~ • ~ • ~ • ~ • ~ • ~

These are all examples of the Adapted Child in action except for example A. The Natural Child loves the nurturing touch.

In example B, Ken is using an avoidance strategy to deal with his unpleasant feelings about calling Mr. Green. This is a favorite Adapted Child technique. In childhood Ken learned to feel deep guilt and anxiety whenever he made a mistake (no matter how small). He, like most of us, is a repeater. In fact, without being aware of it, he may even make mistakes so he can reexperience these old feelings. He may do this because it keeps his world predictable, even if uncomfortable. However, note that these old feelings are now getting in his way and interfering with his ability to solve problems and to work effectively. They also interfere with other people's work.

The Natural Child feels physical pain; the Adapted Child usually feels psychological pain. In C, Nancy's pained expression probably doesn't result from any physical cause, but from what she is saying to herself about the impending meeting with her boss, T.J. (Nancy is afraid T.J. is going to "chew her out" about something.)

In D, Ron is showing patience by waiting. Often this is a positive use of the Adapted Child.

Now that you've had some practice in identifying characteristics that distinguish the Natural Child and the Adapted Child, let's look at the Little Professor. The Little Professor is the "thinking" part of the Child—thinking without knowing all of the facts believed to be needed. It is creative, intuitive, and manipulative. With the Little Professor a child psychs out a situation and seems to have an inborn ability to:

— dream up new ideas;
— "pull just the right strings" to reach a desired goal;
— intuitively sense what to do (or how to solve a problem) as if by magic.

The Little Professor is able to:

— come up with unusual concoctions;
— put familiar things together in new ways;
— imagine new ideas, products, solutions.

Little Professor "thinking" can be free of rigid boundaries. For example, four-year-old Tommy thought nothing of using all of the colors of the rainbow to color a duck or a horse. He loved to make his own dot-to-dot pictures by using a hole punch instead of obediently following the usual preprogrammed numbers. He made pies out of mud and maybe ate them, horses from broomsticks and rode them, cars out of sofas and vroomed them down an imaginary speedway.

Tommy also knew how to "pull a few strings" to get his way. For example, he knew just the right tone of voice to use in saying things like, "I guess I'll just have to go to bed hungry tonight," so that his parents quickly came up with cookies and a glass of milk. He also knew how to increase the probability of being served his favorite jam by dropping "subtle" compliments like:

"Hey, Mom, did you know that I really don't like this jam?"
"What? You don't like it?"
"No, I don't like it—I love it!"

Tommy also had a knack for sensing when his mother was in a mood for giving him permission to stay up late or eat another piece of candy. This ability to psych people out on the basis of subjective feeling is also typical of the Little Professor.

Grownups have Little Professors too. For example, when you're talking to your boss about the weather and suddenly, without anything specific being said, you have a strong gut feeling that "something is up," your Little Professor's sixth sense is at work, tuning into some "vibes" that your Adult can't pin down.[1]

The Little Professor figures out how to manipulate others. For example, as a grownup Tom belittled his own work in hopes that his boss would say, "What do you mean? You did a terrific job on those layouts!" (Of course, it didn't always work!) Similarly, Joyce may well be using her Little Professor when she dreams up a way to get some sympathy from Ed's Nurturing Parent by staggering into his office with a harried look and heaving a sigh as she puts a load of mail on his desk.

APPLICATION

Here's another exercise designed to help you sharpen your skill at recognizing the various parts of the Child. Tell whether each of these items best describes the Natural Child (NC), Adapted Child (AC), or Little Professor (LP). No two person's ego states are identical, so there won't always be one right answer to our questions, but you can make an "educated" guess. Write NC, AC, or LP in the blank before each item.

___ (a)   Smiling with a genuine twinkle in the eye when greeting customers.

___ (b)   Creating a new product at a brainstorming meeting.

___ (c)   Enjoying the feel of the warm sun coming through the window.

___ (d)   Saying words like "please" and "thank you."

___ (e)   Holding a grudge against your boss or a subordinate.

___ (f)   Using intuition to spot a forger passing a bad check.

___ (g)   Experiencing excitement from doing something for the first time.

___ (h)   Holding back a question or comment because it may seem stupid.

___ (i)   Avoiding a co-worker who did something to offend you.

___ (j)   Manipulating subordinates to get them to do what you want without their knowing it.

~.~

Natural Child: (a), (c), (g)
Adapted Child: (d), (e), (h), (i)
Little Professor: (b), (f), (j)

If you disagreed with any of these (or even if you agreed 100%), you might want to read our comments about each item.

(a) NC. A smile with a genuine twinkle in the eye is a natural smile, one that is uninhibited.

(b) LP. It's the Little Professor (working together with the Adult) that is able to create new things.

(c) NC. When you're perceiving feelings that come from uninhibited contact with the environment, you are in your Natural Child. Similar feelings are the feeling of the sand between your toes on the beach, the pleasant feeling you get from looking at an attractive scene, the feeling of warm rain on your face, and so on.

(d) AC. Social skills (like knowing when to say "please" and "thank you") are examples of the positive side of the Adapted Child.

(e) AC. It's the Adapted Child that holds a grudge. The Natural Child lets everything out and so doesn't know how to collect bad feelings.

(f) LP. One of the key features of the Little Professor is its ability to psych out or *intuit* things on the basis of undefined variables.

(g) NC. Everything is new to the Natural Child. It delights in the sights, sounds, smells, and tastes of nature.

(h) AC. Embarrassment is a learned feeling. Often the Adapted Child learns to keep quiet to avoid the embarrassment of looking stupid.

(i) AC. This is a favorite Adapted Child trick. The Adapted Child usually deals with an unpleasant situation by grudgingly going along with it, by avoiding it, by putting it off, or by sulking.

(j) LP. Manipulation is another word for "pulling strings," a favorite method used by the Little Professor to get its way.

GETTING IN TOUCH WITH YOUR EGO STATES

You've learned a lot about ego states and explored your Parent briefly. Now it's time for you to meet all three of your ego states![2]

APPLICATION

1 First, think of an interpersonal relationship problem that you're having on your job. Write down the name of the person and the nature of the problem. (Later we'll ask you to come back here and make some additional observations.)

2 Now, think of a parent or parent figure who had authority over you when you were a young child. You may think of your mother or father or perhaps an aunt, uncle, grandparent, older brother, sister, guardian, or friend of the family. Any such person is acceptable for the purpose of this exercise. However, you will get the most out of this experience if this person was important to you when you were growing up. Write that person's name here. Then continue

reading. _____

3 Think of three things this person frequently did for you, to you, or with you. Go back as far as you can, remembering this person when you were a child. Write them down.

   Note: Sometimes you may not want to write out your answer, but since you will be building on this information throughout our discussion, it's important for you to do so.

4 Now look back at what you wrote. For each behavior you listed, how might a child *feel* in response to that behavior?

5 Now consider the three behaviors you listed. Are they positive behaviors or negative? If you listed negative behaviors (things you didn't like), see if you can list some positive behaviors. If you listed positive behaviors, list some negative ones. Come up with three of each kind altogether.

6 Which were harder for you to remember—positive behaviors or negative ones?

   ____Positive ____Negative

   Many people say they find it harder to think of negative behaviors carried out by their parents (or parentlike figures). Perhaps that's because most people have a strong parental message in their heads that says something like, "Honor and respect your parents!" After all, how can you say something negative if the Child in you is feeling guilty? Others say they find it hard to think of *anything* good about their parents, especially people who were ignored, humiliated, or brutalized when they were children. If you can't think of anything good about what your parents did, try digging a little deeper. Go back to basic questions. Ask yourself: "Did they feed me? Did they give me shelter?" and so on. Often if we hold resentments about our parents, it is difficult to remember their good qualities.

7 Again, think of how a child might feel in response to the last three behaviors that you listed.

8 Next, think of a time when (as a young child) you were sick or injured (or perhaps feeling humiliated or depressed). Imagine the same person at your side. Go back in time and make the picture as vivid as possible. Got it? Describe what this person is doing and saying.

9 Now write down how a child might feel if treated this way.

10 Now think of a time when you got in trouble for some reason or another. (Relax, you don't have to tell what you did!) Imagine the same person walking toward you. Describe his or her walk (for example, striding, thumping the floor with heavy footsteps, walking quietly). What is she or he saying and doing? Describe any body language you can visualize (stance, gestures, facial expressions, and so on). Have fun with your description; make it interesting.

11 How would a child feel in response to what this person did?

12 Write three adjectives that sum up the personality of the person you have been thinking of. (If you are beginning to have some repetition here, that's fine.)

_____   _____   _____

13 How would a child tend to feel around such a person?

Our aim in this exercise was *not* to have you learn more about your mother or your father or your Aunt Karen. Most parents do the very best they know how. Rather our aim is to have you get in touch with your Parent and Child ego states, who *you* are now. Remember, your Parent and Child were shaped by *your early* decisions about your world and your interactions with parent figures. You were very impressionable then but your Parent ego state is *your* responsibility now. It's sometimes too easy to place blame rather than take this responsibility.

Meet Your Parent

Consider for a moment the positive and negative behaviors that you listed for the *parent figure.* (Look at questions 3, 5, 6, 8, 10, and 12 in the preceding application.)

APPLICATION —————————————————————————————

1 Do *you* engage in any of the positive and negative behaviors of your parent figure now? If yes, which ones?

2 Are any of these negative behaviors? ___ Yes ___ No

3 Now study these behaviors and ask, "If I use these now, will they help or hinder

me in my relationship with people?" _____

4 Look back at the interpersonal problem you described in question 1 on page 50.

Are you using any of these behaviors with this person? _____

5 Is there anything you'd like to change in your relationship with this person? ___

If so, what?

6 What do you see yourself doing instead?

Picture yourself using this new behavior.

People are often surprised to find that they do many of the same things that their parents did—*even parent behaviors that they didn't like!*

Example

Tim was often scolded severely by his father whenever he would daydream or watch a cloud drift by. As a child, Tim told himself that when he grew up he would let people have time to relax and just sit and think. But as an adult, Tim frequently caught himself using his father's tone of voice, gestures, and expressions in criticizing his subordinates for not looking busy.

Meet Your Child

Now consider what you wrote about how a child might feel in response to the actions of your parent figure. (Look at questions 4, 7, 9, 11, and 13 in the application beginning on page 50.

APPLICATION ───────────────────────────────

1 Do you ever have any of these childlike feelings today? If yes, which ones?

2 In what situations?

You have just described an aspect of your Child ego state. Perhaps it was part of your Hidden Self or Blind Self, of which you are now aware. Remember, your Child ego state developed when, as a child, you learned to respond in certain ways to your environment. The way you felt when someone scolded you then is probably similar to the way you feel now when your supervisor calls a mistake to your attention. The way you feel *now* when someone compliments you is likely to be similar to the way you learned to feel when your parents praised you. If your parents rarely complimented you, you may be suspicious of compliments now. If you sulked, you may still be sulking. If you were charming, you may still be turning on your charm.

APPLICATION ───────────────────────────────

1 Consider the feelings you listed in the previous application. Which feelings help you now?

2 Which feelings, if any, get in your way now?

If you identified some feelings in your Child that are getting in your way, you may wish to change that. We all have more control over our learned feelings than we believe. Awareness that you are still responding in ways you learned as a child is a first step toward expanding your options.

Meet Your Self-Image

In doing these exercises, you probably flashed on some old scenes, people, and experiences in your life. You made some decisions about yourself a long time ago in response to these scenes. The way you have learned to feel can affect your self-image—what you've come to believe about yourself. Now begin to look at how you see yourself.

APPLICATION

1 What are some elements of your self-image that you are in touch with right now?

2 How would these beliefs about yourself affect your success on the job today?

3 If you find some of your beliefs defeating, picture what you'd like to have different and make some notes here about that picture.

Keep these positive self-images in mind and see them for a few minutes several times a day. Later in this book you'll learn some techniques to strengthen these positive self-images.

Meet Your Adult

You've looked at your Child and your Parent in some detail. Now let's consider your Adult. Think of a time when you faced a problem and were able to calmly work out a realistic solution that made sense to you. Your head seemed clear and you could think without undue stress. Relive that situation for a moment.

APPLICATION

1 What was the problem?

2 What were the physical surroundings?

3 What were your thoughts?

4 What was your body language?

5 What did you decide?

While you were in the situation you just described, you were in your Adult ego state. It's important to be able to tell what ego state you're in at any given time. That's not always so easy to do. For most of us it's easier to talk about others' ego states than to recognize our own. That's why we asked you to try to relive a time when you were problem solving—so that you could get an idea of what it's like to be in *your* Adult.

APPLICATION ────────────────────────────────

1 What ego state are you in now? ___Parent ___Adult ___Child

2 How did you decide which one?

Most readers of the test version of this book answered "Adult." If you've been studying this book seriously and working through the exercises in this chapter, the odds are that your Adult is in action. (Remember, the Adult is the objective observer, the fact seeker, the thinker, the problem solver, the estimator, the decision maker, and so on.) However, if you've been thinking critically of this exercise and thinking something like, "What in the world does this have to do with my job?" you may be in your Parent. Or if you are feeling good or sad or angry about having memories stirred up by this exercise, you may be in your Child.

SUMMARY

In this chapter you've begun to explore your personality. You've seen how the Parent ego state often has two major aspects: the Nurturing Parent and the Controlling Parent. A person's Parent also reflects the various ego states of his or her parental figures. The Child ego state has three main parts: the Natural Child, the Little Professor, and the Adapted Child. You've begun to identify the acts, feelings, and thoughts that characterize your own ego states. In the next chapter you will continue to explore your personality and get an even clearer picture of it.

SOURCE NOTES

[1] For further information, see a series of papers by Eric Berne, *Intuition and Ego States* (San Francisco: TA Press, 1977).

[2] Compare this exercise with Dorothy Jongeward et al., *Everybody Wins: Transactional Analysis Applied to Organizations* (Reading, Mass.: Addison-Wesley, 1976), pp. 85–88.

4

Exploring Your Personality

In the previous chapter you had some practice in getting in touch with your ego states. In this chapter you will explore more fully your own ego states.

OBJECTIVES

When you finish this chapter, you'll be able to:

- draw a special bar graph (called a Dusay egogram) to show the relative amount of psychic energy in each of your ego states;
- draw a similar graph to show how you'd like your egogram to be (if different from what it is now);
- identify what ego state would be most useful for various work situations
- describe some techniques for moving your psychic energy out of an undesirable ego state and into a more useful one.

Now we'd like you to focus on what your ego states are like on a typical day at work. The following exercise will help you do this.

APPLICATION

Show how frequently you do each of the following behaviors by placing a check in the proper column opposite each item.

Behavior on the Job	Frequency				
	Almost Never	Rarely	Sometimes	Frequently	Very Frequently
1. I give people reasons why my work isn't done.					
2. I feel bad about something (about what someone did or said to me, or about something I did or said).					

Behavior on the Job	Frequency				
	Almost Never	Rarely	Sometimes	Frequently	Very Frequently
3. I expect people to do what I say.					
4. I send out a questionnaire or carry out a survey to get needed information.					
5. I do what my boss says to do even when it's difficult.					
6. I feel guilty about something (not getting a job done on time, coming in late, working too hard, and so on).					
7. I play a hunch without bothering to gather factual data.					
8. I smile at other people (co-workers, subordinates, customers, superiors, and so on).					
9. I suggest that an ill person see the nurse or take the rest of the day off.					
10. I insist that things be done my way.					
11. I hear a voice in my head saying something like: "Those people should . . ."					
12. When I know something won't be ready when I want it, I repeatedly ask if it might possibly be ready ahead of schedule.					
13. I find ways to make a boring task interesting.					
14. I attend classes, programs, seminars, and so on, to improve my job skills.					

Behavior on the Job	Frequency				
	Almost Never	Rarely	Sometimes	Frequently	Very Frequently
15. I have a feeling that something unusual is about to happen before it happens.					
16. I plan ways to do things that might be considered harmful, illegal, or unethical.					
17. I say (or think) things like: "What would you do without me?"					
18. I do a little dance step when walking into a friend's office or work area.					
19. I correct subordinates when they fail to perform up to standard.					
20. I cleverly figure out how to get my own way at someone else's expense.					
21. I keep calm when in an emotionally charged atmosphere.					
22. I help my co-workers, subordinates, or boss by going a little out of my way to do something for them.					
23. I feel hurt and go off somewhere to be by myself.					
24. I put people down without thinking.					
25. I take a stretch break and really enjoy the feeling of loosening up my muscles and relaxing.					
26. I say "please" and "thank you."					

	Frequency				
Behavior on the Job	Almost Never	Rarely	Sometimes	Frequently	Very Frequently
27. I say or think things like: "I'll do it for them; they can't be expected to handle it."					
28. I talk about facts when another person is in need of comfort.					
29. I take the last one of the doughnuts or other goodies some-one brought for coffee break.					
30. I gather necessary information and then use my sixth sense to make an accurate interpre-tation.					
31. I help out a co-worker in an emer-gency.					
32. I insist that others take care of them-selves—for example, that they wear a coat on a windy day or carry an umbrella if it looks like rain.					
33. I answer the phone in a well-modulated voice, giving my name or the name of my company (or unit).					
34. I slyly work out a way to avoid doing a job that's been assigned to me.					
35. I set people straight when they aren't doing their job properly.					
36. I set standards for proper performance.					

Now that you've filled out the question-naire, let's score it. Here's how to do it.[1]

1 Give yourself a score for each question, using this formula:

4 points for "very frequently"
3 points for "frequently"
2 point for "sometimes"
1 point for "rarely"
0 points for "almost never"

2 Write your scores in the proper boxes in the chart. For example, if you answered question 1 with "some-times," you would put a "2" in the box indicated for question 1. If you answered "very frequently" for question 2, you would put a "4" in the box designated for question 2, and so on.

3 Add the numbers in each column and enter the totals in the spaces provided.

The total for the first column is your score for your CP (Controlling Parent). The total for the column labeled NP is your score for your Nurturing Parent, and so on.

CP = Controlling Parent
NP = Nurturing Parent
A = Adult
NC = Natural Child
LP = Little Professor
AC = Adapted Child

Question No.	Ego State					
	CP	NP	A	NC	LP	AC
1.			□			
2.						□
3.	□					
4.			□			
5.						□
6.						□
7.					□	
8.				□		
9.		□				
10.				□		
11.	□					
12.				□		
13.					□	
14.			□			
15.				□		
16.			□			
17.		□				
18.					□	
19.	□					
20.					□	
21.		□				
22.		□				
23.						□
24.	□					
25.				□		
26.						□
27.		□				
28.			□			
29.				□		
30.					□	
31.		□				
32.		□				
33.						□
34.					□	
35.	□					
36.	□					
Totals						
	CP	NP	A	NC	LP	AC

This questionnaire is *not* intended to be a precise scientific measuring instrument. These scores give an estimate of the way your ego states function. Take the results of this questionnaire seriously but with a grain of salt.

In developing our ego-state questionnaire, we asked a number of people to fill it out and score it. You may find it interesting to see the scores of a police captain:

Controlling Parent	18
Nurturing Parent	3
Adult	15
Natural Child	1
Little Professor	3
Adapted Child	8

John Dusay, M.D., a creative TA expert, points out that we can make a bar graph to show the relative amount of psychic energy a person has in each ego state. He calls these bar graphs egograms.[2] We have taken the liberty of adding the Little Professor because its function is so important on the job. So our egogram for the police captain would look like this:

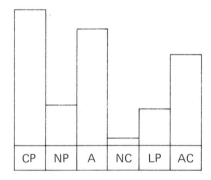

Police Captain

APPLICATION

1 Below are four egograms and descriptions of four different people. Write the letter of each egogram in the blank beside the description it matches.

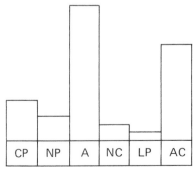

Egogram A

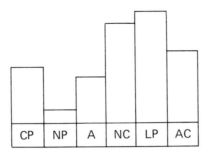

Egogram B

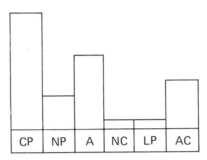

Egogram C

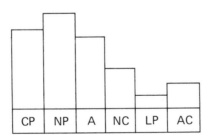

Egogram D

____ (a) Hazel, the librarian, is very scholarly—an expert on literature. She is very polite and proper. Although she knows a tremendous amount about the world, she has experienced little of it.

____ (b) Alfred is a bank manager. He has an intellectual, controlling position. He is so busy collecting data and disciplining employees that he has little time to relax and use his latent intuitive powers.

____ (c) Charlie is a salesperson. He greets customers warmly and shows enthusiasm for his products. He uses his Little Professor to find the right words to say to close a deal with a hesitant customer.

___ (d) Sally, the head nurse, doesn't take any sassiness from her subordinates. She wants things her way. She chose the nursing profession because she's dedicated to helping people.

~ • ~ • ~ • ~ • ~ • ~ • ~ • ~ • ~ • ~ • ~ • ~ • ~ • ~ • ~ • ~

(a) Hazel, the librarian: Egogram A.
(b) Alfred, the bank manager: Egogram C.
(c) Charlie, the salesperson: Egogram B.
(d) Sally, the head nurse: Egogram D.

Note: We are not implying here that all librarians have ego states like Hazel's or that all salespersons have ones like Charlie's. These are fictitious examples to give you practice in working with egograms.

~ • ~ • ~ • ~ • ~ • ~ • ~ • ~ • ~ • ~ • ~ • ~ • ~ • ~ • ~ • ~

2 Now to get a clearer idea of your own ego states, draw your egogram based on the summary of your ego-state scores on page 61. Use these scores as a guide, but include other information (including your Little Professor!) in deciding how to draw it. Start with your highest-scoring ego state and draw a high vertical column for it on the appropriate box below. (Don't worry about its exact height.) Make the columns like this ⊓, not like this ■. (We'll explain why in a little bit.) Next, draw the column for the lowest part of your personality. Finally, draw in the other columns to finish your egogram.

CP	NP	A	NC	LP	AC

(Date) _____

3 Now ask yourself how your egogram relates to the kind of work you've chosen to do and make some notes here:

Every ego state has positive and negative aspects. For example, Margaret was happy with much of her Parent ego state. It gave her firmness when she needed to take a stand with a subordinate and stick to it, and tenderness when a subordinate needed understanding. She felt her Adult was well-informed but that she used it too often in situations where a feeling approach would have been more appropriate. She was happy with most of her Natural Child and Little Professor but was dissatisfied with the way she used her Adapted Child to collect feelings of guilt or anxiety. To clarify her conception of the usefulness of her ego states, Margaret shaded in part of each one to show its *positive* content:

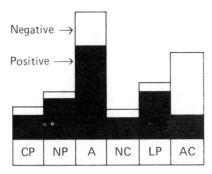

Margaret's Egogram

Think about how you are using your various ego states. Look back at your egogram and shade in the part of each ego state to show the extent to which you are using it positively at work.

APPLICATION ─────────────────────────

You can use this exercise to get in touch with how others see your ego states. Think of a person on the job who knows you well. Picture yourself at work as you think this person sees you. Now write down eight to twelve adjectives that characterize your personality or behavior on the job as you've pictured it in box A below. If you have trouble coming up with eight to twelve adjectives, give yourself a little more time. You may wish to refer to the list of adjectives in Appendix A. You'll get the most from this exercise if you do this before continuing.

Then write down eight to twelve adjectives that describe your ideal self in box B. (If you like a certain adjective in box A, simply put a dash in box B opposite the corresponding number.)

Box A	Box B
1. _____	1. _____
2. _____	2. _____
3. _____	3. _____
4. _____	4. _____
5. _____	5. _____
6. _____	6. _____
7. _____	7. _____
8. _____	8. _____
9. _____	9. _____
10. _____	10. _____
11. _____	11. _____
12. _____	12. _____

Important: Don't read on until you've written out your adjectives or you may pre-
judice yourself.

After Rhoda (one of our test readers) wrote the adjectives in boxes A and
B (dashes show desirable qualities that she didn't want to change), she cate-
gorized them according to what ego states they seemed to go with in her.
Here's how she did it:

Ego States Now	Ideal Self
Box A	**Box B**

Box A	Box B
1. *crabby — CP*	1. *appreciative — AC*
2. *intelligent — A*	2. *——— A*
3. *firm — CP*	3. *——— CP*
4. *decisive — CP*	4. *——— CP*
5. *stubborn — CP*	5. *thoughtful — NP*
6. *quiet — AC*	6. *vivacious — NC*
7. *reserved — AC*	7. *congenial — AC*
8. *helpful — NP*	8. *——— NP*
9. *ethical — CP*	9. *——— CP*
10. *harried — AC*	10. *nonchalant — NC*
11. *rationalizing — A*	11. *rational — A*
12. *manipulating — LP*	12. *perceptive — LP*

Ego state · Number of adjectives associated with each ego state

Ego state	Box A	Box B
CP	= 5	= 3
NP	= 1	= 2
A	= 2	= 2
NC	= 0	= 2
LP	= 1	= 1
AC	= 3	= 2

After summarizing her scores, Rhoda drew two extra egograms—one based
on box A (her ego states now) and one on box B (her ideal self):

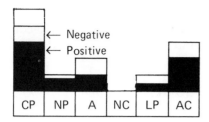

← Negative
← Positive

| CP | NP | A | NC | LP | AC |

Egogram of Rhoda's Ego States Now

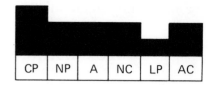

| CP | NP | A | NC | LP | AC |

Egogram of Rhoda's Ideal Self

APPLICATION

Categorize by ego state the adjectives you wrote in boxes A and B in the last application. Then draw two egograms the way Rhoda did.

Ego States Now

Ego state	Number of adjectives
CP =	_____
NP =	_____
A =	_____
NC =	_____
LP =	_____
AC =	_____

Ideal Self

Ego state	Number of adjectives
CP =	_____
NP =	_____
A =	_____
NC =	_____
LP =	_____
AC =	_____

| CP | NP | A | NC | LP | AC |

Egogram of My Ego States Now

(Date) _____

| CP | NP | A | NC | LP | AC |

Egogram of My Ideal Self

(Date) _____

(Don't forget to shade in the *positive* part of each ego state.)

The rest of this book will give you many techniques to help you become your ideal self. Keep this ideal egogram in mind as you read on.

ORGANIZATIONS HAVE EGO STATES TOO

In a certain sense, organizations have personalities just like individuals. For example, an organization that encourages employees at all levels to be creative and spontaneous would have a high Natural Child and Little Professor. An organization in which employees have little freedom to think of better ways of doing things might be thought of as having a high Controlling Parent, low Adult, and high Adapted Child.

Think about your own organization for a moment. Does it encourage employees to be self-reliant decision makers or creative problem solvers? Is anything done to make work fun? Does the organization do anything to take care of its employees? How do most employees respond to directives from management? Are they compliant? Rebellious? Resentful? Cooperative?

APPLICATION

1 With such questions in mind, draw an egogram of your organization. (In drawing it, you may wish to consider how customers perceive your organization.)

CP	NP	A	NC	LP	AC

Egogram of My Organization

(Date)_____

2 How might your organization's egogram affect the egograms of its employees?

3 Now, if you like, draw an egogram of a smaller section in your company such as a department or division or team. You may also want to draw an egogram showing the way you'd like a division, department, or team to be, ideally.

CP	NP	A	NC	LP	AC

Egogram of _____

(Date) _____

CP	NP	A	NC	LP	AC

Egogram of _____

(Date) _____

DEVELOPING EGO-STATE FLEXIBILITY

Each ego state has an appropriate time and place. To realize your potential on the job, it's important to be able to move flexibly from one ego state to another as different situations arise. For example, if you want to think of new and creative ideas to solve a problem, the best ego state is probably the Child, especially your Little Professor. When you want to scrutinize your ideas to pick the best ones, your Adult would be the most appropriate ego state. People who lack ego-state flexibility, however, tend to operate rigidly from one or two ego states and don't use their whole personality, regardless of the situation. The first step in developing more ego-state flexibility is to learn to recognize what ego state is called for in different situations. Here's some practice to help you develop that skill.

APPLICATION

For each of the following situations, show what ego state *or ego states* would most likely be best by checking the proper column(s).

	Ego States					
Situation	Parent		Adult	Child		
	NP	CP		NC	LP	AC
1. One of your subordinates who is usually quite dependable and hard-working has not been performing up to snuff. In talking to him, you discover a close friend of his is seriously ill.						
2. You're unsure of how to advertise a new product. You've narrowed the choices down to either direct-mail advertising or advertising on television.						
3. You want to make a list of some new, way-out ideas to advertise a particular product.						
4. It's time for a break at work. You want to get to know some of your co-workers better but you feel a little anxious about talking to them.						
5. You're walking down a narrow hall-way. Two co-workers are standing in your way carrying on a conversation. They are blocking the entrance to your office, which you are in a hurry to get to.						
6. Some of your subordinates have not been meeting their deadlines.						

~ . ~ . ~ . ~ . ~ . ~ . ~ . ~ . ~ . ~ . ~ . ~ . ~ . ~ . ~ . ~

1. Nurturing Parent: Sympathy and understanding may be the best here. If you do not have a strong Nurturing Parent, you may need to learn appropriate behavior with your Adult. In this case these newly learned behaviors would "sound" Nurturing Parent.
2. Adult: The Adult is good at decision making and in this case may need to collect more information.
3. Little Professor is most likely your best friend here. Your Little Professor, remember, figures things out from many angles. For example, the title of the book *Born to Win* came about from playing with the words "born to lose." The Little Professor doesn't worry about whether ideas are possible, so it's likely to come up with a great quantity of wild, silly ideas. Great! That's exactly what

you want in this situation! Sometimes nutty-*sounding* ideas are winners. The idea for manufacturing razor blades developed when a man named Gillette played with the idea of selling flat, sharpened pieces of metal—an idea that for many years was a big joke to Gillette's friends, but which turned into a gold mine! And the Wright brothers were laughed at for thinking that people could fly.

4. Natural Child and/or Adult: You're using your Adapted Child whenever you have feelings of anxiety about people liking or not liking you. Your Natural Child would clearly be valuable in this situation. In such a situation the problem is that you are using your Controlling Parent to keep your Natural Child locked up. One solution is to activate your Adult by "having a talk" with your Controlling Parent and Adapted Child. Ask the Parent to take it easy and encourage the Natural Child to be expressive.

5. Adapted Child: A simple "excuse me" from your Adapted Child will work fine in this case. Just think what it would be like if your Adult had to solve problems like this anew every time they came up!

6. Adult and Controlling Parent: When people aren't performing as expected, it's important to put your Adult in gear and analyze the situation to discover why.[3] If there's a problem, your Adult needs to check out the reasons and gather information. If the people involved need to be talked to, the firmness most people have in their Controlling Parent comes in handy. But firmness without fairness may not work. So when using your Controlling Parent, check out how effective it actually is. Let your Adult ego state watch your transactions. If your Controlling Parent is arbitrary, authoritarian, and doesn't listen, it needs tempering with your Adult. If it's firm and also fair, you have a useful Controlling Parent.

In this application we've asked you which ego state would probably be best for certain situations. However, although our ego states may have similarities, no two Parent, no two Adult, no two Child ego states are likely to be the same! You can use your Adult and decide which ego state is best for you in a given situation.

Adult as Executive

You can learn to use the qualities of one of your ego states, say your Controlling Parent, while your Adult stays plugged in, carefully monitoring what you do to keep it reasonable and appropriate. This makes the Adult the executive of your personality, which puts *you* in charge. This concept might be diagrammed like this, with the Adult sitting on top of the other ego states:

We'll return to this idea throughout this book.

Raising Your Little Professor and Natural Child

Even when you decide that a particular ego state is best, it's not always so easy to use it. As you progress through this book, you'll learn how to activate various ego states in yourself. This next section will show you how to activate your Little Professor and Natural Child. We'll begin with an example.

Example

Al was a computer-systems salesperson. Around his boss Al tended to use his not-OK Adapted Child more than any other ego state. As a result, he found it hard to assert himself and make his ideas clear. Henry, Al's boss, frequently dismissed Al's ideas as unworkable before allowing him to clarify them. Al's lack of assertiveness also got in the way when his boss made unreasonable demands, requiring him to work overtime without adequate compensation.

One day Al tried something new. Here's what happened. Henry called Al into his office and started to run him into the ground as usual. "You've got a lousy attitude, Al. You waste far too much time helping new customers with their installations. I want you to get rolling. Get out there on the road and make some new contacts. Get some new customers! You hear, boy?"

Al firmly believed that he was doing the right thing by working with new customers and helping them debug their new systems, especially since Henry had decided not to provide these new customers in Al's territory with a service technician to take care of such matters. Usually, Al would sit quietly with butterflies in his stomach, nod passively, make a few weak, defensive statements, and then grudgingly go along with Henry's demands.

But this time Al had a gleam in his eye. He almost seemed to be smiling. Henry was a bit taken aback because Al was not cowering as usual in the face of his demands. He was even more surprised when Al calmly explained his position and asked some intelligent questions that caused him to think that perhaps Al was right.

In the end Al wasn't able to convince Henry, but Al felt good about being able to stand up to Henry and assert himself. He was able to avoid using the not-OK part of his Adapted Child and instead energized his own Little Professor and then plugged in his Adult. How did Al manage this?

Al created a vivid image of Henry sitting before him in only his boxer shorts and socks. Suddenly Henry was no longer threatening! And it was then relatively easy for Al to move psychic energy from his Adapted Child to his Little Professor to his Natural Child and then to his Adult.

APPLICATION ————————————————————————

The ability to plug in your Little Professor the way Henry did can be useful in a wide variety of situations—whether you're in a stressful situation or simply interested in having a little fun during a coffee break or office party. See if you can think of one or more ways of activating your Little Professor and Natural Child (besides the one used by Al).

Other methods for activating your own Little Professor and Natural Child:

~.~.~.~.~.~.~.~.~.~.~.~.~.~.~.~.~.~.~

For activating your Little Professor and Natural Child, you might try
some techniques like these:

— Imagine other people in the nude—a classical technique for
raising one's Natural Child.[4]
— Imagine people as the animals they remind you of. Give them
animal faces. Start dealing with your own false fears by seeing
others in an exaggerated way.
— Elaborate on Al's "underwear analysis" technique in other ways.
You might picture person X with holely (that's holely, not *holy*)
or unusual underwear.

"Far out," you may say. Well, it is—that's the whole idea. It's often more
productive to giggle than to feel inadequate. By creating a bizarre visual image
in your mind, you promote spontaneity and creativity in yourself and unlock
your Little Professor and Natural Child. A nice thing about these techniques
is that no one needs to know that you are using them: you can carry them
out in the privacy of your own fantastic imagination.

SUMMARY

In this chapter you've learned how to draw egograms that reflect the personality of individuals and groups. You can use this to pinpoint where you may want to make a change. You've also learned the importance of flexibility—that ability to change rapidly to fit the situation.

You've been introduced to a few techniques for raising the use of your Little Professor and Natural Child so that you can move energy into your Adult and out of a not-OK space. In future chapters you'll be learning more special techniques for activating positive parts of your other ego states. You'll also be learning techniques for energizing the positive parts of other people's ego states.

SOURCE NOTES

[1] We'd like to thank Wallace Bloom, Ph.D., for suggesting this self-scoring chart.

[2] For a detailed discussion of egograms, see John Dusay's informative book, *Egograms* (New York: Harper & Row, 1977).

[3] An excellent way to activate your Adult when thinking about employees' poor performance is to read Robert Mager and Peter Pipe, *Analyzing Performance Problems* (Belmont, Calif.: Fearon, 1970).

[4] Dorothy Jongeward, *Everybody Wins: Transactional Analysis Applied to Organizations* (Reading, Mass.: Addison-Wesley, 1976), p. 53.

5

Stroking for Doing and Being

In this chapter we'd like to try something a little different. We will *begin* with an exercise. To get the most from it, find a quiet place where you can be alone and relax for a few moments before you begin . . . Ready? OK, go.

STROKELESS-DAY EXERCISE

Part 1

Imagine that it's morning. You jump out of bed. As your feet hit the floor, you realize that something is different. Your feet feel sort of numb, almost as if they're not there. You look down to reassure yourself. You wiggle your toes. You're not quite sure if everything is all right. Something seems strange. Later, as you're leaving for work, you see your new neighbor, Sam, backing his car out of his driveway. You raise your hand to wave. He doesn't respond but drives off with a blank expression on his face. "I guess he didn't see me," you say to yourself, "I guess he was preoccupied with something."

On your way to work you stop as usual at the corner newspaper stand to buy a paper from Barney. "Nice morning, isn't it?" you say as you hand Barney a crisp dollar bill. Barney slaps your change into the palm of your hand, looks at you for a moment, but says nothing. You turn away and walk toward your office wondering, "What did I do to Barney?"

Just as you arrive at work, the elevator doors are about to close. You dash for the elevator. As the doors close in front of you, you get a glimpse of half a dozen people staring expressionlessly past you.

You decide to take the stairs. On the way to your floor, you meet a co-worker. Determined to be friendly despite the cold reception that you've gotten so far, you smile warmly and say brightly, "Good morning, Nina!" Nina continues by you without a word, without looking up.

Finally you reach your floor, eager to see the friendly faces. But when you walk in, no one looks up. Except for the clickety-clack of typewriter keys, you hear nothing. When you close your office door, silence surrounds you. Throughout the day the silence continues: no one listens. no one responds. No one seems to know you're alive. You begin to wonder too.

Now close your eyes and imagine that this is actually happening to you. Imagine it as vividly as you can. Be aware of your thoughts and feelings.

If you are taking this exercise seriously, chances are that you are feeling a bit angry, fearful, or depressed. Perhaps you have experienced the same sort of feeling as a customer. Have you ever stepped up to a counter in a store and nobody waited on you because they were too busy with paper

work at their desks? Have you ever bought groceries from a fast, efficient clerk who didn't look at you, smile, or greet you, but merely said coldly, "That will be $31.58." If this has happened to you, you know what it feels like to be a stroke-deprived customer. In fact, if you really got into this exercise, you may have wondered if you really do exist. If so, you can look forward to the next part of this exercise.

Part 2

Imagine that it's morning. You jump out of bed. You wiggle your toes and realize you're still alive. You make your way to the shower. It feels great as the warm stream of water gently caresses your body. Later, as you're leaving for work, you see your new neighbor, Sam, backing his car out of his driveway. You catch his eye. He smiles brightly and waves at you. You return the wave and feel good about the contact with another human being.

Later you approach the corner newsstand. This time Barney greets you with a snappy handshake. He beams at you and says warmly, "Beautiful day today, isn't it? Look how clear it is—not a cloud in the sky."

As you arrive at work, the elevator doors are about to close. You dash for the elevator, but Neal spots you and quickly catches the door. As you step inside you see half a dozen faces. They're grinning, happy that you were able to make it this trip.

As you walk in the main entrance to your office, the receptionist greets you with a cheery smile. As you pass by a number of desks on the way to your office, you exchange greetings. As you reach your desk, someone comes up to you and says, "Gee, I could hardly wait till you got here this morning. You're really going to like what I've done."

Later, during a coffee break, you laugh and have a good time with your co-workers, telling and listening to jokes.

Part 3

Now imagine the same situation again. This time see yourself receiving even more strokes than in Part 2. For example, see yourself greeting your neighbor warmly, offering Barney a handshake, smiling, talking to the people in the elevator, talking briefly with the receptionist, saying things like, "This report needs some polishing, but there are really good ideas in it." Close your eyes and imagine these scenes now. Then continue reading.

Did you notice how different you felt as you imagined each of these scenes? If you can feel so different simply from imagining these things, just think how much better you and others will feel on the job if you give and receive even more warm fuzzies. Think how good your customers will feel when they're acknowledged and taken seriously. Learning to pass out more warm fuzzies is a major goal of this chapter.

OBJECTIVES

When you finish this chapter, you'll be able to:

- analyze a situation in which employees are not performing as desired and suggest a solution that involves applying certain rules of stroking;
- identify statements that stroke an employee's Adult ego state;
- identify stereotyped stroking patterns on the job;
- identify how you are now using the methods to stroke others and consider whether you wish to expand your repertoire.

THE IMPORTANCE OF STROKES
IN THE BUSINESS WORLD

Good strokes humanize and improve the quality of work life. When companies are relatively small, strokes can come easily. Employees are more often able to talk over their problems with executives, sometimes in the casual atmosphere of the back room. They can bring up problems and chat about how they're doing. They can get more or less direct feedback on the quality of their work.

As companies grow larger, however, employees become farther removed from one another, and people begin to feel smaller. "Nobody listens, nobody cares," they complain. These feelings can usually be traced to a change in the stroke economy. As the organization gets larger, strokes become fewer and more remote. Informal strokes get formalized into things like award banquets and performance appraisals. Such strokes are all right, but they often lack the personal and genuine quality of more spontaneous strokes. Also, formalized strokes often mean fewer strokes.

People need strokes for their sense of survival and well-being on the job. In fact, strokes are a basic unit of motivation. As a general guide:

— The quantity and quality of strokes serves as either positive or negative motivation for employees.
— A good share of the satisfaction we get from work depends on the strokes available from other people.

— We can even get strokes from the activity of work itself—especially if what we're doing really "fits" and we can take responsibility for it.

For positive results on the job, it's crucial to give people positive strokes.[1]

In some organizations, when things are running smoothly, the strokes are few and far between and life at work seems boring—there's no excitement. A crisis offers the only time that people are able to give and get enough strokes. So to get the strokes they need, employees may unwittingly perform poorly so that a crisis develops. Then they get exciting strokes in the process of helping to quell the crisis. What might managers and supervisors do to avoid this situation?

This complex problem has no simple answer. We think the solution lies in setting up a system whereby employees are able to get a lot of positive strokes when things are going well. That will be the focus of this chapter and of much of this book. Allowing workers more autonomy can also be very effective. We'll touch on some ways of doing that in Chapter 17.

GUIDELINES FOR STROKING PERFORMANCE

We've seen that effective stroking is essential to success and satisfaction on the job. Now let's look at some guidelines for stroking performance.

Avoid Stroking Undesirable Behavior

People who conscientiously come to work on time and do a good job may never hear about it for years. For example, Fritz Ritter, a doorman at a huge apartment building on Manhattan's upper West Side, was a top-notch employee but he wasn't stroked for his consistently good performance. Fritz says:

> In 41 years, if I [said I] took 5 days off for foolishness, I would be a liar. Oh, I never take off. I betcha I wasn't late 5 times in 41 years. I'm very on the ball . . . A new guy comes in. He doesn't know nothin', he gets the same pay I do.[2]

Typically, people like Fritz who do a good job don't get stroked, but people who arrive late and goof off get lots of attention. This situation tends to perpetuate mediocrity: *what you stroke is what you get.* Following this principle, avoid stroking a person for undesirable behavior. Instead, think of the *positive* behavior you want and stroke it. It's not uncommon for those of us in organizations to invest 90% of our energy on the negative and only 10% on strengthening the positive.

APPLICATION ————————————————————————

Let's say you would like Frank, a co-worker, to share his communications to head-quarters with you. On Monday you go to Frank and ask him to do just this, explaining why. Tuesday Frank sends you a carbon copy of a memo he sent to headquarters. You discover that he also sent two other memos that he did *not* share with you. Following the rule of thumb we just gave, what would you do?

____(a) Tell Frank you appreciate his sharing one of his memos. Then tell him angrily that you want him to do the same with *all* such memos. Explain why it's important to you.

____(b) Tell Frank that you are upset because he didn't share all his communications to headquarters with you as you asked.

____(c) Tell Frank you appreciate the fact that he shared his memo to headquarters with you. Explain why it's important to you.

~ • ~ • ~ • ~ • ~ • ~ • ~ • ~ • ~ • ~ • ~ • ~ • ~ • ~ • ~ • ~ • ~

(c). Refrain from complaining about Frank's undesirable behavior. Instead, focus only on what he did right, stroke him for that, and then stop. This would likely leave Frank with a good feeling and also increase the likelihood that he would share more memos with you. If you complain, you are, in effect, stroking Frank for *not* doing what you asked him to do. Remember people will often unconsciously work to get cold pricklies, especially if they aren't getting their share of warm fuzzies.

Time Your Strokes

In addition to staying positive, it's also important to time your strokes carefully. To be most effective in motivating a person, *a stroke should come as soon as possible after desirable performance.* For example, if Shirley is going to stroke Priscilla for a good job of making out the stock report, she should do it just as soon as she decides that the report is well done. If Shirley waits until the end of the day (even worse, the end of the week), the stroke will lose its effectiveness. If immediacy is impossible, however, it certainly doesn't *hurt* to say to a person, "I never got around to telling you this when it happened, but I want you to know that . . ."

Stroke Approximations

Chances are that some people who report to you have difficulty in meeting agreed-to standards of performance. In these cases it's usually a good idea to stroke positively for slight approximations of the final desired performances you expect. We're using the word "approximation" in a special sense here, meaning a behavior (or result of a behavior) that is approaching a desired standard.

When an infant flails its arms in the direction of a rattle, it is making an approximation of grasping the rattle. Similarly, the cooing and gurgling of a three-month-old is an approximation of the animated speech that may be pouring from its mouth at age two. Although muscle development is important to speech, positive feedback is equally important even for small changes. What would have happened if our parents had waited for us to talk fluently before they stroked us for those cute sounds that came out of our mouths? We would probably still be babbling, gurgling, and cooing. We might even be entirely mute.[3] The important point here is that *it is often vital to stroke approximations!*

Instead of waiting for perfect or near-perfect performance, we can all motivate people by stroking them for *successive approximations*, each of which comes closer to our desired standard of performance.

On any job, a beginner's rate of work is likely to be less than that of an experienced worker. But whatever the beginner's rate, it should be recognized as an approximation of the typical rate and given positive attention. Many people have a fear of failure, a "be perfect" Parent tape that plays in their heads even when they are just starting to learn a new skill. By stroking them for approximations, you'll put them more at ease and help them along the road to success.

APPLICATION ─────────────────────────────────

Suppose Mary, a new bank teller, is working with Lee who is giving her some one-to-one training. She is accurate, fast, and efficient, but too brusque with customers. She rarely smiles, greets customers, or says "thank you" or "good-bye." Lee tells Mary he is happy with her accuracy and efficiency. He then goes on to say that her performance would be even better if she were more courteous and polite to customers. Lee agrees with Mary that he'll give her a lot of feedback on this until she begins to master the desired performance. Mary wants to improve her performance and thanks Lee for his concern. Later, as Lee watches Mary, he notices that she is now greeting customers but still not smiling or thanking them or saying "good-bye." What should he do?

___ (a) Criticize Mary for not being friendly enough even after having been instructed how to do so.

___ (b) Let Mary know that he's happy that she is greeting customers.

___ (c) Avoid stroking Mary for her performance until she learns to be friendly to customers in an acceptable manner.

___ (d) Stroke Mary's improvements and then immediately point out what else she needs to do.

~ · ~ · ~ · ~ · ~ · ~ · ~ · ~ · ~ · ~ · ~ · ~ · ~ · ~ · ~ · ~ · ~

(b) Lee should give Mary positive feedback for greeting customers because that's an approximation of what both Lee and Mary really want; it's a step in the right direction. Ideally, Lee should avoid complaining about her inadequate performance. However, he might take notes on her performance and talk to her about it later, making positive suggestions.

Note: If you wait until people perform at the mastery level, you may never stroke them and they may never know they're going in the desired direction. Stroking approximations is especially important when an employee will probably be unable to perform a complex procedure right the first time. However, sometimes you can't afford to make approximations—performance must be up to standard the minute people start to work. In such cases supervisors must give employees plenty of practice under training conditions, where it's perfectly legal (and desirable!) to stroke approximations.

Raise the Criteria for Stroking

Of course, it's not enough just to stroke approximations. Eventually you want to be stroking mastery performance, so you must gradually raise your criteria for stroking. A criterion is a rule or guideline for deciding whether something is acceptable. In Mary's case, Lee correctly decided that if Mary made any improvement at all in her dealings with customers, he'd let her know he noticed the improvement. In other words, he set a low criterion for stroking. But as Mary becomes more adept at greeting customers, Lee can raise his criterion. That is, he can wait until Mary not only greets customers verbally, but also smiles and perhaps thanks them before he compliments her for her good performance. As Mary improves, Lee will be encouraging higher levels of performance.

We'd like to stress that when Lee withholds or gives out strokes, he is not doing it to manipulate Mary: Lee and Mary are both working toward the same objective. Recall that Lee openly discussed the situation with Mary and that they agreed that he would be giving her special feedback as he saw her meeting their goals.

Pace Your Strokes

When people are learning something new, they are likely to be a bit shaky and need reassurance. So it helps to stroke them consistently each time they perform well. This clarifies standards—with feedback they know how they're doing and where to concentrate their efforts.

Once people are on their way and are getting more strokes for the activities they are performing well, they begin to need fewer strokes from their supervisors for particular performance. When this happens, gradually phase out your *consistent* stroking and begin to offer strokes intermittently as follow-up or reminders. As you gradually make the interval between these strokes longer and longer, improved performance will be likely to continue at a high level. For example, when Mary first masters the art of dealing with customers courteously, efficiently, and accurately, Lee should stroke her *each time* she demonstrates this high level of performance. But as time goes on, he can gradually stroke her for it less frequently. (After all, Lee can't afford to stand behind Mary forever, and Mary would soon be bored or angry with him if he did.) Even after Mary is working on her own, however, Lee should continue to let her know he notices and appreciates her high-level performance. The more spontaneous Lee can be with this feedback, the better.

Remember, the purpose of stroking performance is not to control people like puppets on a string but to help them reach mutually agreed-on goals. If strokes are not given sincerely and honestly, if they are given only to manipulate other people into performance they don't want to give, they usually won't have the desired effect. People sense when strokes aren't genuine and tend to reject them.

So stroke consistently at first, then intermittently. Don't just suddenly stop offering strokes simply because you feel they're not needed anymore. If you do this, performance may suddenly stop!

APPLICATION ────────────────────────────────

1 Let's see if you can apply some of the guidelines you've learned about stroking.
   One telephone company had a rather high absentee rate among 38 operators,
   about 12%. Usually individuals or groups who had *perfect* attendance records
   were given special recognition at the end of the month by their supervisor, Bob.
   They were called into Bob's office for fifteen minutes and told how good they
   were. This was supposed to happen every month, but actually it didn't. Sometimes two or three months went by before Bob called employees in for this
   fifteen-minute chat. Some employees commented that if they missed a day early
   in the month, they had already messed up their attendance record, so it made
   little difference if they took a day off later. Employees who had poor attendance
   records were also called into the boss's office and talked to for fifteen minutes
   about how they had to improve. Which of our guidelines was Bob following?

___(a) Stroke immediately after desirable performance occurs.

___(b) Stroke approximations.

___(c) Raise your criteria for stroking.

___(d) Stroke consistently at first, then intermittently.

___(e) Avoid stroking undesirable behavior.

___(f) None of these.

   ~•~•~•~•~•~•~•~•~•~•~•~•~•~•~•~•~•~

   (f) Bob wasn't following any of our guidelines.

   ~•~•~•~•~•~•~•~•~•~•~•~•~•~•~•~•~•~

2 What might Bob do to follow each of the guidelines?

   (a) Stroke immediately after desired performance occurs.

   (b) Stroke approximations.

   (c) Raise the criteria for stroking.

   (d) Stroke consistently at first, then intermittently.

(e) Avoid stroking undesirable behavior.

3 Before giving you possible answers to the previous question, we'd like to discuss an actual solution to the attendance problem that was developed by Daniel Grady, a division manager.[4] Grady suggested that the attendance records be put on a weekly basis, and that Bob make *only* brief (fifteen-second) *positive* comments to operators on their good attendance records. Before, with the monthly record-keeping, an employee had to have perfect attendance a full month before being stroked. By changing the recordkeeping to a weekly basis, Grady made it easier for employees to get feedback and to be successful. Under this system, the absentee rate dropped from 12% to 4.5–5%. When the new system was suddenly stopped, the rate shot up to 12%. When it was restored, the absentee rate settled back to 4.5–5%.

Which principles did Grady's system apply?

___ (a) Stroke as soon as possible after desirable performance.

___ (b) Stroke approximations.

___ (c) Raise the criteria for stroking.

___ (d) At first stroke consistently, then intermittently.

___ (e) Avoid stroking undesirable behavior.

~ • ~ • ~ • ~ • ~ • ~ • ~ • ~ • ~ • ~ • ~ • ~ • ~ • ~ • ~ • ~

The new system applied principles (b) (stroke approximations) and (e) (avoid stroking undesirable behavior). By changing the recordkeeping to a weekly basis, Grady was stroking approximations. Perfect attendance for a week is an approximation of perfect attendance for a whole month. In limiting comments to positive remarks on good attendance, Bob avoided stroking undesirable behaviors. (Remember, cold pricklies can sometimes actually serve to maintain the very behavior that is unproductive. *What you stroke is what you get!*)

Dan Grady's system applied two of the guidelines we've listed for improving performance through more effective stroking. Let's look at how the other guidelines could be applied to this situation. (Compare your answers to question 2 with these.)
  — *Stroke desired behavior immediately after it occurs.* Bob might stroke each person on a daily basis instead of at the end of the month or week. This might be done by greeting employees cheerfully when they arrive with something like, "Good to see you, Hank," or "Bill, am I glad you're here today. We really need you."
  — *Stroke approximations.* One way to stroke approximations would be to give people strokes for perfect attendance for a week as Grady did. You may have thought of other ways to stroke an approximation of the desired behavior of near-perfect attendance.

For example, another approach might to be stroke employees for slight improvement in their attendance records. Gladys, who had a record of coming to work seventeen times a month, might be stroked for coming to work eighteen times in one month.

— *Raise the criteria for stroking.* Bob might gradually require better attendance records from people before giving them special strokes for attendance, especially with employees who started with poor attendance records. Gladys, who typically came to work only seventeen days a month, could be given positive strokes for coming eighteen days during the first months of the program. In later months the criterion for giving Gladys special strokes could be raised so she would get recognition for increasingly better attendance. Finally, she would be stroked only for perfect or near-perfect attendance. You could raise the criteria in other ways, too. Consider your answer correct if you said something about gradually waiting for a higher level of performance before stroking.

— *At first stroke consistently, then intermittently.* Bob could apply this principle by stroking employees regularly every week for perfect attendance for, say, the first six weeks of the program. Once a high rate of attendance was established, he could begin to give the special strokes for attendance intermittently (sometimes after two weeks, sometimes after three weeks, sometimes for two weeks in succession, and so on).

— *Avoid stroking undesirable behavior.* Bob could apply this principle by paying attention only to the employees' good attendance records and not focusing on poor attendance. Notice that in Grady's approach, Bob was instructed to comment very briefly— for fifteen seconds or less. This was done because in fifteen seconds it's fairly easy to limit one's strokes to warm fuzzies. (Supervisors who are learning how to give positive strokes— perhaps for the first time—may also find this fifteen-second rule useful.)

Earshotting

Another useful technique for stroking performance is thirdhand stroking. When you give a thirdhand stroke, you don't talk directly to the person you're stroking; instead you talk to a third party when the person you intend to stroke is within earshot. Hence the term *earshotting.* [5]

Often earshotting strokes are used negatively with negative results. Many parents use earshotting in a negative way when they talk about their children's misdeeds in their presence. Husbands and wives may also negatively earshot each other. For example, John uses negative earshotting with Martha when he talks about her to his friends in a negative way in her presence:

John: "Yeah, she can't walk through a grocery store without falling for every trick Madison Avenue dreams up."

Martha may do the same thing:

> Martha: "Yes, and every time he walks through a camera store, he has to pick out a new expensive toy to play with."

Earshotting strokes can be very effective, however, when used positively. For example, Mrs. Labonchi, a sixth-grade teacher, made a point of positively earshotting at least one of her students whenever a visitor came into her room. Her students beamed when she said things like, "Oh, Mr. Green, come over here. Let me show you what Megan is doing," or "Mrs. Samuels, have you seen the fine work Ronnie has done on his science project? Let me show it to you." Positive earshotting can be a useful way to give strokes on the job.

APPLICATION ————————————————————

1 List some on-the-job situations in which positive earshotting might be used.

2 Why do you think positive earshotting might be more effective for some people than direct stroking?

3 Here's another problem situation. Bonnie's job was to talk to customers over the phone and to answer their questions. She often had to call other departments to get needed information and then call a customer back. She was pressured by her supervisor to call customers back within ninety minutes. Many times she wasn't able to do this because Alan's department wasn't calling *her* back soon enough. Usually she had to call Alan's department three times before getting a response. What could Bonnie do to improve this situation, using each of the six guidelines we've discussed?

~ . ~ . ~ . ~ . ~ . ~ . ~ . ~ . ~ . ~ . ~ . ~ . ~ . ~ . ~ . ~ . ~

1 Answers will vary. You might use positive earshotting in any one of these situations:

   — When introducing someone: for example, when introducing Wade to Ben you might stroke Wade by telling Ben about some special skill that Wade has.
   — When speaking in a meeting: for example, when speaking at a staff meeting where Pat is in attendance, you might point out her special qualifications or achievements.
   — When a VIP visits your work area: for example, you might make a point of telling the visitor about the especially good job Steve is doing (as Mrs. Labonchi did).

You may have listed other ways to use earshotting in your situation.

2 Sometimes an earshotting stroke is more intense than a direct stroke. All of us like to hear good things being said about us. Because a third person is involved, the stroke may seem especially sincere. By the same token, a negative earshotting stroke can be particularly devastating.

3 Bonnie could do a number of things to apply the six principles we've discussed. Basically her approach would involve stroking Alan's department in some way for prompt callbacks. She might call them on the phone to compliment them, go to meet them in person, or send them a series of complimentary memos. In this actual situation Bonnie used the techniques described below to improve her situation.[6]

   — *Stroke the desired behavior immediately after it occurs.* Bonnie sent a thank-you note to Alan's department as soon as she got a callback from them that showed an improvement in response time. The notes were effective, partly because she sent the notes immediately. If she had waited until the end of the week, the people involved might not have remembered what the note referred to.
   — *Stroke approximations.* Bonnie didn't wait until Alan's department was returning calls promptly (within ninety minutes) before she sent them a note. When Alan's department returned a call to her after she called them twice, she thanked them for their help. (Typically she had to call three times!) Responding to her *second* call was an improvement and an approximation of responding to her first call.
   — *Raise the criteria for stroking.* Later, Bonnie waited until she got a callback from Alan's department after the first request before sending them a thank-you note. Even later she raised the criterion higher by sending a note only when the callback came within two hours. She continued to raise the criterion until she was stroking them for calling her back with the needed information within ninety minutes.

— *At first stroke consistently, then intermittently.* Once Alan's department was in the habit of calling her back within ninety minutes, Bonnie continued to send them notes after each call-back for a week or so. Then Bonnie gradually began to withdraw the special strokes. But she continued to stroke Alan's department occasionally.

— *Avoid stroking undesirable behavior.* When Alan's department failed to respond to a request for information, Bonnie did *not* complain, either verbally or in writing. Instead she firmly repeated her requests for information in a calm voice using her Adult ego state. In this way she avoided giving Alan's department any cold pricklies for failing to perform.

— *Earshotting.* We don't know whether Bonnie actually used earshotting in this case. But she might have done so by telling others about the fine job that Alan's department was doing at, say, a group meeting where someone from Alan's department was present or maybe even in front of Alan's manager.

Reminders for Stroking

Another effective way to stroke others is to display a record of their performance. A displayed checklist, assignment sheet, or chart that shows people are performing at a high level can be a reminder to stroke them. (It can also remind people to stroke themselves.) Such a record gives both supervisor and subordinate a clear idea of what is expected. This helps to avoid psychological game playing (see more about games in Chapter 6). Here are some examples of performance records:

Achievement Checklist		
Milestone	Due Date	Date Completed
1. Draft of advertising copy.	10/10	(10/8!)
2. Advertising copyedited.	10/24	(10/21!)
3. Rough layout of artwork.	11/15	
4. Artist's composition approved.	11/30	
5. Camera-ready copy ready for printer.	12/13	
6. Brochures printed.	1/10	
7. Brochures mailed.	1/22	

←—— *Supervisor has circled these dates and added exclamation marks to express delight at seeing milestones achieved ahead of time.*

Assignment Sheet				
Date Assigned	Person Responsible	Assignment	Due Date	Date Finished
1/7	Pat	Develop new training program for sales force.	7/15	
1/7	Sue	Prepare a set of performance standards for loan-processing department.	2/8	
1/8	John	Make FNMA bid.	1/15	
1/8	Alfred	Find a lender willing to make a reverse repo agreement.	1/10	
1/9	Jeff	Fix price for FHA package.	1/16	

Productivity Chart

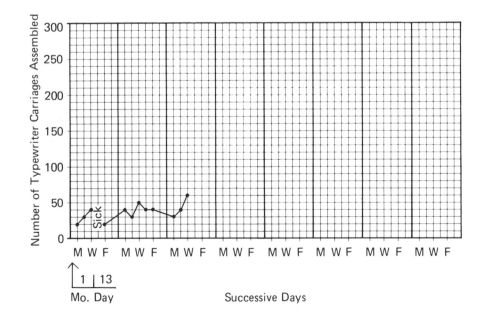

APPLICATION ——————————————————————

A company adopted a procedure of packing small packages into large containers as a way of cutting handling and delivery times to airlines.[7] Managers had exhorted the dock workers to use the large containers as described above. The managers assumed that containers were being used 90% of the time when possible. However, when they collected actual data (plugged in their Adult), they found that the containers were being used only 45% of the possible time. The dock workers were skilled: they did not need instruction on how to use the containers. Using some of the ideas we've just discussed, describe what you might do to motivate the employees to make better use of the containers.

~ • ~ • ~ • ~ • ~ • ~ • ~ • ~ • ~ • ~ • ~ • ~ • ~ • ~ • ~ • ~ • ~ • ~

This problem might be handled in many different ways. Compare your ideas with what was actually done in this situation. Dock workers were given checklists and asked to mark each time they used a container. At the end of each shift, workers totaled their results to see if they hit a goal of 90%. Managers avoided criticizing when performance was not satisfactory. Instead, supervisors and regional managers looked over the checklists and complimented workers for *any* improvement in performance. If workers made no improvements, supervisors looked for *something* else they could compliment them for. For example, they praised workers for keeping an honest record of their use of containers. This approach worked! Nine out of ten times it was used, container use increased from 45% to 95% in a single day! The improved performance has been maintained for several years. Because of these procedures the company saved more than $3,000,000 in three years!

Notice that the checklists served as *reminders* for *positive stroking.* Managers and supervisors avoided negative stroking. Instead they stroked *approximations* by complimenting workers for improvements and honest recordkeeping.

WAYS OF STROKING

Stereotyped Stroking

When stroking performance, it's also important to be aware of our pattern of stroking the ego states of others. Sometimes we don't distribute strokes equally—one ego state may get all the strokes and the others none. If we're fixed in a stroking pattern, we are often unaware of its consequences. One example of a stereotyped pattern is illustrated by the following application.

APPLICATION

Suppose that Lisa and Ted both have the same job and carry out similar tasks equally well. Without knowing them or their supervisors, take a guess at these questions.

1 Ted probably gets stroked most for being:

_____ (a) Intelligent

_____ (b) Decisive

_____ (c) Controlling

_____ (d) Self-reliant

_____ (e) Cute

_____ (f) Dependent

_____ (g) Nurturing

_____ (h) Decorative

_____ (i) Aggressive

2 Lisa probably gets stroked most for being:

_____ (a) Intelligent

_____ (b) Decisive

_____ (c) Controlling

_____ (d) Self-reliant

_____ (e) Cute

_____ (f) Dependent

_____ (g) Nurturing

_____ (h) Decorative

_____ (i) Aggressive

3 Which ego states in Ted probably get the most strokes?

4 Which ego states in Lisa probably get the most strokes?

~ • ~ • ~ • ~ • ~ • ~ • ~ • ~ • ~ • ~ • ~ • ~ • ~ • ~ • ~ • ~ • ~

Although we don't know Ted and Lisa and their job situation, from our experience with these questions in training groups we would say that Ted is *most likely* being stroked for (a) intelligent, (b) decisive, (c) controlling, (d) self-reliant, and (i) aggressive behaviors; Lisa, for (e) cute, (f) dependent, (g) nurturing, and (h) decorative behaviors. Ted's *Adult* and *Controlling Parent* are probably getting stroked the most, while Lisa's *Child* and *Nurturing Parent* are probably getting stroked the most.

Traditionally women commonly have gotten strokes for such things as appearance, cuteness, niceness, neatness, quietness—strokes for their Adapted Child ego states. In contrast, men have gotten strokes for such things as performance, leadership, decision making, achievement—strokes for their Adult ego states. These cultural patterns for stroking continue in many organizations today even though the roles of men and women have changed. Since everyone can use *all* their ego states, it's a good idea to become aware of stereotyped stroking and to move toward more balanced stroking of ego states.

Sometimes supervisors complain that female employees are not as self-reliant, decisive, or logical as they should be. Sometimes men are described as insensitive, without feeling. Can you see how this might happen if the stroking patterns are stereotyped, if only part of each personality gets recognition? It works like a self-fulfilling prophecy.

APPLICATION ─────────────────────────────

Tim, a supervisor, became aware of the stereotyped way in which he stroked women. He expected an adult's day's work but rarely stroked for achievement, goal setting, performance, or decisiveness. He teased the women in the office and stroked them for being attractive. He directed lots of strokes toward the Child. He is now trying to encourage the women who work for him to use their *Adult* ego states more. Which of these strokes would be most appropriate for this purpose?

____ (a) A warm smile and a wink.

____ (b) A cheery "Hello."

____ (c) "I like the way you always do such a good job of making the coffee, straightening up my desk, and taking care of the mail distribution."

____ (d) "Thanks for ordering an extra supply of these catalogs. You showed good judgment in doing that."

____ (e) "Would you reflect on this and then let me know how you think we might reach that goal?"

___ (f)   "I really appreciate your vivaciousness; it's fun to work with you."

~ • ~ • ~ • ~ • ~ • ~ • ~ • ~ • ~ • ~ • ~ • ~ • ~ • ~ • ~

Items (d) and (e) would be most appropriate for stroking the girls' Adult ego states. (Just kidding. We mean the *women's* Adult ego states. That really makes the point, doesn't it?) You might have noticed that some of the other strokes may be quite appropriate or helpful in certain situations. If a person is vivacious, for example, there's nothing wrong with stroking that person for his or her Child—the Child is valuable in many work situations. It's the appropriateness and productiveness of the strokes that count.

Nonverbal Stroking

So far we have focused on verbal stroking—stroking with *spoken* words. But we can also stroke others in nonverbal ways (including *written* words). Let's discuss a few.

Physical Touch

The most direct and often the most powerful stroke is the kind that involves physical touch—a pat on the arm, shoulder, or back, a hearty handshake, or a warm hug. Every group has rules for what kind of touch seems appropriate, but all too frequently we hold back on even those contact strokes. There are times, however, when physical touch is OK on the job. When it is appropriate and genuine, it adds an important dimension to the quality of contact between people.

Body Language

Our body language also delivers our messages without spoken words. For example:

Eyes turned up through batting eyelashes convey something different than downcast eyes.

Folded arms convey something different than relaxed, open arms.

A tightly set jaw conveys something different than a broad, warm smile.

Often our body language is part of our Blind Self. We don't realize we are *constantly* sending messages with our bodies by the way we use:

— gestures,
— posture, and
— facial expressions.

Eye contact is an important aspect of body language. Often eye contact alone results in either a warm fuzzy or cold prickly. Have you ever felt chilled to the bone after someone gave you an icy glance or happy when someone beamed at you with a twinkle in the eye?

When we give verbal strokes and body-language strokes together, the messages should jibe with each other. For example, if you intend to give Hal a warm fuzzy by complimenting him, yet you frown and look away, your intended compliment may well be perceived as a cold prickly. Similarly, a cold "Yes, you do write good reports" doesn't motivate more good reports.

It's not always so easy to make one's verbal and nonverbal messages fit each other. People who find it difficult to express themselves face to face may give better strokes through written messages.

Written Messages

If you find it hard to say anything warm or complimentary, consider expressing your appreciation through the written word.

For example, Martha, a fourth-grade teacher, wanted to start positively stroking Tommy, a "problem" student, for making improvements in his classroom behavior. But she felt so resentful toward Tommy that she was afraid that her attempts at giving warm fuzzies would come across as sarcastic cold pricklies. She solved her dilemma by writing Tommy notes complimenting him for his improved behavior. Tommy kept every note she wrote, and in the long run these notes broke the ice between them. Similarly you may wish to stroke co-workers, subordinates, or even bosses with brief handwritten notes. One added value of a handwritten positive stroke is that the person who gets it can save it and reread it from time to time. More on that later.

On the job, a memo or printout that *shares information* with employees can be an effective written stroke. Hoarding information is a common management problem. For example, one company had scads of computer-generated information about sales but its national sales force of sixty people got none of it. Much of the information was useless to management but meant a great deal to the individual sales representatives. When the decision was finally made to send out regional printouts, the sales representatives had detailed feedback on their work they'd never had before. Besides getting valuable feedback, the sharing of this information increased the sales representatives' trust in management because now they felt more a part of a team effort.

Gifts

Another nonverbal way to stroke a person is to give a gift. We're not talking about buttering up or bribing someone, but rather a spontaneous act of thoughtfulness or a planned honor for service or an outstanding performance. For example, one hospital staff member gave another a poster to hang on his filing cabinet. Such gifts tend to feel good to the Child. They say in an important way, "I like you" or "I like your work." You may remember how good it felt when someone brought you a trinket because they were thinking of you.

APPLICATION

Now that we've explored various ways of effective stroking, try exploring your own stroking patterns.

1 Think of a person who depends on you for strokes. _____

2 How do you stroke this person—with spoken words, physical touch, body language, written messages, gifts, or what?

3 Are the strokes positive or negative? _____

4 If you were this person and getting the kinds of strokes that you give, what would they feel like?

5 Looking at it from the other person's point of view, do you see more productive methods to stroke this person? ___ Yes ___ No

6 If so, what are they?

7 Visualize yourself giving these more productive strokes. How would you look?

Sound?

Feel?

Organizational Stroking Patterns

Not only do individuals have stroking patterns, but so do groups.[8] Business organizations are no exception—they reward certain kinds of behavior and criticize or even ignore other kinds. Just like individuals, groups have blind spots and may not be clearly aware of their stroking patterns.

For example, company X rewarded being young in an effort to put forth a youthful, aggressive image. One fifty-year-old male employee whose productivity showed a whopping 50% increase was passed up for a raise.

Corporation Y rewarded climbers and put down people who had found their niche and liked it. As a consequence, they had several managers who had moved up to their "level of incompetence" and got stuck.[9]

Organization Z gave positive strokes to people who devoted their lives to their work to the detriment of their personal lives and health (a game called *Harried*), even though encouraging this bent defeated the person and eventually the organization.

Notice that organizations have another basic way to stroke people on the job: they can pay a fair salary or wage. Bonuses and raises can be effective strokes for motivating employees to be *responsible* and *productive*. Of course, people need money to meet their basic needs. Often, however, money paid to employees is a *maintenance stroke*. Once basic needs are met, other values and other kinds of recognition become more important. To be most effective, money needs to be accompanied by strokes for personal worth and an honest challenge to the unique potentials of the individual. These are best achieved when personal and organizational goals mesh.

APPLICATION ─────────────────────────────

The leaders of another corporation analyzed their stroking pattern and realized that they were stroking people merely for putting in time rather than for skills and productivity. This was causing some definite problems in production, because proper production depended on the work of certain skilled people who were in short supply. Company policy, however, dictated that before people could be promoted to meet the shortage, they had to go through a mandatory three-year apprenticeship training program no matter how quickly they learned the skills. How might this organizational stroking pattern be changed so that there would no longer be a shortage of highly skilled workers?

~・~・~・~・~・~・~・~・~・~・~・~・~・~・~・~・~・~

The actual solution arrived at by the IBM Corporation was to stop requiring the three-year apprenticeship program. Instead managers told workers, "We'll promote you into this advanced job and raise your pay just as fast as you learn it and improve your productivity."[10] Results were dramatic. For most people, the three-year training program was cut to six months! Shortages of skilled people disappeared. (You may have had some other ideas for eliminating the shortage.)

STROKES FOR BEING

So far we've stressed stroking performance almost exclusively, but it's also important to stroke people simply because they're there, because they exist. Such stroking is not only reassuring but it also feels especially good. It tells others that you know they're there and that you care about them as people. People need both kinds of strokes. If you stroke others *only* when they have carried out some specific performance, your strokes may be interpreted as plastic (people see right through them), manipulative, or cold.

Subordinates who consistently get only performance strokes often say things like, "The only time Don ever comes to talk to me is when he wants me to work an extra night. That man just doesn't give a hoot about people." What they are really saying is, "I'd sure like some strokes for my Child. Work seems better when it feels good to be here."

In many work situations people are stroke-deprived. As a result such people tend to be grouchy, lethargic, unproductive, and sometimes even sabotaging. But in work situations where people stroke each other freely just for being, people feel better about themselves and each other and are likely to put more energy into their work. In one elementary-school principal's office, such an atmosphere prevailed. In a tape-recorded, unpublished conversation, the principal described it like this:

It's small. It's close. We enjoy being around each other all the time. We do a lot of joking, a lot of kidding. Never a putdown. We have fun. Like we all got together and decided what color to paint the building. Someone said, "Let's have a mural." There's constant brainstorming around here. Not formal, but a discussion will turn into a brainstorm. We decided to have trees painted on the side of the building.

It's a neat place to be. We go on hikes together. See, we have the land. I'll go out with one of the teachers or my secretary. Have you noticed I lost a lot of weight? I lost 17 pounds! We're on a diet together. Every Wednesday we weigh in. We're like a family. We even give each other backrubs.

You know, when people know each other at the gut level, and really care about each other and touch each other, they work together smoothly because the communication is like electricity. There are a lot of things you don't have to say because you know people: just by looking at them, they know what you want.

Stroking others for being is rewarding simply because it feels good to do it. If we stroke others with one hand while holding out the other for a return stroke, we will probably feel disappointed. Although it's unwise to expect strokes in return for those we give, strokes do tend to boomerang. Often you get more back than you give. Here's an example from *Try Giving Yourself Away* by David Dunn:

It did not take me long, after I took up giving-away as a hobby, to discover that it is virtually impossible to give yourself away without getting back more than you give—*provided you give away with no thought of any reward.* As Seneca, the Roman philosopher, wrote: "There is no grace in a benefit that sticks to the fingers."

Usually the return comes in some wholly unexpected form, perhaps long after you have forgotten the giving-away episode.

For example, one Sunday morning an important special delivery letter was delivered to my home, though it was addressed to me at my office and the post office would have discharged its obligation by attempting to deliver it there. I wrote the postmaster a note of appreciation.

More than a year later I was in pressing need of a post office box for a new enterprise I was starting. The clerk at the window told me there were no boxes available, that my name would have to go on a long waiting list.

I appealed to the assistant postmaster, who told me the same thing. As I started to leave, keenly disappointed, the postmaster appeared in the doorway of his adjoining office. He had overheard the conversation and my name had caught his ear.

"Are you the David Dunn who wrote us that nice letter a year or so ago about our delivering a special delivery to your home one Sunday morning?" I said I was.

"Well, you don't know what a letter like that means to us. We usually get nothing but kicks. You are certainly going to have a box in this post office if we have to *make* one for you."

A few days later I had a box. Bread upon the waters.[11]

One of the things that makes it fun to stroke others for being is that we never know when a boomeranging stroke will come sailing our way.

An excellent way to stroke others for being is to show them our appreciation without any thought of "modifying their behavior." David Dunn expresses this well when he says:

In our working relations we should try to remember that the girl at the next counter, the man at the next bench or machine, the person at the adjoining desk or in the next office, is a human being first of all, and after that a salesperson, machinist, cost accountant, or department head. And all human beings hunger for appreciation.

Leaving a friendly train of little sparks of appreciation is largely a matter of cultivating the habit of reflecting your happiness by expressing it to the people around you. It will prove a heart-warming habit—for them and for you.[12]

APPLICATION ───

Mike was business-minded and didn't seem to have time for anything that wasn't directly tied to increased productivity. He was applying all the principles he knew regarding stroking subordinates for performance. Yet they didn't seem to respond. They even seemed to resent it when he would compliment them for doing a job well. What might be the problem? What might Mike do to improve his relationship with his subordinates?

~ • ~ • ~ • ~ • ~ • ~ • ~ • ~ • ~ • ~ • ~ • ~ • ~ • ~ • ~ • ~ • ~

Mike seems to be stroking his subordinates only when they perform up to standard. Perhaps if he would warm up and stroke them just for being around—just because they're people—they might be more receptive to strokes he gives them for performance.

We've discussed the importance of strokes and when and how to stroke. But to put these ideas to use for yourself, you may wish to gather some information (for your Adult) about your personal stroking patterns as well as those of your organization. Try the following exercise and see what you discover.

APPLICATION: Stroke-Awareness Exercise ─────────────────────

Part 1: Your Early Childhood Strokes

Often the way you are stroked and the way you stroke others *today* is related to the way you were stroked as a child. The following exercise should help you get in touch with your early childhood strokes so you can better understand your present patterns.

1 Think of a parent or parent figure who had authority over you when you were

 a young child. Write that person's name here: _____

2 What percentage of the strokes that you got from this person consisted of warm

 fuzzies as opposed to cold pricklies? _____

3 Of all the strokes that you received from this person, about what percentage was directed toward your own:

Nurturing Parent? _____

Controlling Parent? _____

Adult? _____

Natural Child? _____

Little Professor? _____

Adapted Child? _____

4 So you can visualize your answers to question 3, make a bar diagram to show the relative number of strokes different parts of your ego states got.

NP	CP	A	NC	LP	AC

Then decide how much of each bar represents negative and positive stroking. Shade in the positive part of each bar, like this:

Negative

Positive

5 Of the strokes that you get now on the job, what percentage does each of your ego states get?

Nurturing Parent: _____

Controlling Parent: _____

Adult: _____

Natural Child: _____

Little Professor: _____

Adapted Child: _____

6 Jot down some notes about the way your parent figure stroked you with:

Physical touch:

Body language:

Written messages:

Gifts:

Money:

7 Of all the strokes that you received, about what percentage of them were for specific performances as opposed to strokes for being? _____

8 Think about the strokes you got for performance. Write down an example for each kind of stroke you got.

Were you stroked immediately after performance? _____

Were you generally stroked for approximations or only for a major accomplishment? (For example, were you stroked only for getting a good grade at semester's end or for making improvements in daily assignments? Were you stroked for an approximation of keeping your room neat, such as making your bed, or only when everything was neatly in place?)

Did this person gradually expect more and more from you before he or she stroked you? _____

Did this parent figure continue to stroke you intermittently after you mastered the skill you were being taught? _____

9 Of all the strokes that you received, about what percentage of them consisted of firsthand strokes as opposed to thirdhand (earshotting) strokes? _____

10 Make some notes about how you felt about the various kinds of strokes that you got as a child.

11 While this information is fresh in your mind, relate it to the kinds of strokes you get today. Does anyone on the job give you the same kind of strokes this parent figure did? _____

If so, what kind?

How do you feel?

Are you aware of any ways you might provoke these strokes? If so, explain.

12 Now think back about what this parent figure taught you about strokes, either by what was said or done. What did you learn about:[13,14]

Giving strokes—Did you learn that it's good to share good feelings and enthusiasm or that it's not-OK to go around saying nice things to people?

Accepting strokes—Were you taught to savor a good feeling or to put yourself down immediately after being given a compliment? Were you taught to return a compliment immediately?

Rejecting strokes—Were you given permission to reject uncomfortable strokes or taught to just stand there and take them, always being polite?

Giving yourself strokes—Were you taught that it's OK to say and think good things about yourself or that patting yourself on the back for a good job is wrong?

Asking for strokes—Were you taught that meaningful strokes must be given spontaneously or that it's OK to ask for what you want?

Part 2: Strokes You Give

Now that you've increased your awareness of the strokes that you received as a child, and the parent messages you got about strokes, let's consider the strokes that you now generally *give* to others on the job.

1 Of all the strokes that you give on the job, roughly what percentage of them involves warm fuzzies as opposed to cold pricklies?

Warm fuzzies = _____ %   Cold pricklies = _____ %

How would you like these percentages to be?

Warm fuzzies = _____ %   Cold pricklies = _____ %

Are there people you ignore whom you could give positive strokes to? _____

If yes, who are they?

2 Think of a particular person you'd like to get along with better. Make a bar graph showing the percentage of strokes that you now give to various ego states in this person. Then if you're not entirely satisfied with the way you're stroking this person, make another bar graph to show how you'd like the percentages to be.

CP	NP	A	NC	LP	AC

(How you stroke this person now.)

CP	NP	A	NC	LP	AC

(How you'd like to stroke this person.)

3 Make some notes about how you might begin to stroke this person more the way you'd like to ideally.

4 Assess the various aspects of your stroking of this person. Then list your planned improvements. Throughout this exercise, be specific when listing your planned improvements. Write down an example of what you will do, such as: "When Wendell turns in a progress report on time, I'll thank him right away." What would you say about:

The timing of your strokes now?

Planned improvements:

Your stroking of approximations?

    Planned improvements:

Raising your criterion for stroking? (Can you think of any examples of situations where you've done this?)

    Planned improvements:

Consistent stroking for new behaviors?

    Planned improvements:

Intermittent stroking for established behaviors?

    Planned improvements:

Your use of reminders to give positive strokes (charts, graphs, checklists, progress reports)?

    Planned improvements:

Your use of earshotting?

    Planned improvements:

5 Of all the strokes you give, about what percentage involves strokes for specific behaviors as opposed to strokes for being?

Strokes for specific performance = _____%   Strokes for being = _____%

How would you like these percentages to be?

Strokes for specific performance = _____%   Strokes for being = _____%

6 Of the strokes that you give for performance, about what percentage is given directly to the person as opposed to earshotting strokes?

Direct strokes = _____%   Earshotting strokes = _____%

7 Describe how and when (if at all) you stroke people with:

Written messages:

    Planned improvement:

Gifts:

    Planned improvement:

Money:

    Planned improvement:

Body language—facial expressions, gestures, posture, gait, and so on (ask a friend if you're not sure):

    Planned improvement:

Part 3: Vivid Visualization of How You'd Like It to Be

In working through Part 2 of this exercise, you described in detail how you have been giving strokes and how you'd like to improve. Now pick out one or two of the items you'd like to work on most. Then vividly visualize yourself doing what you want to do, the way you want to do it. Doing this will help you to get a clear mental image of your goal. The clearer you make the image, the more likely you will be successful in achieving your goal.

What do you see?

Think?

Say?

Feel?

Hear?

How do you move?

How do others react?

Part 4: Your Organization's Stroking Pattern

1 To get a feel for the stroking patterns where you work, describe how your organization strokes in each of the following subject areas.

Attendance:

Quality of work:

Creativity:

Competition:

Cooperation:

Longevity:

Youth:

Looking busy:

Customers:

Compliance:

Education:

People in their niche:

Climbers:

2 Describe some positive results of these stroking patterns:

3 Do you see ways to improve the strokes in your organization? If so, put down some of your ideas here (be specific):

SUMMARY

People need strokes—negative or positive. For positive results on the job, it's crucial to give people positive strokes. In this chapter you have learned some guidelines for stroking for performance, as well as stroking for being. You've also identified various stroking patterns on the job. Finally, you explored how you are now stroking others and what changes you would like to make in your own stroking patterns. In later chapters we will discuss more fully how you can put those changes into effect. However, in Chapter 6 we will turn our attention to games—destructive patterns that lead to negative pay-offs. But first collect fifty warm fuzzies for having finished this rather long chapter!

SOURCE NOTES

[1] N.H. Atthreya makes this point very well in his poems "Other Compensations Apart," "Not Enough If You Approve," and "If You Don't." They are found in his book *The You and I in Business* (Bombay: K. Venkataraman, MMC School of Management), pp. 24–29.

[2] Studs Terkel, *Working* (New York: Random House—Pantheon, 1974), p. 129.

[3] Before the end of the first year of life, a typical infant has developed all the muscles needed to make every sound in human speech. See Kathleen Speeth and Donald Tosti, *Introductory Psychology* (San Rafael, Calif.: Individual Learning Systems, 1973), p. 79. But when infants are not stroked for babbling, they soon stop and lie listlessly in their cribs, making few if any sounds. See Geraldine Harvey, *Child Psychology* (New York: Wiley, 1975).

[4] Philip J. Hilts, *Behavior Mod.* (New York: Harper's Magazine Press, 1974), p. 103.

[5] Jim Evans (Federal Reserve Bank, San Francisco) and Lloyd Homme (San Rafael, Calif.) originated the term *earshotting.*

[6] Hilts, *op. cit.,* p. 101.

[7] *Organizational Dynamics,* 1973, 1(3): 41–50.

[8] Also see Dorothy Jongeward et al., *Everybody Wins: Transactional Analysis Applied to Organizations* (Reading, Mass.: Addison-Wesley, 1976), Chapters 1 and 4.

[9] Laurence J. Peter and Raymond Hull, *The Peter Principle* (New York: Morrow, 1969).

[10] Clair F. Vough with Bernard Asbell, *Tapping the Human Resource* (New York: AMACOM—a division of American Management Associations, 1975), p. 29.

[11] David Dunn, *Try Giving Yourself Away* (Englewood Cliffs, N.J.: Prentice-Hall, 1970), pp. 18–19.

[12] *Ibid.,* p. 62.

[13] Dorothy Jongeward and Dru Scott, *Women as Winners* (Reading, Mass.: Addison-Wesley, 1976), p. 101.

[14] Claude M. Steiner, *Scripts People Live: Transactional Analysis of Life Scripts* (New York: Grove Press, 1974), pp. 114–117.

6

Games Workers Play

☆ Do you ever say to yourself, "Oh, no—not this again," as you suddenly find yourself going through the same old motions with the same person?

☆ Have you ever been fouled up by someone's advice and then have the person look at you innocently saying, "I was only trying to help you"?

☆ Do you often end an encounter feeling trapped, with a sinking feeling in your gut?

☆ Have you ever found yourself gleefully bawling out someone who finally made a mistake?

☆ Do you feel you make stupid mistakes more frequently than you'd like?

☆ Do you sometimes lament, "I tried my best to be finished on time but everything went wrong. I don't know why things like this always happen to me"?

If so, you've probably been involved in psychological games. Since we all play them at times, let's explore the world of games.

OBJECTIVES

When you finish this chapter, you'll be able to:

- identify at least one game that you play;
- use a technique called "the Game Plan" to analyze a psychological game;
- understand the phony roles various people are playing in a game;
- identify some of the important reasons why people play games.

THE WORLD OF GAMES

As we've seen, a psychological game is a series of ongoing transactions with an ulterior message—a hidden agenda. These transactions conclude with an emotional payoff—a hurtful stroke—which in turn reinforces an old decision that someone is "not-OK": either "I'm not-OK" or "you're not-OK." Games are usually played outside our awareness, in our Blind Area. When we feel bad as a result of games, we may smolder or pout and store our feelings in the Hidden Area.

We can look at games in many ways.[1] John James has formulated five key questions, the Game Plan, that can help us analyze when we're playing games:[2]

— What keeps happening over and over that leaves someone feeling hurt?
— How does it start?
— What happens next?
— How does it end?
— How does each person feel when it ends?

Let's see how these questions help us to recognize when a game is occurring.

Example

Dick approaches Brad, one of his subordinates, and says, "Say, Brad, I'm having lunch with the vice-president of the board tomorrow. We'll be discussing your proposal. Perhaps it would be a good idea for you to join us."

"That's great. I'd really like to do that," says Brad.

The next day Brad looked forward to the luncheon with Dick and the vice-president. Brad expected Dick to approach him sometime that morning to discuss plans for lunch, but he didn't. About five minutes before noon, Brad became a bit antsy and decided to approach Dick. "Well, Dick, are you about ready to go to lunch?"

"Oh, yes, . . . lunch. I've been meaning to talk to you about that, but I've been really busy with the Anderson project. You know how it is. Well, anyway, I don't think you need to come along today. I've got to do some preliminary talking with Mr. Jenkins."

Next week Dick again approached Brad. "Brad, we're having a staff meeting next week. Would you like to give a report on the progress you people have been making in the design of that relay system?"

"Sure, I'd be glad to," said Brad.

When the time came for the staff meeting, Brad was prepared to give his presentation and was a bit on edge. As the meeting progressed, Brad waited for Dick to introduce him. He waited and waited. Before he knew it, the meeting was over.

"I thought you wanted me to give a progress report on the relay system," Brad said.

"Oh, that. Yes, Brad, I had considered doing that but as you saw we got involved in discussing the budget for this coming fiscal year. Perhaps you can give that report next time."

Sometime later . . . "Brad, as you know, the national convention is coming up next month, and I think you've earned the right to attend it this year."

"Thanks, Dick. I'd really like to go."

Next month when the time for the convention came, Brad overheard the office secretary asking two of Brad's co-workers about their travel plans for the convention. "Alice hasn't gotten around to talking to me yet, I guess," he said to himself. But after awhile it became plain that Alice *wasn't* going to ask him about his travel plans to the convention. "This is the last straw," he said to himself.

Brad exploded at Dick. "You *told* me I could go to the convention. You had no right to set me up and then pull the rug out from under me. You're nothing but a —."

"Now, wait a minute, Brad. You don't need to lose your temper like that. You know, you look awfully foolish standing there ranting and raving over a little thing like this."

APPLICATION ——————————————————————————

Analyze the preceding example by answering the following "Game Plan" questions.

1   What keeps happening over and over that leaves someone feeling hurt?

2   How does it start? (This is the first move in the game.)

3   What happens next? (This is the second move.)

4   How does it end?

5   How does each person feel when it ends?

~ • ~ • ~ • ~ • ~ • ~ • ~ • ~ • ~ • ~ • ~ • ~ • ~ • ~ • ~ • ~ • ~

1   Brad is not given the opportunity to do something that he was previously asked to do.
2   It starts when Dick approaches Brad and asks or invites him to have lunch, make a proposal, attend a convention, etc.
3   Brad accepts the invitation even though his experience tells him the deal may not come off. He makes no effort to set a clear contract.
4   It ends when Brad finds out at the last minute that the event he had keyed himself up for will not take place. Dick has just finished his game of *Sorry About That.* (In this game someone who has made a promise or an agreement doesn't renegotiate or inform another of a change.)
5   As each episode ends, Brad feels disappointed and depressed. He may have been playing *Kick Me,* getting himself put down or put off. Dick feels self-righteous and perhaps later he feels guilty for having treated Brad so poorly.

Phony Roles

To learn more about how to identify games, let's analyze them in more detail. Game players usually assume one of three basic roles: Victim, Persecutor, and Rescuer. We have capitalized these phony, playacted roles to distinguish them from genuine situations. Some people are victimized in a very real way by others. For example, they may be victimized personally or politically, or discriminated against on the job. In such cases they are *real* victims. However, when referring to a person who plays a part and manipulates others to help fulfill that part, we capitalize "Victim" to show that we're talking about the role, not the reality.

Here are descriptions of the three basic roles:

Persecutors are people who:
- make unrealistic rules;
- enforce rules in cruel ways;
- pick on "little guys" rather than people their own size.

Victims are people who:
- provoke others to put them down, to use them, and to hurt them;
- send "helpless" messages;
- forget conveniently;
- act confused.

Rescuers are people who:
- offer a phony helpfulness to keep others dependent on them;
- don't really help others and may actually dislike helping;
- work to maintain the Victim role so they can continue to play Rescuer.

Steve Karpman[3] points out that players of psychological games often switch back and forth in their roles. For example, sometimes the person playing Victim will tire of being stepped on and will suddenly become the Persecutor. Similarly a person who enters as a Rescuer may suddenly find that she or he is the Victim. Karpman diagrams this tendency as follows:

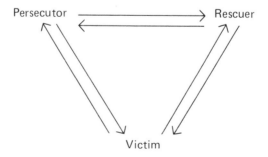

The Karpman Triangle

APPLICATION ───

In the following example, the characters are switching back and forth among the roles of Persecutor, Victim, and Rescuer. As you read each item, identify the role that is being played.

1 T.J. (training director—yells at Duane, the administrative assistant): "Duane, why did you order these expensive hand calculators? You must know they're a terrible waste of money."

____ Persecutor   ____ Rescuer   ____ Victim

2 Duane: "Gee, I thought they were what you wanted. Everything I do lately seems to be wrong."

____ Persecutor   ____ Rescuer   ____Victim

3 Nancy (director of personnel—quietly): "Hey, T.J., you don't have to shout. Duane was just doing what he thought was right."

____ Persecutor   ____ Rescuer   ____ Victim

4 Nancy (sarcastically): "By the way, T.J., you authorized the purchase of that model last month." (Her voice gets louder): "Next time you feel like griping about something, I suggest you take the time to check your facts first." (Nancy turns on her heel and leaves. Duane excuses himself and T.J. is left alone.)

____ Persecutor   ____ Rescuer   ____ Victim

5 T.J. (sitting alone in his office): "I try to do my job, I don't get any support. She wants me to keep control of Duane. But when I try to supervise him, she puts me down. Boy, I'm always getting it in the neck around here."

____ Persecutor   ____ Rescuer   ____ Victim

6 Duane (returns to T.J.'s office): "T.J., don't feel bad about what Nancy said earlier. I remember you were really busy when you authorized that purchase last month. It probably just slipped your mind. That can happen to anyone."

____ Persecutor   ____ Rescuer   ____ Victim

7 Duane (now entering Nancy's office): "Nancy, you were too harsh with T.J. You know he doesn't respond to that kind of talk."

____ Persecutor   ____ Rescuer   ____ Victim

8 Nancy: "Gee, Duane, I was just trying to help you and you come back at me like this. Boy, I can't win."

____ Persecutor   ____ Rescuer   ____ Victim

9 T.J. (steps into the doorway of Nancy's office): "Let's just forget the incident. Nancy has been working awfully hard lately. She was just blowing off a little steam."

___Persecutor   ___Rescuer   ___Victim

~ . ~ . ~ . ~ . ~ . ~ . ~ . ~ . ~ . ~ . ~ . ~ . ~ . ~ . ~ . ~ . ~

1   T.J. comes on as a *Persecutor* when he yells at Duane for ordering the expensive calculators. (Duane is playing *Kick Me* and luring T.J. into the complementary game, *Now I've Got You, You SOB.*)
2   Duane responds as a *Victim* to T.J.'s complaints.
3   Nancy plays *Rescuer* to Duane.
4   Nancy then turns on T.J. and switches from *Rescuer* to *Persecutor*.
5   T.J., alone in his office, plays the *Victim* role.
6   Duane becomes the *Rescuer* as he comforts T.J.
7   Duane then switches to the *Persecutor* role as he attacks Nancy.
8   Nancy responds in the *Victim* role, as she plays *I'm Only Trying to Help You.*
9   T.J. returns as the *Rescuer* as he defends Nancy.

Why We Play Games

As we have discussed, we usually learn our game patterns in childhood. We watch our parent figures and copy their games. We also learn to believe certain things about ourselves and about others, and act accordingly. As grown-ups, we play games for a variety of reasons. Some of the most important are:

— *to get strokes.* We need strokes. If our work situation offers few warm fuzzies, we'll settle for cold pricklies. Remember that playing games is a sure way of getting cold pricklies.

— *to strengthen psychological positions.* Games ultimately are played to put ourselves down or to put others down. Most of us occasionally assume an "I'm not-OK" position and arrange our worlds to confirm it. For people who think of themselves as not-OK, *Kick Me* games provide a powerful way to reconfirm negative expectations. This can become a downward spiral: the more often and the harder a person plays *Kick Me*, the more intense the not-OK psychological position becomes; the more intense that not-OK position becomes, the harder and the more often *Kick Me* gets played. People who have assumed "you're not-OK" will tend to strengthen other people's feelings of not-OKness by blaming them, picking on them, and catching them making mistakes.

— *to avoid or control intimacy.* Games put distance between people. They can be used to control or block intimacy, keeping us from open and honest encounters. People who fear openness, accountability, and responsibility in relationships play games as an avoidance. Sometimes organizations also encourage an avoidance of honesty. When honesty turns out not to be the best policy, people feel compelled to play along with the company politics rather than to express their real feelings.

APPLICATION

1 Jim has difficulty expressing his feelings. For example, he was given a clerical assistant, but was not given any say on this assistant's work location. When the assistant's desk was located on the opposite side of the building, Jim was unhappy about these arrangements yet he didn't share this with his boss. He kept his feelings hidden and lamented to his neighbor about the situation, saying, "Why does this always happen to me?"

From the information presented here, it appears that Jim was playing a variety of a *Poor Me* game (*Why Does This Always Happen to Me?*) mainly to:

___ (a)   avoid or control intimacy;

___ (b)   spend more time in authentic transactions;

___ (c)   keep things smoothed over.

2 Wendy has a negative self-image. Whenever she is on the verge of doing something well, her Adapted Child insists on leaving some important detail unattended. This prompts others to put her down for her carelessness.

It appears that Wendy is playing *Kick Me* mainly to:

___ (a)   get positive strokes;

___ (b)   reaffirm a negative psychological position;

___ (c)   avoid negative strokes.

3 Clyde has a lonely job. He seldom has an opportunity to interact with other workers exeept when he finds errors in subordinates' work. He plays a perse- cuting game of *Now I've Got You, You SOB* by making his directions sufficiently vague so that when subordinates fail to meet his unexplained criteria, he can call them on the carpet.

Based on this information, it seems that Clyde is playing this game to:

___ (a)   give and get negative strokes;

___ (b)   keep a high standard of quality control;

___ (c)   promote intimacy.

~ • ~ • ~ • ~ • ~ • ~ • ~ • ~ • ~ • ~ • ~ • ~ • ~ • ~ • ~

1 (a); 2 (b); 3 (a).

Some Common Games

Before we can stop playing games, we must become aware of when they are happening. We will look at some common games played on the job. As you become familiar with them, you will learn to recognize them if they occur in your organization. Recognizing a game is the first step to giving it up. We've mentioned some games already. You can probably recognize many of these games just from their names.

Games that attack or put others down include:

— *Blemish*
— *If It Weren't for You (Him/Her/Them/It)*
— *Now I've Got You, You SOB*
— *Rapo*
— *Psychiatry*
— *Let's You and Him (Her/Them) Fight* (discussed in Chapter 2)

Games that we use to put down ourselves include:

— *Wooden Leg*
— *Kick Me*
— *Stupid*
— *Schlemiel*
— *Lunch Bag*
— *Harried*

Let's look at these games in more detail.

Blemish

Blemish players are the office nitpickers. They pick on small, inconsequential details. They love to pettifog, bicker, or quibble over trifles when more important matters need attention. The payoff is a false sense of superiority that comes when the Victim (the person being criticized) feels uncomfortable, inadequate, or angry.

Blemish players seldom see the big picture—they are too busy attacking piddling details. As a result they rarely give out warm fuzzies like, "That was a really good job," or "Your approach to the problem was terrific!" *Blemish* players seem unable to allow others to feel good for very long and are more likely to point out the mispronounced word, the comma instead of a colon, the unmatching tie.

Some *Blemish* players try to give warm fuzzies but seem to be unable to let go of them. For example: "That's great the way you whipped this letter out so fast, Shirley. It really looks neat, but next time remember Anita has a doctor's degree so the letter should be addressed to *Dr.* Cortez."

If It Weren't for You (Him/Her/Them/It)

People who play *If It Weren't for You* (*IWFY* for short) often unconsciously feel incapable, unhandy, or inadequate. Rather than admit these feelings, they blame others for their plight. They find one scapegoat after another. When one situation is corrected, another is found to explain away their unsatisfactory performance. The payoff comes when the person who starts the game collects feelings of self-righteousness and purity, while the Victim (the one who is blamed) feels bad.

Note that just because a person says, "If it weren't for . . . ," doesn't mean the person is playing a game. But if someone says it again and again, a game is likely. How many times have you heard, "If it weren't for the boss, I would have had that . . . ;" "If it weren't for this lousy territory, my sales would be up to . . . ;" "If it weren't for my family, I could . . ."?

Now I've Got You, You SOB (NIGYSOB)

NIGYSOB players lay booby traps. They set impossible goals, give ambiguous directions, fail to provide subordinates with needed job aids, or give hazy standards. When a subordinate fails to measure up, these players pounce on the Victim and indulge in angry explosions. The payoff comes when the Persecutor feels justified in working up a "righteous" anger. The Victim is likely to play *Kick Me*, feeling stupid or inadequate. The two are a perfect fit and may live unhappily ever after.

Barbara, for example, had cruel parents. As a child she frequently heard comments like, "You're so slow. You're always late. You never pay attention." Barbara came to believe that she was born with these personality traits and that they couldn't be changed. Later in life, when Barbara became a nurse, she often played a game of *Kick Me* with Cora, the head nurse. Cora played *NIGYSOB* with Barbara.

Barbara worked the night shift. Cora expected Barbara to arrive at least ten minutes early every day so that the nurse on duty could discuss with Barbara what had happened during the day with her patients. This procedure would allow the nurse on duty to leave right on schedule. But Cora merely told Barbara that it was important to arrive early. When Barbara frequently showed up only five minutes early and sometimes showed up late, Cora pounced on her.

Barbara also collected kicks from Cora by giving patients their medicine just a few minutes off schedule. Cora set a trap by not making clear what deviation from the medication schedule could be tolerated.

Rapo

Women who play *Rapo* have learned to distrust or dislike men and have taken the position that "men are not-OK." To confirm this position, the *Rapo* player sends sexy "I'm available" messages to the men around her. Her objective is to lure a man into approaching her, thus setting a trap. But when a man responds, she puts him down with a comment like, "What kind of a woman do you think I am?" or "You're nothing but a dirty old man."

Men who take the position that "women are not-OK" also play a variation of *Rapo*. Such a man lures and charms a woman with fancy words and special attention. Then, when she responds, he suddenly drops her and turns his attention to another woman. This form of *Rapo* is often called *Kiss Off*.

Needless to say, sexually oriented games are disruptive and especially inappropriate on the job. In addition, they tend to reconfirm role stereotypes. This is particularly defeating to women seeking higher positions in an organization and to men who are adjusting to the new roles of men and women.

Psychiatry

Having discovered the language of TA, you may be tempted to analyze your boss, your co-workers, your subordinates, and everyone in your personal life. Because you know TA jargon, you may be tempted to throw the language around in front of people who don't know it. However, the result may be to put them down, causing them to feel uncomfortable and "out of it." A *Psychiatry* player hurts other people with special psychological language. Guard against playing this game.

In an article on the value of TA training, B. L. Stroud points out the danger of *Psychiatry:*

> The training can also produce the obnoxious "sophomore syndrome." This is the tendency for personnel to become enamored with the PAC model for describing behavior. They actually "bug" their associates by continually pointing out when they are coming on "Parent" or have had their "Child" hooked.[4]

To make sure that you're not playing *Psychiatry*, be sure that whenever you use a TA term, everyone within earshot not only understands it but also agrees to its use. If they don't, don't use it. You can always put the meaning of a TA term into everyday language. That's the beauty of TA.

But language can be a shortcut. So if a work team, for example, agrees to use TA language, it can be very helpful. That's not *Psychiatry*.

Wooden Leg

A person who plays *Wooden Leg* wants to be excused from work and responsibility. These players often have a burden of some kind such as a physical or social handicap. But they take advantage of their burdens and use them to excuse themselves. *Wooden Leg* players are often heard to say such things as, "What can you expect from a person with my background?" or "How can you expect me to operate that machine? You know:

- I'm too short."
- I'm too tall."
- I wear glasses."
- my ears are too sensitive to loud noises."
- I never learned to read very good."
- I've never done that before."
- I come from a poor home."
- I've always had a bad memory."

To play this self-defeating game, players must put themselves down or see themselves unnecessarily as fragile or dependent. They use their situation dishonestly, pleading their afflictions to manipulate others into doing their work. *Wooden Leg* players also often get themselves put down by others who will eventually get fed up and strike back.

For example, one *Wooden Leg* player avoided tasks such as making deliveries of important documents by saying, "You can't expect me to run all over town making deliveries like that and still do my job. I just don't have the energy for it." She used the same ploy to extend her lunch hours, claiming that she needed to walk several blocks to the only "health food" restaurant in the area. Her co-workers got back at her one day when a package of candy from an old boyfriend arrived at work while she was on vacation; they held a private party, ate her candy, and justified their action by proclaiming, "All this sugar wouldn't be good for her health."

Kick Me

Kick Me players provoke other people to put them down. They do this in a variety of ways—for example, by:

— drinking excessively;
— doing sloppy work;
— violating company policies or procedures;
— taking drugs;
— failing to carry out important tasks;
— consistently missing deadlines.

Kick Me players like being kicked; it's what they've learned to expect and accept. A hard game of *Kick Me* on the job often results in the star player being fired.

For example, Sid played *Kick Me* in a very cool fashion. He spoke rationally and reasonably to his boss while giving a thoroughly prepared proposal on what he thought was the best sprinkler system for the data-processing section. (This was his plausible Adult–Adult transaction.) However, all the while he was making his presentation, he puffed smoke in his nonsmoking boss's face. This ulterior transaction turned out to be a sure way to get his ideas criticized.

We can also play *Kick Me* all by ourselves. In such games players kick themselves by how they talk to themselves in their own heads—hence this is called a "skull game"! These players often say things like: "How could I have done such a terrible thing? I could kick myself." "Why did I say that?" People acting from an "I'm not-OK, you're not-OK" position sometimes set booby traps for subordinates and play *NIGYSOB*. They pounce on their victims and indulge in angry explosions. Then later they feel guilty for having treated their subordinates so roughly and kick themselves saying, "How could I have been so mean to . . . ?"

Stupid

The game of *Stupid* (which we discussed in Chapter 1) is a type of *Kick Me* game in which players make special arrangements for putting their brains down. They seem to compulsively make mistakes so that they can make a fuss and proclaim, "How could I have done such a stupid thing? Where was I when the good Lord passed out brains?"

For example, Tim was playing *Stupid* when he mailed important documents outside the country which were supposed to go to New York. He also did such things as dial incorrect long-distance numbers, order the wrong-colored stock, and frequently fail to fully complete file folders needed for company training sessions. These acts provoked the Persecutor role in his supervisor, who'd come down on him hard (*Now I've Got You, You SOB*) for doing so many dumb things. Then Tim beat himself emotionally for being such a stupid oaf.

Schlemiel

Although *Kick Me* players want kicks, *Schlemiel* players do many of the same things but seek a different kind of ending to their game—forgiveness. *Schlemiel* players want to be reassured that they are OK, that they are accepted no matter what they do. To get reassured, the *Schlemiel* player compulsively makes clumsy mistakes like:

— spilling coffee on the final draft of a manuscript;
— dropping a delicate piece of equipment;
— spilling typing correction fluid on a new rug;
— burning a desk with a cigarette.

Each time *Schlemiel* players goof, they become highly upset and plead for forgiveness until someone reassures them by saying, "That's OK. Don't worry about it. Everybody makes mistakes." Let's look at an example.

Sarah balanced her cigarette on the edge of Ralph's desk. It burned away as they talked over the agenda for the next day's staff meeting. When they discovered the burn, Sarah became extremely upset and, with a pleading look on her face, lamented, "Oh, Ralph, look what I've done. How could I have been so careless? You've only had this oak desk for a week and now I've practically ruined it. You must think I'm terrible. Only last week I broke your calculator. I feel just awful."

If Ralph played his expected part, he would say something like, "Now don't feel bad, Sarah. It was just an accident." However, this had happened to Ralph before and he'd learned a little about games people play, so this time he tried something different: "You're right, Sarah. It's a shame to have such a mark on my brand-new desk. I'd appreciate your checking with supplies and seeing that it gets touched up."

Lunch Bag

Executives who compulsively collect self-righteous feelings about themselves like to play *Lunch Bag*. They often bring their lunch (last night's leftovers) to the office in a wrinkled bag saved from the corner drugstore. By staying in their offices and working through the lunch hour, *Lunch Bag* players put on a phony, humble front.

Lunch Bag players try to make others feel too guilty or too fearful to come to them with their proposals and requests. The object of playing *Lunch Bag* is to feel self-righteous and to encourage others to think, "How can I come to this humble person with a request for a new dictaphone when he/she doesn't even eat a good hot lunch?"

The *Lunch Bag* game also allows players to avoid contact with co-workers who don't get a chance to talk over lunch about their needs and interests.

If you're working in a situation in which someone is playing *Lunch Bag*, you can refuse to feel guilty or fearful! Whenever you feel negatively in response to someone else's action, you just might be letting them have unwarranted power over you.

Harried

Harried is a dangerous game that can structure a whole lifetime. These players play the role of superman or wonderwoman to hide an underlying psychological position of "I'm not-OK." They work extremely hard so that they can keep up a false sense of "OKness." Often they're the first ones to arrive at work and the last ones to leave.

As *Harried* players advance in an organization, they take on more responsibilities and do more work under excessive pressure to maintain their superperson front. Stress takes its toll, and eventually *Harried* players may collapse from nervous tension. Common payoffs are depression, ulcers, colitis, and even heart attacks.

In an extreme case one executive died after 27 years of "dedicated" service during which he often bragged, "My kids think the mailman's their dad." He died falling facefront into an unfinished report. He was working late on this report at home one Saturday night—a classic ending to a tragic script.[5]

Harried players need to get a handle on their priorities to ask, "If I keep doing what I'm doing now, where will I end up? When I'm on my deathbed, what are the things I'm going to be glad I did? Sad I didn't do? What's really important?" They can learn to structure their time in ways that relax them, bring them pleasure, and strengthen their friendships and family ties. In the long run this helps both the person and the organization.

As we mentioned in Chapter 4, some organizations tend to stroke *Harried* players by encouraging people to work under excessive stress even at the risk of employees' personal lives and health. Although the immediate benefits to the company seem great, such organizations are blind to the long-term harmful effects to people and to the organization itself.

Now that you've been introduced to some common games, try your hand at recognizing them.

APPLICATION ————————————————————————————

For each of the following situations or remarks, indicate what game is probably being played, if any.

Situation or Remark	No Game Likely	Likely Games						
		Schlemiel	Wooden Leg	Blemish	NIGYSOB	IWFY	Harried	Psychiatry
1 "Overall, I'm impressed with your work, Bill. I see how you may well boost sales with this plan."								
2 Roger checks over 15 pages of design specifications for a new product and says, "I may be wrong, and I'll have to check it out, but I think this part can be made of a cheaper material and still do the job."								
3 Bernice checks over a 15-page report and says only, "This word should be spelled with two 'm's,' not one."								
4 "Not again! How awful of me. Why do I always do such clumsy things, spilling coffee all over your final report. I'm sorry. I'm so very sorry. You must think I'm a clod."								
5 "There's no use trying as long as Ted's in charge. As soon as he is replaced, we'll be able to start meeting our quota," said Russ. Later, when Ted is replaced, Russ is heard saying, "You know our only problem now is George." Later, when George begins carrying his fair share of the load, Russ is still not meeting the quota. "You know, our only problem is that our department is overcharged by the shipping department," Russ is heard saying.								
6 "I haven't taken a day off in three years. My family's forgotten what I look like."								
7 "Jane, I've noticed that you seldom speak to me lately. I sense that you are upset with me about something. Am I right?"								

Situation or Remark	No Game Likely	Likely Games						
		Schlemiel	Wooden Leg	Blemish	NIGYSOB	IWFY	Harried	Psychiatry
8 Terry does *not* clearly present rules for purchasing company supplies and equipment. Then, when Ben violates a purchase rule, Terry "calls him on the carpet" and sets him straight.								
9 "What can you expect from an old person like me? I'm close to retirement, you know."								
10 "Oh, you're just playing a game. Why don't you stop collecting red stamps . . . what are red stamps? You mean, you're not into TA?"								

~ • ~ • ~ • ~ • ~ • ~ • ~ • ~ • ~ • ~ • ~ • ~ • ~ • ~ • ~

1 No game likely. This looks like a good-hearted warm fuzzy.
2 No game likely. If you took this for a *Blemish* game, note that the speaker is pointing out a rather significant issue in the design specifications. *Blemish* players tend to pick on trivial mistakes. Also, note that Roger clearly indicates that what he is saying is an opinion that needs to be checked out.
3 This is a classic example of a *Blemish* player's comment.
4 *Schlemiel* is the game. There's a strong plea for forgiveness.
5 This is a variation of *If It Weren't for You.* Notice that the speaker is constantly blaming someone or something else for his problem. Note that each time his scapegoat is eliminated, he finds a new one.
6 *Harried* players sometimes make comments like this in jest as if bragging about their dedication to their job. Often they don't realize the seriousness of this game.
7 No game likely. The speaker is being direct and asking for clarification, which is not compatible with playing a game.
8 *NIGYSOB.* Terry withholds needed information. Then later he catches subordinates who are unaware that they may be pounced on.
9 *Wooden Leg.* Here old age is the wooden leg. Other conditions and situations may be used as wooden legs: allergies, backaches, cultural deprivation, return from vacation, and so on.
10 *Psychiatry.* Be careful that you don't play this game; it hurts.

Games Organizations Play

As we have seen, organizations sometimes play games too. Without really understanding what they're doing, they often continue policies that hurt people or even discriminate against them.

One organization adopted a policy of advancing people who were less qualified than other members of the same minority group. When these people failed on their jobs, the company's attitude was *I Told You So*—a hurtful game.

Another organization gave positive strokes only to those women who lived up to the stereotyped feminine image. A forty-year-old, aggressive woman was considered an "over-the-hill, pushy broad," while forty-year-old, aggressive men were management material. Women were thus *Cornered*—damned if they were and damned if they weren't.

Still other organizations play *Bear Trap*. They lay the bait by:

— giving a starry-eyed description of the job;
— promising lifetime security;
— encouraging a person to believe such things as "I can do pure research here" or "In five years I'll be area supervisor."

The trap springs when the person realizes:

— the job is loaded with drudgery;
— security is for people under fifty;
— pure research and fast promotions are a myth.

Then the employee is trapped and faces a serious decision. "Do I stay, knowing what I know now, or do I risk what I've built up so far and move on?"

Games Use Up Time and Energy

Games make up repetitive scenes in our life script. We know the dialogue and the roles; the outcome seems certain. They provide ways of filling up our time. Some games take only a few minutes while others take a lifetime. For example, we can provoke someone to call us "stupid" and thus play the game of *Stupid* by doing one quick "dumb" thing. Or we can live a life of slow suicide by playing *Harried*.

Games also can be played at different levels of intensity. For example, some *Kick Me* players may provoke only playful jibes about always missing deadlines, while others may play for keeps, provoking the boss to fire them. Intense games for serious consequences are indeed *hard* games.

Psychological games can damage our chances for success on the job. They sap our psychic energy, sometimes leaving us nervous, frustrated, depressed, and feeling falsely triumphant or superior. At best, they consume our valuable time and add some excitement to an otherwise strokeless work day. At worst, they may lead us to the prison or the graveyard. While we invest our time in games, productivity goes down the drain. Problems go unsolved. Decisions remain unmade. And important tasks wait for our attention. Games not only eat up work time but, more important, they cost us our life's time.[6]

For all these reasons it's important to get a handle on our own games.[7] But be patient with yourself. It certainly is easier to see what others are doing first! If you do see someone else's game, ask yourself: "Am I playing that game?" Also ask: "What's the complementary game?" You will find that many games do indeed fit together. For example, if others seem to pick on you (play Persecutor) or overprotect you (play Rescuer), you just may be playing Victim. You might be into *Kick Me, Stupid,* or *Schlemiel.* It's courageous and useful to check out your own contribution to a bad or hurtful relationship. Once you clarify what's happening, you can use your energy for positive change. Here is an exercise to help you identify your own games.

APPLICATION ————————————————————————

1   Put an "X" on each of the lines below to show how you feel about yourself and others most of the time.

	OK	Not-OK
Yourself	├————————┼————————┼————————┤	
Others	├————————┼————————┼————————┤	

2   What games might you be playing to strengthen the feelings about yourself and others you listed in item 1?

3   Take a moment to review the stroking-analysis exercise you did on pages 98 through 105. Then list any games you may be playing to get these kinds of strokes.

4   How many people are you open and honest with on the job?

5   Are you perhaps playing any games to avoid leveling with others? If so, which ones?

6   What games and roles do you notice others playing? Show roles by checkmarking (√) appropriate columns.

GAMES	ROLES		
	Persecutor	Rescuer	Victim

7 Now look again at the games you listed in item 6. Consider whether you play
these games too. Also are you perhaps playing a complementary role? (For
example, if another person is playing a Persecutor role, you may be playing
Victim, and so on.) Show any complementary roles in the chart by putting an
"X" in the appropriate columns.

Remember, if you suspect that a set of transactions may be a game, apply
the five key Game Plan questions:

— What keeps happening over and over that leaves someone feeling hurt?
— How does it start?
— What happens next?
— How does it end?
— How does each person feel when it ends?

Now that you've had more practice in identifying games, you're probably
anxious to learn how to stop them. In the next section we'll give you an over-
view of some ways for stopping games. Later chapters will help you develop
skills in using these methods.

WAYS TO STOP GAMES

Give an Unexpected Response

The classic way to stop games is to give an unexpected response to the first
move or as early in the game as possible. Remember, since games involve
repetitive situations, the players' moves are often predictable. For example,
in the game *Yes, But,* the person starting the game usually states a problem
from the Victim role. The Rescuer predictably responds with a series of
reasonable suggestions. Each suggestion in turn is dismissed with a phrase
such as "Yes, but." The Rescuer can avoid this game simply by giving an
unexpected response. One such response is to turn the problem back to the
initiator: "That's quite a problem. What are you going to do?" In Chapter 15,
we'll explain some effective transactional techniques, such as active listening,
for stopping games.

Caution: If a person is used to playing a game and you suddenly refuse
to play it, you are depriving that person of his or her usual supply of strokes.
When this happens, the game player may respond almost like a drug addict
going through withdrawal symptoms. Just as a drug addict may frantically
scramble to get a fix, the game player may try harder and harder to lure you
into a game.

Children may respond the same way in certain situations. For example,
many children whine to get attention. Parents often play along by responding
very quickly and strongly when a child whines. If the child's parents suddenly
decide to ignore whining, the child is likely to whine more intensely and
more frequently in the hopes of getting some attention. If the parents are

consistent *and if they supply positive strokes in place of the missing negative strokes,* the whining will eventually stop.

So when you give up a game be prepared. If you notice that the other person intensifies his or her game playing, take heart. The fact that the other person is reacting strongly may well mean that you succeeded in refusing your part in it.

APPLICATION

1 Anne was having difficulty with her subordinates. She frequently came to Sally asking for help. No matter what solution Sally would suggest, Anne would say, "Well, that's a good idea. However, that won't work because . . ."

(a) What game was Anne playing? _____

(b) What might Sally do to break up this game?

2 Suppose Sally tries the technique of giving an unexpected response. But Anne persists and presses Sally for her ideas about solving her problems. The situation seems to be getting worse instead of better. What do you think Sally should do in this situation?

~ • ~ • ~ • ~ • ~ • ~ • ~ • ~ • ~ • ~ • ~ • ~ • ~ • ~ • ~ • ~

1 (a) The game is *Yes, But.*
   (b) Sally might break up the game in a number of ways. One effective approach might be for Sally to make an unexpected response to Anne's request for help. For example, instead of offering a solution, she might ask, "How do you see the way things are going? How would you like things to be?"
2 It's probably best for Sally to persist in giving unexpected responses. But because she is depriving Anne of her usual supply of strokes, Sally should probably go out of her way to stroke Anne positively. For example, if Anne makes any attempt at coming up with a solution herself, Sally might say enthusiastically, "Hey, now *there's* an idea! You might consider that, Anne." Or she may stroke her in positive ways about other issues.

Stop Putting People Down

One key feature present in all games is a *putdown*. When we play a game, we either collect or give negative strokes. By decreasing the frequency with which we carry out putdowns, we automatically will decrease our game playing: no putdown, no game. Chapter 15 on effective transacting techniques will give you some specific skills you can use to relate to people in a positive way—to build them up rather than put them down. You don't have to put others—or yourself—down.

Build Self-Confidence

One way out of an ever-growing collection of not-OK feelings is to increase our self-esteem and build an even sounder sense of "I'm OK." We can learn to appreciate our true natures and care about ourselves. We accept that we deserve success. Chapter 12 has some practical suggestions you may wish to use to boost your self-confidence and self-esteem, so you'll have less use for games like *Kick Me* that provoke putdowns. In addition, whenever we operate from a core of confidence, we can allow other people their success without envy—others are OK, too.

Stop Playing Phony Roles

Since phony roles are always part of psychological games, if we stop playing phony roles, we can stop playing games. For example, when we stop "acting" like Victims, we also stop attracting Persecutors and Rescuers. When we stop acting like Rescuers, we no longer need Victims.

Give and Receive More Warm Fuzzies

If we're not giving and receiving warm fuzzies on the job, we're likely to be playing games to get some kind of attention—even if negative. One way to avoid games, then, is to dramatically increase the time we spend giving and getting warm fuzzies as suggested in Chapter 5. Such behavior is incompatible with game playing: we can't consistently exchange genuine warm fuzzies and play games at the same time. In Chapters 9 through 14, we'll go into detail on some "self-care" techniques you can use to step up your warm fuzzy economy if you choose to.

Risk Authenticity

Many of us play games because we do not know how to establish open, honest relationships with other people. So another way to avoid games is to risk authenticity. If we can transact more openly and honestly with people on the job, our game playing will decrease since game playing is incompatible with authenticity. The first step toward establishing more open relationships involves surrendering our resentments against other people. In Chapters 7 and 17 you'll learn some basic skills for doing that.

Being open and game-free can lead to intimacy. True intimacy involves the releasing of feelings of warmth, tenderness, and caring for another person. Such transactions can happen with people at work and usually feel very good.

Example

Ron's hands shook slightly with anticipation as he opened a tightly sealed envelope marked "Personal." His heart sank as he read the words, "Therefore,

we regret to inform you that your request for a promotion has been denied."
Because Ron had a close relationship with Greg, one of his co-workers, he
was able to go to him and express his feelings of disappointment. In this
exchange, Ron and Greg experienced a moment of real closeness: they
weren't afraid to touch each other, to really look at each other. They showed
and expressed their feelings and felt better for it.

Keep Your Sense of Humor

You may be able now to spot a game you play. If so, try to see yourself
acting it out as if you're in the movies, acting on the big screen. If you really
do this, you may find it's difficult not to chuckle at some of the antics you
go through. Some of the maneuvers we go through when we play games are
pretty funny!

SUMMARY

Most people play psychological games. A series of questions called the Game
Plan can help us analyze games. When we play games, we also playact roles.
Victims, Rescuers, and Persecutors are the classical characters in human
dramas. Victims play to collect bad feelings but they also encourage others
to feel angry, frustrated, guilty, or pure. Rescuers and Persecutors play to
give bad feelings yet also collect arrogance, purity, superiority, exasperation,
and hostility.

Some people play games at a light, social level to put a little distance
between themselves and others—like a coquettish game of *Rapo* that titillates
but hurts no one seriously. Others, however, play more intensely for greater
stakes, such as a hard game of *Kick Me* that ends with getting fired or a hard
game of *Harried* that ends with a heart attack. Games divert people's energy
and often cost money. They distract us from decision making, problem
solving, and productivity.

Once we identify our games, we can gradually learn to give them up (or
lighten them) in favor of better feelings and more productivity. We can learn
to attract fewer putdowns and to pass out better feelings, to be "real" more
of the time rather than to act out roles, to do more good things for ourselves,
to risk sharing more of ourselves with people on the job, to laugh at our
games.

Every time we take a positive step to use our time better and to exchange
warmer, more positive feelings, we increase our chances of choosing success.

SOURCE NOTES

[1] For further information on game analysis, see Eric Berne, *What Do You Say After You
Say Hello?* (New York: Grove Press, 1973), p. 24; Claude M. Steiner, *Games Alcoholics
Play: The Analysis of Life Scripts* (New York: Grove Press, 1971); and Muriel James and
Dorothy Jongeward, *The People Book: Transactional Analysis for Students* (Reading,
Mass.: Addison-Wesley, 1975), pp. 131-134.

[2] John James, "The Game Plan," *Transactional Analysis Journal*, 1973, 3(4):14–17.

[3] Stephen B. Karpman, "Fairy Tales and Script Drama Analysis," *Transactional Analysis Bulletin*, April 1968, 7(26):39.

[4] B. L. Stroud, "Is TA O.K.?" *Journal of European Training, MCB Journal*, 1976, 5(4): 208–209. Our thanks to J. I. Gathiawala for alerting us to this article.

[5] See Dorothy Jongeward, *Everybody Wins: Transactional Analysis Applied to Organizations* (Reading, Mass.: Addison-Wesley, 1976), pp. 44–46.

[6] Because they are ulterior, we consider games to be primarily negative transactions. For a discussion of "good games," see Eric Berne, *Games People Play* (New York: Grove Press, 1964), pp. 163–168; and Robert Zechnich, "Good Games: Therapeutic Uses and Four New Ones," *Transactional Analysis Journal*, 1973, 3(1):163–168.

[7] For more information on games played in organizations, see Jongeward, *op. cit.*; and Muriel James and Dorothy Jongeward, *Winning with People: Group Exercises in Transactional Analysis* (Reading, Mass.: Addison-Wesley, 1973).

7

Good-bye Gray Stamps

☆ Have you ever felt put down by a co-worker, subordinate, or boss?
☆ Do you often feel fear in the face of authority?
☆ Have you ever wanted to tell a co-worker or a client something
important and yet couldn't do it because you felt too embarrassed,
angry, or resentful?
☆ Have you ever blown up at someone for some little thing and then
wondered why you did it?

If you've answered "yes" to any of these questions, then this chapter will
interest you.

OBJECTIVES

When you finish this chapter, you'll be able to:

- explain what is meant by "stamp collecting";
- distinguish between gray and gold stamps;
- identify situations in which you are collecting gray stamps;
- distinguish between racket feelings and genuine feelings;
- distinguish between recommended ways of handling racket feelings as
  opposed to genuine feelings;
- track down your own racket feelings;
- describe a variety of techniques for dealing with rather than collecting
  bad feelings;
- increase your share of gold stamps by accepting more positive strokes,
  monitoring your collection of good feelings, and nurturing your Child.

Let's begin with a discussion of stamp collecting.

STAMP COLLECTING

The term "stamp collecting" is borrowed from the practice of collecting
trading stamps when buying goods and later cashing in these stamps for mer-
chandise. In TA those stamps are feelings—positive or negative. Gold stamps
refer to our collection of good feelings that can be cashed in for good times.

Collecting gold stamps is a constructive activity; we'll discuss in later chapters how and when to cash them in. Collecting gray stamps (negative feelings), however, is *un*constructive. If we collect enough gray stamps and our book is full, we cash it in—that is, we feel justified in indulging in a dramatic, emotional outburst or in feeling depressed and sorry for ourselves. Does this remind you of psychological games? One of the reasons we play games is to collect and cash in stamps—gray stamps in particular.

Gray stamps are any negative feelings we repeatedly attract and collect. Such negative feelings are also rackets[1] because they're dishonest. Racket feelings are a repeat of past learned feelings from the Adapted Child rather than spontaneous, genuine feelings in the present. To collect them we set up and create rackets—situations in which we can experience depression, anger, or guilt. We might even imagine that someone sneers at us and thus collect a *counterfeit* gray stamp. We humans can be avid repeaters. Even if what we're repeating feels bad, it's what we are used to.

Examining our rackets and gray-stamp collections can be rather painful. They often reflect rather negative experiences in our early lives, times when we couldn't be completely honest. Some people use their sense of humor and, for fun, think of racket feelings not as gray stamps but as stamps of specific colors. Are you ever red with anger, green with envy, pure white with self-righteousness, or blue with woes? If so, and most of us are at times, you've been collecting your own colorful book of old, bad feelings.

When bad feelings are held in, they result in resentment. When enough resentments build up—when people say to themselves, "That's the last straw"—they may cash in their stamps by deliberately performing poorly. They may:

— slow down production,
— sabotage production,
— feel justified in feigning illness,
— bad-mouth a manager, supervisor, subordinate, or co-worker.

Such cashing in of stamps may be so undermining that a manager is finally fired.

Sometimes instead of collecting stamps and cashing them in later, people pass on stamps.

Example

Lou storms into Tim's office with his hands on his hips, frowns, and peers over his glasses. "The parts for Bixby's computer haven't arrived yet. Where is your brain—did you leave it home last month? You should have ordered them then. If you had done that, we wouldn't be in this mess." Lou does a military about-face and walks briskly down the corridor before Tim can reply. A moment later, Tim's secretary enters his office: "Tim, I have a question about the letter you dictated this morning to Dr. Green. I was wondering if..."

"Can't you do anything by yourself without always coming up with some dumb question? OK, what is it this time?"

At lunch time the secretary bawls out the waitress with: "I don't see why you can't serve a meal hot. This is awful. Take it back. Why should I put up with this?"

And so on . . . .

Notice that when Lou struts into Tim's office he is probably cashing in a book of stamps that he has been saving up. Tim feels bad about what Lou says to him and momentarily collects a stamp. He quickly passes it on to his secretary, who passes it on to the waitress, who is probably still wondering what she did to deserve such a tongue-lashing. They all displaced their feelings.

APPLICATION ——————————————————————————

Here's an exercise you can use to test your understanding of the concept of collecting psychological stamps. Read each of these descriptions and tell whether a gray stamp is being collected. (Or, if you prefer, specify a particular color.)

1   Ben was really mad when he discovered that upper management had given one of his clients a price break after he had told the client that such a price break was impossible. He contronted the management officials, expressed his anger, and explained how their action was undermining his client's confidence in him. Having cleared the air, he felt better about the matter.

Did Ben collect a stamp?   ___ Yes   ___ No

2   The staff of a mail-order company is meeting to try to think of ways to increase efficiency. Early in the meeting Barry suggests this: "I know, let's hook up an answering device to the telephone. You know, the kind where a tape-recorded message comes on and then the caller can leave a message."

"That's a dumb idea," said Leah. "What a waste of time. We'll just have to call the people back and that costs money."

Barry got a familiar sick feeling in his stomach when he heard Leah's words. He was silent for the rest of the meeting. The next day, when he met Leah in the hallway, he greeted her as usual even though he still had bad feelings about what she had said.

Did Barry collect a stamp?   ___ Yes   ___ No

3   Sarah was extremely angry and resentful because she was not given a promotion she thought she deserved, even though she knew that the person who got the job was highly qualified. She recognized her angry feeling as familiar and out of proportion to the situation. That evening at home she found a private place, put a pillow in her lap, and then repeatedly swung her fists down into the pillow as hard as she could. She said whatever she felt like saying. By carrying out this exercise she was able to dissipate her feelings of frustration to the point where she could talk to her boss about the situation the next day without a tremor in her voice. She explained that she felt bad about the situation and listed reasons why she believed she should have gotten the promotion. Her boss didn't agree and the promotion stood, as first made. However, Sarah still felt better for having asserted herself.

Did Sarah collect a stamp? ___ Yes ___ No

4 Jim's office was always a mess. He had no workable filing system. He repeatedly became angry at himself for his lack of organization when he needed a particular document. He frequently scolded himself by saying things like, "How stupid of me to lose those product specifications. I'll never learn, will I!"

Did Jim collect a stamp? ___ Yes ___ No

~ • ~ • ~ • ~ • ~ • ~ • ~ • ~ • ~ • ~ • ~ • ~ • ~ • ~ • ~ • ~ • ~

1 No, Ben didn't collect a stamp. Had he not dealt with his anger, however, he would have collected a red stamp.
2 Yes, Barry collected a stamp—a blue one—by holding onto the hurt he had at the meeting.
3 No, Sarah did not collect a stamp. If she had not dealt with her feelings, however, she would have collected a red stamp.
4 Yes, Jim collected a stamp. His racket was to repeatedly arrange things so he would have an excuse to become angry with himself. Notice that he collected his red anger stamp all by himself—no one else was involved.

Collecting gray stamps is bad medicine. When you collect stamps, you end up carrying a burden around inside of you, which you may eventually unload on someone—maybe yourself. For example, collecting stamps can contribute to such things as:

— headaches,
— gastrointestinal problems,
— respiratory problems,
— nervous-system disorders,
— skin disorders, and
— hypertension.[2]

The practice of stamp collecting doesn't always result in such dramatic observable symptoms. But when we collect gray stamps by:

— repressing anger,
— feeling hurt or inadequate, and
— carrying grudges,

we usually become less effective, less whole, and less able to do our job.

Ken Olson does an excellent job of explaining why it's harmful to hang onto resentments. Here's what he says:

> I believe in hanging loose emotionally. The art of hanging loose emotionally is an art because few people do it naturally. Most of us have to work very hard learning how to turn off our negative tapes and cut loose the bad memories, hurts, disappointments, and bitterness of yesterday. It's hard to walk away from the bad memories of yesterday because, for some strange reason, individuals believe if they can spend enough time on yesterday's mistakes and hurts that yesterday will be different. But we cannot get from here to yesterday and do a remake of it, so why hang onto the

bummers of the past? They'll just drag you down emotionally. I discovered that in my life I could not afford the distinctive luxury of hate or bitterness. It's far too expensive a price for me to pay.

When I was about four or five I discovered that tomorrow never comes. When I would ask my mother for something she would reply, "Well, maybe tomorrow we can do it," but the next day wasn't tomorrow, it was today. So, if you and I can't go back to yesterday or live in tomorrow, I believe we should spend more energy in living more fully and completely the day that we have.[3]

Everyone has collected stamps at one time or another. Yet we can learn to give up stamp collecting and set ourselves free from the burden of carrying around resentments.

You can start spending more energy in living in the present if you give up collecting gray stamps. The first step is to become aware of just how you do it now. The following exercise is designed to help you figure that out.

APPLICATION

1 Let's go back to an exercise you did in Chapter 3. Think of a time when you got into trouble for some reason. Remember what your parent figure did? Now imagine that whole scene again as if it were on a TV screen. Describe what you see and hear, including voices, body language, the setting, and so on.

2 How did you feel in response to what the parent figure did?

3 What did you do with your feelings? Hold them in? Work them out in some way? Express them?

4 If you expressed your feelings in some way, what did the parent figure do or say in response?

5 Today, do you generally express your feelings right away or do you collect them and let them fester?

6 Do you sometimes unload your feelings by exploding at someone or at yourself?

7 Write down some bad feelings that you've had on the job fairly recently.

8 Is the feeling in item 7 anything like the one you listed in item 2 of this exercise? If yes, perhaps you've identified a racket feeling.

9 If you have any ideas now about how you might unload feelings in a positive way, write them down. Later, after you've finished this chapter, you may wish to return to this page and jot down any additional ideas you've come up with.

10 Now recall several incidents from your childhood when you felt bad. See each incident happening and get in touch with your feelings at the time. Look for the occurrence of these feelings in your life now. Which ones seem to be favored now?

GIVING UP GRAY STAMPS

The rest of this chapter is about how to give up collecting gray stamps. We will show you a step-by-step procedure for dealing with your feelings. As we proceed, we will gradually build a flowchart to help you visualize and recall the basic steps.

GOOD-BYE GRAY STAMPS

(Situation: You are feeling bad. You want to get rid of these bad feelings rather than hold them inside.)

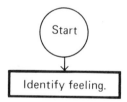

Identify Your Feelings

The first step in dealing with a feeling is to recognize it. Many of us have bad feelings without even being aware of them. For example, we may know we're unhappy, but we aren't aware of *specific* feelings underlying our unhappiness. Our lack of awareness may result from Parent tapes like:

"Big people don't cry."
"Don't feel bad."
"Wipe that frown off your face."
"You shouldn't feel that way."
"You should be ashamed of yourself for feeling that way."

As young people, we don't have the needed experience to put such slogans into proper perspective. Consequently, we may well have interpreted these messages to mean: "Don't feel." As a result, many of us have become numb to certain feelings, sometimes even denying that they exist.

APPLICATION ───────────────────────

From what we've just said, which of these actions would be the most helpful first step toward saying good-bye to gray-stamp collecting?

___(a) Frequently ask yourself how you're feeling: happy, sad, angry, envious, fearful, and so on.

___(b) Ignore your feelings.

___(c) Involve yourself in your work and forget about your feelings.

~•~•~•~•~•~•~•~•~•~•~•~•~•~•~•~•~

(a) is the best choice, we think. The first step in saying good-bye to gray-stamp collecting is to get in touch with your feelings. A good way to do that is to question yourself: use your Adult and listen to your Child.

GOOD-BYE GRAY STAMPS

(Situation: You are feeling bad. You want to get rid of these bad feelings rather than hold them inside.)

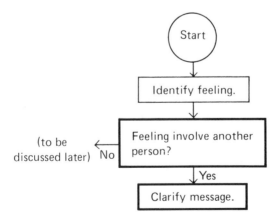

Clarify the Message

Next, ask if your feelings involve another person. On pages 152 and 153 we discuss what to do if your feelings do not involve another person. If your feelings *do* involve another person, your next step is to clarify the intent of the other person's message. You might simply say, "I don't understand. Would you mind repeating that?" You might find the person said something entirely different from what you had thought. Or if the person *did* something (such as wrinkling her nose), you might ask something like this, "Did I say something that you disagreed with? I noticed you were wrinkling your nose." You might find that the person simply has an allergy!

If you are feeling bad in response to criticism, ask for details. For example, suppose that your boss has criticized a project that you have recently finished. You might say, "I don't understand. Would you go over that with me again? What do you see wrong with the way I handled this project?"

If you feel hurt by what you think is an ulterior (hidden) message, consider expressing your interpretation of the hidden message to the other person. You might say: "I don't understand. Are you saying . . . ?"

When clarifying a message, be sure to use your Adult. At this point you are still gathering information. It's probably best not to express your feeling until you're sure you've clarified the message.

APPLICATION ———————————————————

1   Oscar burst into Norma's office. "What's going on in this department? I don't believe it!"

Norma felt a stabbing pain in her stomach. She thought, "Oh, no, what's he complaining about now?"

What should Norma do now?

___ (a)   Remain quiet and wait to see what Oscar does next.

___ (b)   Say, "I get upset when you criticize me like that."

___ (c)   Say, "I don't know, Oscar. What's happening?"

2   Shane, an aspiring pianist and a member of a dance band, received a gift from Barbara, another musician.

"Hey, Shane, look what I got you. It's the sheet music for 'Evergreen'—you know, the love theme from *A Star Is Born.* It's a great piece and it's real easy to play."

"What a putdown," Shane said to himself, "I guess she thinks I have lousy technique—that I can't play anything a little difficult."

Following our guidelines, what might Shane say to Barbara?

~ · ~ · ~ · ~ · ~ · ~ · ~ · ~ · ~ · ~ · ~ · ~ · ~ · ~ · ~

1   The last choice is best. Norma's best move is to gather more information before taking Oscar's comments too seriously. In this case it turned out that Oscar was delighted with Norma's department's production record for the past month. He just had an unusual way of showing it at first.

2   Shane might simply repeat Barbara's statement in his own words— for example: "Yeah, I'll bet it's easy to sight-read." This response encourages Barbara to expand on her statement. For example, she

> might say, "Yeah, I enjoyed just sitting down and playing it right
> away without having to practice it. I thought you'd enjoy doing that,
> too." Shane might also take a more direct approach and simply say,
> "I don't understand. Why did you point out that it's easy to play?"
> Any such response by Shane that would encourage Barbara to am-
> plify her statement would be useful here.

After you've clarified the message, do you still feel bad? If not, great!
You've just given up a stamp. If you still feel bad, do you suspect that you
are experiencing a racket feeling? If so, the next step is to track your feelings.
(We'll discuss the alternative on pages 149–151.)

GOOD-BYE GRAY STAMPS

(Situation: You are feeling bad. You want
to get rid of these bad feelings rather than
hold them inside.)

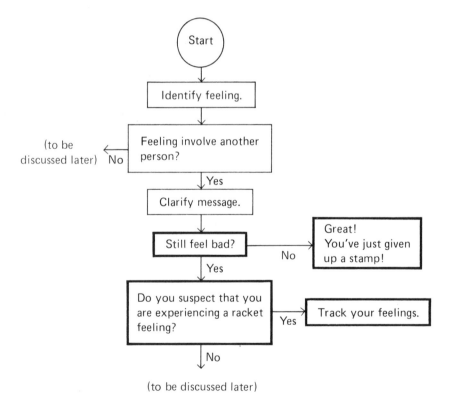

(to be discussed later)

Track Your Feelings

If your response to a situation seems irrational—if you are overreacting or
overdoing—you may be dealing with a racket feeling. That is, this feeling
may be a repeat of a past learned feeling, rather than a genuine feeling in the
present. If so, you need to track down the original learned feeling.

The first step in learning to track your feelings is to realize that *you* own them. We have been led to believe that people, things, or events cause us to feel bad. Phrases such as "You made me feel bad when . . ." are common expressions in our language. But we are actually responsible for our own feelings. If we feel glad, mad, scared, or sad, we feel that way because of what we say to ourselves (consciously or unconsciously).

For example, if someone insults you and you feel bad, it is *not* the insult that directly triggers (starts) your feeling. It is your *perception* of that insult and what you think about it that serves as the trigger. Often your perception of an insult is colored by a Parent tape. Here's how this concept might be diagrammed:

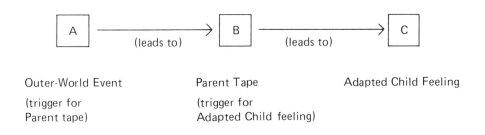

Outer-World Event	Parent Tape	Adapted Child Feeling
(trigger for Parent tape)	(trigger for Adapted Child feeling)	

Another way of saying this is that unless we are *physically* injured by an event, we cannot be hurt by it. If we *are* hurt, it is because *we* use the outer-world event to hurt ourselves. In this case, A does *not* cause C. Instead we allow A to start B (the Parent tape). When B plays, it stirs up C (the Adapted Child feeling).

Another way to look at this is shown by this ego-state diagram:

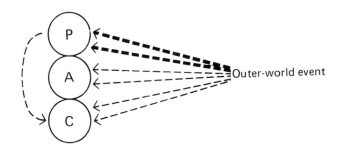

This diagram shows that even though an outer-world event is broadcast to the whole personality, we tend to filter it through our Parent values. Our Child ego state, then, *feels* in response to our Parent thoughts about the event. For example:

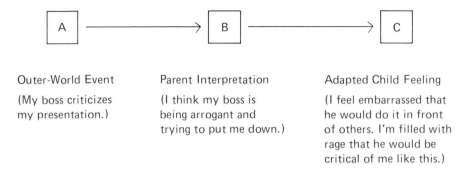

Outer-World Event	Parent Interpretation	Adapted Child Feeling
(My boss criticizes my presentation.)	(I think my boss is being arrogant and trying to put me down.)	(I feel embarrassed that he would do it in front of others. I'm filled with rage that he would be critical of me like this.)

We can, however, filter outer-world events through the Adult ego state:

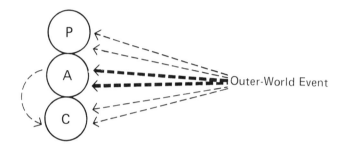

For example, here's how an employee might react differently to criticism when the filtering is done through the Adult:

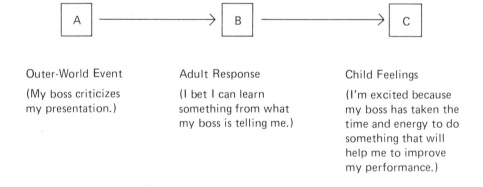

Outer-World Event	Adult Response	Child Feelings
(My boss criticizes my presentation.)	(I bet I can learn something from what my boss is telling me.)	(I'm excited because my boss has taken the time and energy to do something that will help me to improve my performance.)

APPLICATION ─────

Here are some statements about feelings. Which one(s) show(s) that the speaker "owns his own feelings?"

____ (a) "John makes me jealous when he talks about his new office."

____ (b) "I can't help feeling this way."

____ (c) "It embarrasses me when you talk about me like that in front of my boss."

___ (d) "I feel put down when you talk to me like that."

___ (e) "These people make me sick."

~ • ~ • ~ • ~ • ~ • ~ • ~ • ~ • ~ • ~ • ~ • ~ • ~

> Statement (d) only. In statement (a), the words "makes me" show that the speaker is projecting blame on someone else. This is a very frequent phrase in our language and shows how we have been convinced that other people can control our feelings by their actions. In statement (c), the speaker is projecting the blame for his or her embarrassment on some indefinable force called "it." In (e), the key word, again is "make."

Often the way we talk is a reflection of our philosophy, so it pays to listen to how we are phrasing our sentences. One way to gain more control of feelings is to avoid statements that project responsibility on someone or something. For example, we can avoid saying things like, "John makes me jealous when he talks about his new office." Instead, we can say, "I get jealous when John talks about his new office," or even better, "I make myself jealous when I hear John talking about his new office."

APPLICATION

Using this idea, rewrite the following statements. Show that the speaker is taking responsibility for his or her feelings.

1 "It embarrasses me."

2 "You hurt my feelings when you yelled at me."

3 "These people make me sick."

4 "That really bothers me."

~ • ~ • ~ • ~ • ~ • ~ • ~ • ~ • ~ • ~ • ~ • ~ • ~

Here are some possible revisions:

1 "I feel embarrassed," or "I embarrass myself."
2 "I felt bad when you yelled at me."
3 "I feel sick in front of these people," or "I make myself sick in front of them," or "I'm using these people to make myself sick."
4 "I'm bothering myself about that."

After you accept responsibility for your feelings, the second step in tracking a feeling is to ask yourself certain key questions:[4,5]

— *When have I had this feeling before?* Often a bad feeling is one that recurs. If you are having a feeling repeatedly, you may be unwittingly using this feeling as a payoff.

— *Does another feeling underlie the feeling that I'm having now?* Am I covering up a hidden feeling with my current feeling? For example, when children feel anger or resentment, often they have a hidden feeling of fear, which they're not aware of. They may fear rejection, abandonment, neglect, physical punishment, or any number of things. As grown-ups we may do the same thing. We may feel angry and not be aware that deep down we are fearful. Because we perceive fear as a sign of weakness, we tend to push it into the background. Instead of getting in touch with our fear, we sense only a "more respectable" feeling such as anger or resentment.

— *What Parent tapes am I using to bring on the feeling?* Remember that people, things, and events don't *make* us feel bad; we feel bad in response to our thoughts, which are often Parent tapes. The tricky thing about this is that our Adapted Child may respond negatively to these Parent tapes while our Adult is not even aware that they're playing. That's why the outer-world event, rather than our own thoughts, *seems to be* causing our feeling. So the next time you're feeling bad, listen for the Parent tapes you are using to trigger the bad feeling. Once you identify those tapes, you may be able to let go of a whole fistful of gray stamps that you have been fiercely collecting for some time.

Example

Amy, who worked for a mail-order company, often got upset when angry customers would call complaining about the company's products and slow delivery times. By tracking her feelings, Amy became aware of a Parent tape that was saying, "You're so slow! You should be ashamed of yourself." Once she became aware of this tape, she began to understand that she was upsetting herself, that the customers weren't responsible for her feelings. She turned off that old irrational Parent tape and found that she was more relaxed and more able to help customers who had problems.

But it isn't always that easy. After all, you may have been listening to a tape and collecting bad feelings for years, so it may take some time and effort to get rid of it. (We'll discuss some methods for doing this in Chapter 12.)

GOOD-BYE GRAY STAMPS

(Situation: You are feeling bad. You want to get rid of these bad feelings rather than hold them inside.)

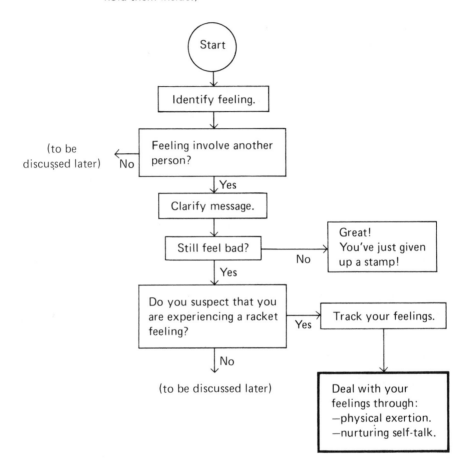

Deal with Your Feelings

If your Child clings to the racket feeling after you've tried tracking it, your next step is to try dealing with it in some other way. Two good techniques are physical exertion and nurturing self-talk.

Physical Exertion

Often when we upset ourselves about something, our body is ready to fight or to flee. Adrenaline flows; blood vessels dilate. But even though our body primes itself for an aggressive attack, we may choose to act calmly and not show our emotions. Sometimes that may be the best thing for us to do, especially if our feelings of aggression are racket feelings, yet we feel frustrated.

We need to do *something* to deal with our feelings and the mobilization of our body. Otherwise we are likely to collect gray stamps and perhaps cash them in on some unsuspecting bystander. Going for a swim, jogging, skipping rope—these are all good ways of exerting ourselves physically to release the tension of racket feelings. You might also go off by yourself and beat on something soft. For example, you can do what Sarah did (as described on page 132): slam your fists into a pillow as hard as you can until you are exhausted. If no one else is around, you might want to scream and say whatever comes to your mind without censoring it. Because you are giving your Child permission to express feelings, it's important that your Adult protect you from hurting yourself, destroying important property, or unduly disturbing others.

Nurturing Self-Talk

Another good way to deal with a bad feeling is to use your Nurturing Parent to talk to your Child. If you don't have a good Nurturing Parent, you can learn self-nourishing through your Adult. As the Nurturing Parent, some people find it useful to look down at their toes and talk out loud. Then they respond from their Child while looking up. Looking down and then looking up helps them to switch ego states as they give themselves a pep talk.

For example, Scott used this technique to stop collecting some *Kick Me* stamps. Scott had the habit of procrastinating and then kicking himself for being late with things. He was late to meetings, late making progress reports, and late finishing projects. Here's how he carried on a dialogue between his Nurturing Parent and Child ego states to move from fear to action.

After finishing an internal Nurturing Parent/Child dialogue like this, you may find that your racket feeling has dissipated. If it hasn't, experiment with something else, like jujitsuing the feeling.

GOOD-BYE GRAY STAMPS

(Situation: You are feeling bad. You want to get rid of these bad feelings rather than hold them inside.)

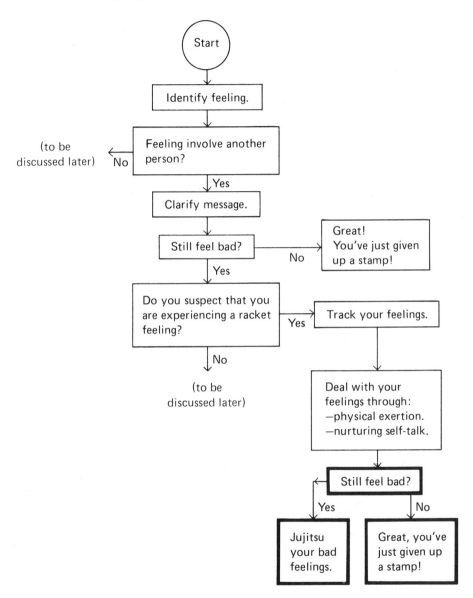

Jujitsu Your Feelings

Still feel bad? If not, congratulations! You've just given up a stamp. If so, your next move is to try jujitsuing your feelings. Jujitsu is an art of self-defense. One of the important principles used in jujitsu is balance. If a person much bigger and stronger attacks you, you can turn that person's strength to your advantage by keeping your balance and using jujitsu tactics. Suppose

Bush Cavendish (a big bruiser) attempts to push you. If, instead of trying to push back, you suddenly yield and move back more quickly than Bush is moving forward (while keeping a hold on him), you can force the bully off balance using his own strength to your advantage.

You can do the same thing with bad feelings! You can suddenly yield to them and turn the energy you've stirred up to a useful purpose. You can say to yourself, "OK, I'm feeling bad right now and there's nothing much I can do about that. But is there something I can do for myself that is more positive? Can I learn something from this experience? Can I treat myself in some OK way?" Keep your balance. Don't try to fight your bad feelings. Instead take the energy you are putting into feeling bad (it takes a lot of energy to be depressed, angry, or frustrated!) and put it to work for you.

Example

Dick, a sales representative for an elementary-school supply company, jujit-sued his feelings to good effect when he was calling on a retail teachers' supply store that also sold by mail order. "Oh, I see you have a new catalog now," Dick said to the store owner as he picked up the catalog and looked through it quickly to see how his company's products were being displayed. Just then a customer asked the owner a question and Dick stepped aside. Suddenly Dick realized his products weren't in the catalog. An unpleasant tension swept over him. He was angry.

Instead of letting his anger get the best of him, he yielded to it and began asking himself, "How can I make something positive out of this situation?" Just then he remembered that a friend of his was presenting a seminar for teachers of gifted students. "Sam, would you like me to distribute some of your catalogs for you?" Dick asked. "I have a friend who can give them out to some teachers of gifted students. Those teachers have a special budget, you know, and have money to spend on special supplies."

Sam was pleased. "Thanks, Dick. I really appreciate that. Oh, by the way, Dick, I need six dozen of your math workbooks."

By doing something for Sam instead of complaining, Dick got a good order and increased the probability that his products would be listed in the next printing of Sam's catalog. He did inquire about the omission but not in anger. The explanation he got satisfied him, and he agreed to check with Sam just before the spring printing.

GOOD-BYE GRAY STAMPS

(Situation: You are feeling bad. You want to get rid
of these bad feelings rather than hold them inside.)

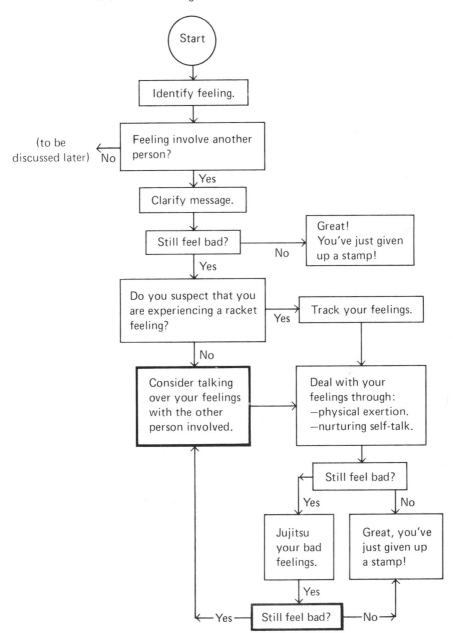

Expressing Your Feelings

If you still feel bad even after dealing with your feelings on your own, you
might consider talking your feelings over with another person—perhaps the
person involved, a trusted friend, or even a counselor.

There is a caution to remember, though, when we speak directly to the person involved: If our feelings are racket feelings, they aren't necessarily rational and tend not to be fully appropriate to the situation. If our feelings were never distorted, they would be complete[6] and genuine. We would experience a sensation, give it meaning, and then act on it. It is characteristic of a healthy, genuine feeling that it is appropriate to the situation. Also, others accept and understand it more easily because it is real and immediate.

But few of us escape twisting at least some of our feelings and, as a result, sometimes they just don't make sense. For example, Hank and Matt were both invited to the same office birthday party during an afternoon break. Hank got excited, looked forward to the party, and bought a small package of nuts and tied them in a big purple ribbon as a gift. Matt, however, became uneasy, feeling anger and even envy. He grew cross and irritable and, although he attended the party, his actions were stiff and he appeared sullen. Hank's feelings seemed appropriate to the situation. Given the context, his feelings "fit" what was happening. Matt's, however, were incongruent. They didn't match what was going on at the time.

When our feelings, like Matt's, seem out of proportion or irrational—out of tune with the circumstances—we can often ease the situation by openly *stating that possibility* and expressing to the other person that our feelings may not add up. In fact, talking to someone about our anger, sadness, disappointment, hurt, or whatever, and listening to what we ourselves say is one way to get in touch with the possible inappropriateness of our feeling response. It also allows us to discharge the feelings to some degree while not forcing someone else to take responsibility for them.

If your situation seems extreme, if you find your feelings get in the way of having the rewarding communication you'd like, if you find that your feelings *frequently* seem to be out of tune—unrealistic and out of proportion to the situation—you might consider professional counseling.[7] This would give you an opportunity to release your Hidden Self, uncover more of your Blind Self, and expand your Open Self.

If our feelings are a *genuine* response to a situation, expressing them to the person involved may be the most expedient thing to do. Yet even when our feelings are genuine and aren't snapping back like rubber bands to some earlier experience, it's often hard to talk about them directly to another person. Yet being able to say openly what we're feeling encourages authentic relationships and good communication. Most of us know intuitively that it's better to get things out, to lay our cards on the table, and to let people know how we're feeling—whether it be negative or positive. As you've seen, holding feelings inside and storing up a warehouse full of emotional bundles is likely to be self-defeating.

For most of us, expressing either genuine or racket feelings involves a degree of risk. We could be rejected. We could be told that it's silly to feel that way. We could even be told that our feelings don't count. The risk seems greater, however, when we have few skills.

If expressing feelings is difficult for you, strengthening your use of "I" messages helps. Then you're not accusing someone else, thus activating defensiveness; instead you're taking responsiblity for what's happening to *you.* You'll learn some useful skills for more open expression in Chapter 15, "Tips on Transactions," and for learning to level in Chapter 17, "Transacting Authentically."

APPLICATION ────────────────────────────────────

Which of these is probably the best way to express a *racket* feeling?

___ (a) "You really hurt my feelings when you . . . ."

___ (b) "Hey, I know that this may sound strange—it doesn't make any sense—but here's what I'm feeling about the situation . . . ."

___ (c) "I'm feeling really nervous about the fact that you don't take your breaks in the lounge with the rest of the workers."

~ • ~ • ~ • ~ • ~ • ~ • ~ • ~ • ~ • ~ • ~ • ~ • ~ • ~ • ~ • ~ • ~

The best choice is (b). The words, "I know that this may sound strange," help to convey the idea that the speaker is taking responsibility for the feelings to be expressed.

(Flowchart continues next page.)

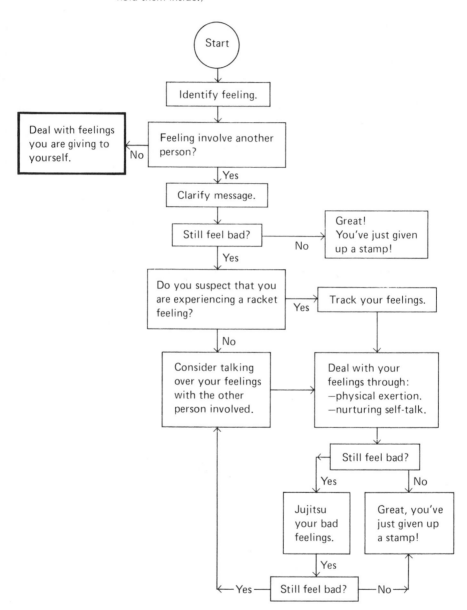

GOOD-BYE GRAY STAMPS

(Situation: You are feeling bad. You want to get rid of these bad feelings rather than hold them inside.)

Face Your Feelings

What if your feelings don't involve another person? Up until now we have focused on stamps that we decide to collect when another person does or says something. But you can collect stamps all by yourself.

For example, see if you are giving yourself *Kick Me* gray stamps in any of these ways:

— I procrastinate and then feel guilty or anxious because I haven't started on an important project.
— I repeatedly make a certain kind of mistake and call myself "stupid" each time I do it.
— I feel bad for making promises I don't have time to keep.
— I worry needlessly when working on a major project and bring on feelings of frustration, anxiety, or fear.
— I make "to do" lists and then scold myself for losing them.
— I blow up and then feel guilty.

We usually give ourselves *Kick Me* gray stamps when we are infected with self-doubt and our sense of self-esteem sags. If you collect gray stamps in this way, you can use the same approach that we have just outlined to check out your collection.

First, you can clarify the messages that you are giving to yourself. For example, if you're frequently making mistakes, the message you're giving yourself may be: "I'm stupid."

You can also track down the feeling. For example, if you're playing "stupid," begin tracking the feeling by realizing that you are compulsively arranging your outer world so it's likely that you'll do stupid things. You could track down the feeling by asking the self-inquiry questions we mentioned earlier:

— When have I felt this way before?
— How did I feel as a child when things went wrong in my family?
— What am I doing to sabotage myself?
— What Parent tapes am I using to trigger these bad feelings in myself? (Once you identify the offending Parent tapes, you can begin to counter them.)

Sometimes when you collect gray stamps, you may want to tell sympathetic listeners about them. The problem in expressing your bad feelings about yourself to sympathetic listeners is that you may just be creating an opportunity to bask in self-negation. Examples of this are people who feel compelled to tell everyone they meet about their stupid mistakes. For this reason, we suggest you avoid talking about your *Kick Me* stamp collection. Every time you tell someone how stupid you are, you strengthen your negative payoff.

An alternative is to talk about the *good* feelings that you've been getting and how you got them. This approach tends to strengthen your good feelings. If you're having good feelings most of the time, you won't be having bad ones!

Collect Gold Stamps

People who choose success make a habit of attracting and collecting gold stamps. Gold stamps, remember, represent good feelings that we savor, such as self-appreciation and confidence.

One way to build more good feelings is to put energy into your gold-stamp collection. An important skill in this regard involves being able to accept positive strokes.

APPLICATION ——————————————————————————————————

Here are some examples of ways to respond to various strokes. Identify each as winning or losing responses.

Positive Stroke	Response	Winning	Losing
1. "That was a great speech, Anne!"	"Oh, you think so? I didn't think it was so good."		
2. "Your sales are up this week, Max. Good work!"	"Thanks. I'm feeling good about some of the new sales techniques I'm using."		
3. "Thanks for all the help you gave me in hiring that new employee."	"Well, you did almost everything."		
4. "That letter you wrote to B.J. did the trick! He's giving us a fantastic order."	"Yeah, well thanks. He probably would have given us that order anyway."		

~ • ~ • ~ • ~ • ~ • ~ • ~ • ~ • ~ • ~ • ~ • ~ • ~ • ~ • ~ • ~ • ~

Only item 2 is likely a winner's response. Notice that each of the other responses amounts to a rejection of the stroke that was offered.

~ • ~ • ~ • ~ • ~ • ~ • ~ • ~ • ~ • ~ • ~ • ~ • ~ • ~ • ~ • ~ • ~

Now, rewrite each of these loser responses and change them into winning ones by *accepting* the positive stroke.

Positive Stroke	Old Losing Response	New Winning Response
1. "That was a great speech, Anne!"	"Oh, you think so? I didn't think is was so good."	
2. "Thanks for all the help you gave in hiring that new employee."	"Well, you did almost everything."	
3. "That letter you wrote to B.J. did the trick! He's giving us a fantastic order."	"Yeah, well thanks. He probably would have given us that order anyway."	

~ . ~ . ~ . ~ . ~ . ~ . ~ . ~ . ~ . ~ . ~ . ~ . ~ . ~ . ~ . ~ . ~

1 You might say, "Thanks, I'm pleased you liked it," or "Thanks, I enjoyed giving it."

2 You might say, "I'm glad I was able to help," or "I'm happy my input was useful."

3 You might respond with, "Thanks, I really appreciate hearing that," or "I'm glad the effort I put into that letter paid off."

These are just sample winning responses. Yours may be quite different. Count them correct if they revealed a gracious acceptance of the positive stroke, rather than a rejection.

By accepting positive strokes, you enable yourself to collect and savor good feelings. You give power to yourself. Sometimes people are able to accept a positive stroke momentarily, but they are not able to enjoy it for very long. They feel compelled to return it immediately to the person who gave it. For example:

Don (a truck driver): "Say, Roy, that's really great the way you've been staying ahead of your schedules lately and you haven't gotten any tickets lately either."

Roy: "Thanks for the compliment, Don. You've been moving those tomatoes pretty fast yourself. I understand you hold the record for the shortest time for the run to Pittsburgh."

One way to break yourself of the habit of not hanging onto a gold stamp is to practice responding differently. For example, after thanking a person, you might express your good feeling about the compliment. Also you might say a word or two about how you achieved the particular accomplishment that you were just stroked for.

APPLICATION

Phyllis, a receptionist, is being complimented by Terry for her outstanding work in handling an important incoming phone call. As we look in on the scene, Terry is just finishing up his positive stroke.

Terry: ". . . and that was just great, Phyllis, the way you put Thatcher on hold while you called the airport and contacted Mr. Thornbottom. Most people would have just said, 'I'm sorry, he is out. Can I take a message?' "

Which of these ways of responding to Terry's positive stroke is consistent with what we recommend?

___ (a) "Yeah, I was just doing what's expected of me."

___ (b) "Thanks. It feels good to hear that. You know, getting our clients in touch with the right people is a part of my job I really like. And I knew Mr. Thornbottom was eager to talk to Thatcher."

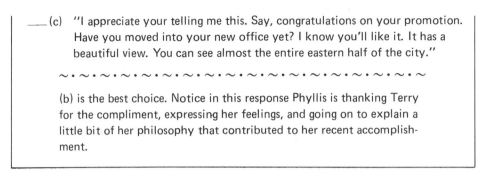

____ (c) "I appreciate your telling me this. Say, congratulations on your promotion. Have you moved into your new office yet? I know you'll like it. It has a beautiful view. You can see almost the entire eastern half of the city."

~ . ~ . ~ . ~ . ~ . ~ . ~ . ~ . ~ . ~ . ~ . ~ . ~ . ~ . ~

(b) is the best choice. Notice in this response Phyllis is thanking Terry for the compliment, expressing her feelings, and going on to explain a little bit of her philosophy that contributed to her recent accomplishment.

We can collect and savor gold stamps by accepting and enjoying the positive feedback that comes our way. We can collect them in other ways, too. For example, Anne Morton keeps a gold-stamp calendar.[8] To start a gold-stamp calendar of your own, first invent some kind of simple figurative design that represents your positive self. Think of it as your own personal logo, your symbol. You might want to use something like a star, a heart symbol, a happy face, or whatever strikes your fancy. Dorothy's symbol is

. Phil's is . You might want to doodle for awhile before you settle on your final design. Here are some ideas to get you started.

Once you've decided on a logo that you like and feel good about, you can use it to reward yourself for attracting gold stamps. For example, you might have a special calendar on which you draw in your logo each day that you feel you've made progress toward one of your goals. At the end of a month, you can look back on your accomplishments and remember your good feelings.

A related approach is to keep a special place for recording your achievements and good feelings. You might want to have a file folder in which you keep such things as complimentary notes from others, photographs, letters, certificates, and so on. Whenever something works out particularly well on the job, make a record of what happened, how you achieved it, and what special qualities you made use of in yourself. Or you may want to make yourself a handy Warm Fuzzy Bag. Stuff it with the many good things that come your way. On occasion reach inside and pull out something that helps you reexperience a good feeling. In these ways you can build on your successes and take delight in your achievements. It's OK to do that!

Just as we save up anger and then cash in by blowing off steam, we can also cash in our collections of good feelings. When you've saved up enough gold stamps, you'll feel good about redeeming them by doing things such as these:

— Go to a special place for lunch.
— Arrange time with a close friend.
— Sit outside and watch the sky, trees, and birds.
— Go to that movie you've wanted to see.
— Get a new plant for your desk.
— Ask for a promotion.
— Do something terrific for yourself!

You might ask: "Doesn't this show a lack of self-confidence—to go to so much trouble to bask in past accomplishments? If people have inner contentment, wouldn't this be unnecessary?" Yes, if people have inner contentment, they will not feel a strong need to collect stamps, gray or gold. But as is pointed out in *Born to Win*, "It's a rare person who can achieve this degree of independence. Most of us find it comforting to have a few gold stamps for a 'rainy day'—even winners."[9] Many of us need practice in treating ourselves well and accepting that we deserve an abundant life.

SUMMARY

We collect stamps to strengthen old feelings learned in our childhood. Negative feelings that we repeatedly attract or collect are racket feelings or gray stamps. They're called rackets because they're dishonest repeats of past learned feelings. We collect stamps (like trading stamps) and cash them in through an emotional outburst, a dramatic action such as quitting a job, firing an employee, or even a heart attack. Plainly, stamp collecting is unhealthy emotionally, physically, and psychologically. People who give up stamp collecting often remark that they feel set free, as if a great weight has been lifted from their shoulders.

You can do a number of things to avoid collecting gray stamps. If you feel bad in response to what someone has said or done, first clarify the message. If you still feel bad, next consider whether the feeling is a racket feeling. If you decide your feeling is genuine, it's generally best to express it in some tactful way so that it doesn't turn into a grudge. (We'll discover techniques for expressing feelings in Chapter 17.) However, if your feeling seems to be a racket, you can deal with it in a number of ways. You can exert yourself physically or nurture yourself. If the unpleasant feeling persists, you can jujitsu it. These are all corrective techniques to help you avoid collecting an unpleasant feeling. Once you've done this, it's important to switch your focus to good feelings. Accept positive strokes, collect and savor your gold stamps. Start a gold-stamp calendar or file.

In coming chapters we'll discuss other techniques for building self-confidence and enhancing the ability to attract and collect gold stamps. These include:

— meditation,
— deep relaxation,

— systematic desensitization,
— frequency modification, and
— vivid visualization.

In the next chapter, you'll take a look at how you use your time and gather some ideas on how to use it even better. Before going ahead to that chapter, we'd like to close this one with a poem by Sharla Lee Donahue. We suggest you read it now and review it whenever you're hooked by a racket feeling. Then say, "Good-bye gray stamps!"

Here I Stand, Myself

Here I stand in the early morn,
Hearing the rushing water sing its continuous song.
Watching the morning sun rise, awaking the sleepy valley,
Stroking the shimmering reflectors of dew,
The sun almost seems to be saying,
"Awaken, I've come to renew!"

Here I stand, breathing in the fragrance of pine,
Hearing a sweet song which is so sublime.
How my mind clears, like using a large broom,
Sweeping a dusty room.
I can see now in my mind so far and clear.
I feel infinity very near.

Here I stand, myself, at last.
My eyes are washed with fresh clear air and mist.
The warm sun soon dries the mist from my freshened face,
While happily knowing it's not a disgrace
Of feeling free and content;
I no longer hold a burden of my past.[10]

SOURCE NOTES

[1] Claude M. Steiner, *Scripts People Live: Transactional Analysis of Life Scripts* (New York: Bantam, 1975), p. 50.

[2] Leo Madow, *Anger* (New York: Scribner, 1974).

[3] Ken Olson, *The Art of Hanging Loose in an Uptight World* (Greenwich, Conn.: Fawcett Crest, 1974), pp. 191–192.

[4] Muriel James and Dorothy Jongeward, *Born to Win: Transactional Analysis with Gestalt Experiments* (Reading, Mass.: Addison-Wesley, 1971), p. 209.

[5] Muriel Schiffman, *Self Therapy: Techniques for Personal Growth* (Menlo Park, Calif.: Self Therapy Press, 1967).

[6] For a more detailed discussion of complete feelings, see J. Hart and R. Corriene, *Going Sane: An Introduction to Feeling Therapy* (New York: Dell, 1976).

[7] If you want the names of counselors in your area trained in TA, write to the International Transactional Analysis Association, 1772 Vallejo Street, San Francisco, Calif. 94123.

[8] Anne Morton, president of Careerwise, Inc., in San Francisco, uses several different colors of ink to make what she calls her "rainbow of success" calendar.

[9] James and Jongeward, *op. cit.*, p. 186.

[10] Unpublished poem by Sharla Lee Donahue, Concord, Calif.

8

Structuring Your Time

In this chapter we'll explore various ways of structuring time and see how they relate to Parent tapes, stroking patterns, and life script.

OBJECTIVES

When you finish this chapter, you'll be able to:

- identify from a description how a person is structuring time;
- draw a diagram to show how you structure your time on the job;
- analyze your stroking pattern in terms of how you structure your time;
- examine a situation in which people or organizations are structuring their time in unproductive ways and suggest improvements;
- identify Parent tapes you have about time and explain how they may be affecting job performance;
- describe your script as it relates to your job;
- make a tentative plan for enhancing the way you spend your life's time.

As we grow up, another basic hunger besides stroke hunger emerges: the desire to fill our time. If we have nothing to do, we become bored. This boredom can, like a lack of strokes, bring on physical and emotional deterioration, so we search out ways to fill our hours. Eric Berne observes that people structure their time in relation to other people in six basic ways. They:

- *withdraw* from others,
- carry out *rituals*,
- engage in *pastimes*,
- work together (carry out *activities*),
- play psychological *games*, and
- experience feelings of *intimacy* (feelings of tenderness, openness, closeness, affection).

STRUCTURING TIME

Let's begin by discussing the different ways we structure our time and the kinds of strokes each way encourages.

Withdrawal

You withdraw when you remove yourself from a situation either physically or psychologically. Physical withdrawal involves actually walking out and removing yourself from other people. Psychological withdrawal occurs when you turn off awareness of your surroundings and perhaps go off on a fantasy trip. Both kinds of withdrawal can be positive or negative.

Withdrawal is not helpful when it results in extended savoring of cold pricklies or continued avoidance of responsibility. Focusing on your inner awareness can be negative if it interferes with your ability to function effectively. Have you ever found yourself "coming to" halfway through a stoplight? Focusing inside could also be dangerous if you're working around machinery or chemicals or if you're involved in important transactions where you need to be listening to your outer world.

We all talk to ourselves—positively and negatively—inside our heads. If you strengthen negative tapes by allowing them to play repeatedly, you may put energy behind those thoughts and bring them to life. Listen to how you speak to yourself. Make sure you're affirming yourself and not putting yourself down. Remember, thoughts have power to influence your chances for success.

Withdrawal can be positive. We can withdraw to go for a walk, read a thriller, ponder a problem, listen to music, or check out how we feel. If we can relax or engage in productive mental activity, we can give ourselves positive strokes while we are alone. Sometimes we simply need time to sort things out, to integrate what's happening to us. Sometimes we need time alone to *still* our minds so that we can recoup our energies and allow our bodies to heal. In Chapter 12 we discuss some techniques for using withdrawal in a positive way: focusing on deep relaxation, vivid visualization, and clearing the mind.

When you engage in withdrawal you give strokes only to yourself. But the other ways of structuring time usually involve exchanging strokes with other people. Rituals, for example, are fixed, group-approved ways of interacting.

Rituals

Carrying out rituals gets us strokes. For example, when we meet an acquaintance for the first time during the day, we usually engage in a greeting ritual. We briefly catch the other person's eyes and say something like:

"Hi"
"Hello"
"How are you?"
"Good morning"

When we part company, we do the same:

"Good-bye"
"So long"
"Take it easy"

"Good evening"
"Have a nice night"
"Sweet dreams" (and so on)

Such informal rituals tend to involve light, superficial strokes, but since they are "maintenance" strokes, they are sorely missed if they're absent. Depending on the situation and the manner of delivery, however, ritual strokes can range from superficial to intense. Most of us also engage in other rituals, such as in marriage and funeral services, that involve a highly intense interchange of strokes. They go deeper and are felt longer than a simple "Hi."

Although rituals develop to meet real needs, they tend to become "set in stone." If rituals are not updated, they often lose their original value and can become a waste of time. For example, a company picnic for an organization of a hundred employees may be quite useful in promoting good relationships, but a company picnic for 20,000 could become just a clumsy attempt to maintain a false "family" feeling. Similarly, weekly staff meetings, performance appraisals, and other such scheduled activities can lose their original value, unless they respond to changing needs.

APPLICATION ———————————————————————————

1 Name a ritual that your company engages in.

2 What is the purpose of this ritual?

3 Is it useful?

4 If this ritual is a waste of time, what might you do to make it worthwhile?

5 In understanding rituals, it's helpful to relate them to ego states. When you are carrying out a ritual, what ego states are you likely to be using?

～•～•～•～•～•～•～•～•～•～•～•～•～•～•～•～•～

When engaging in a ritual, we are most likely using our Adapted Child and Parent ego states. When we carry out a ritual, we usually respond almost automatically, the way we've learned to.

～•～•～•～•～•～•～•～•～•～•～•～•～•～•～•～•～

6 Stan, a division manager in an electronics firm, didn't have time for "empty" greetings. He often passed others in the hallway without saying a word, his mind being on "more important" company matters. Stan often complained that his subordinates did not have the proper cooperative spirit. He even accused them at times of sabotaging his efforts.

Which of these is probably the best explanation of Stan's apparent "stuck up" or uncaring attitude?

___(a)　Stan is operating from an I'm OK, you're not-OK position.

___(b)　Stan is prejudiced against his subordinates.

___(c)　Stan's parents weren't great for observing greeting rituals.

What might Stan do differently to get more cooperation from his subordinates?

~ . ~ . ~ . ~ . ~ . ~ . ~ . ~ . ~ . ~ . ~ . ~ . ~ . ~ . ~ . ~ . ~

Any of the answers is a possible explanation. The simplest is that Stan's parents weren't much for giving ritual strokes and Stan incorporated their behavior in his Parent ego state.

Stan might improve his relationship with his subordinates by paying more attention to some simple greeting rituals. (Other measures might be needed, but this would be a good start!)

Because people carry out rituals more or less automatically, almost as if to comply with their traditional Parent, they *may* tend to discount rituals, dismissing them as being of little or no value. On the contrary, it's important to realize, as Berne points out, that "they offer a safe, reassuring, . . . and often enjoyable method of structuring time."[1]

One advantage of rituals is that they give us an easy starting point and enable us to move to more meaningful ways of structuring time. For example, people may begin with a ritual and then move into a pastime.

Pastimes

Pastimes are comfortable ways to *pass* our *time.* A pastime is defined as a "series of semi-ritualistic, simple, complementary, open transactions arranged around a single field of material whose primary object is to structure an interval of time."[2] When you give a person pastime strokes, you fill the time between you with a commonplace subject like the weather, a recent political event, sports, cars, bosses, subordinates, and so on.

Eric Berne supplies some witty labels for different pastimes, such as:

— General Motors (discussion about cars)
— PTA (usually a discussion about what's wrong with schools)
— Who won (sports)
— Ever been (to some nostalgic place)

Pastimes frequently heard at work include:

— Why don't we (do it this way)
— Did you hear (the latest gossip)
— Nowadays . . . (it ain't what it used to be)
— If only . . . (they would do their jobs)

Ain't It Awful (about . . .) is a favorite pastime. Who hasn't filled the time at lunch break talking about the awful weather, the awful young people we hire nowadays, how awful company politics is—all with no intention of doing anything except talking.

A certain amount of pastiming is beneficial because it helps people get to know one another better. Also, some research suggests that 20–30 minutes of pure Adult activity is about as much as we can manage without the need for a break.[3,4]

Pastiming can give us a needed break and a chance to relax. If carried to excess, however, pastiming can take an overwhelming amount of time away from our productivity. Pastimes usually don't go anywhere. They are not goal-oriented; they can go on and on without producing any meaningful product or service.

Example

Bill, a sales representative for a textbook company, called on isolated teachers in the boondocks. Because many of these teachers felt stroke-deprived, they were delighted to see Bill coming. However, he was easily hooked into a pastime of Ain't It Awful, often talking vehemently with the teachers about the awful things happening: how students can't read, how parents don't support the schools, how kids are allowed to stay home to work on the farm, how voters vote down tax bonds, and so on. Doing this felt good to Bill and he believed it helped him establish a friendly relationship with his clients. Instead he often got so carried away that he failed to cover important selling points and didn't make all his calls. The problem multiplied because Bill, being alone on the road, often felt stroke-deprived himself. When he learned what he was doing, Bill cut down the time spent in pastiming and stepped up the time spent making sales points. He also stopped using his clients to fill his stroke bucket and started looking for other ways to get the strokes he needed.

APPLICATION ───────────────────────────────

Doug manages a group of traveling sales representatives who have problems similar to Bill's—that is, they travel alone a lot and tend to carry pastiming strokes to excess. What might Doug do to alleviate this problem?

~ • ~ • ~ • ~ • ~ • ~ • ~ • ~ • ~ • ~ • ~ • ~ • ~ • ~ • ~ • ~ • ~ • ~

There are many possible solutions to this problem. Doug might arrange for his people to get a lot of strokes. For example, he might make himself available for phone calls and chat with them about their day. Members of one such sales force who had learned TA simply called and

announced, "I need some strokes. Things are lonesome out here!" One
pastime session with the manager took the place of several with clients.

Another approach might be to install CB radios in the salespeople's
cars, so they could exchange ritual and pastime strokes with other
CBers while traveling from one client to the next. They might also use
the CB radios directly in their work and consequently increase their
share of activity strokes.

The main idea of any solution should be to reduce stroke deprivation, so the sales force will no longer satisfy their stroke needs by
excessive pastiming with customers.

Although pastimes can get in our way, they can sometimes be a valuable
use of time because:

— They allow us to get strokes without getting too involved with people.
— They give us information for deciding whether to continue, expand, or
  end relationships.
— They help keep conversations going until it's appropriate to exchange
  more meaningful strokes.

Some people find it easy to exchange pastime strokes; they have the
"gift of gab." But others are shy. They have not learned pastiming skills and
feel awkward even if they do have many subjects they could talk about;
they just don't feel comfortable about looking someone in the eye and
talking about things like the weather or where they went last vacation. If
you have difficulty giving and receiving pastime strokes, you may be happy
with that. On the other hand, you may wish to make it a self-management
project.[5] (See Part II, "The Self-Care Program.")

Being able to give and receive pastime strokes easily is an important skill
for many working people. For example, supervisors who can't pass a little
time in small talk may have difficulties with their subordinates simply
because subordinates view them as cold and impersonal.

Example

"The man just doesn't know how to relate to people. He never comes to
talk to me about anything, unless he's asking for the weekly sales report.
Sure, I do my job, but I'm *not* going to break my back for him when he
doesn't seem to care about me."

APPLICATION

From what you know about pastimes, which of these statements do you agree with?

____ (a)   It's best to avoid them.

____ (b)   They are an OK way to give and get strokes.

___ (c)   The ability to give and receive pastime strokes is useful for meeting new people and making friends.

___ (d)   Most salespeople would benefit from learning to be skillful at engaging in limited pastimes.

___ (e)   A pastime is another word for a psychological game.

___ (f)   Pastimes can be counterproductive.

~ • ~ • ~ • ~ • ~ • ~ • ~ • ~ • ~ • ~ • ~ • ~ • ~ • ~ • ~ • ~ • ~ • ~

We agree with (b), (c), (d), and (f). Pastimes can be useful on the job. They are often a fun way to spend time and get to know customers, co-workers, subordinates, and bosses. But when carried to excess, pastimes can hinder productivity. A pastime is quite different from a psychological game. For one thing, psychological games always involve ulterior messages; pastimes do not.

Activities

Activity strokes are strokes you give and get while working on a project by yourself or with others. A distinguishing feature of activity strokes is that they result in some form of a product or service, in getting a job done: discussing a planned project, putting a product together, serving a customer. Activities are goal-oriented and have a definite purpose. Activities often provide a setting for many other ways of structuring time to occur. For example, we may pastime in the middle of a project, take a ritualistic break, or experience a sense of closeness when an experiment clicks. Also, activities can be carried on outside the job. Some people carry out their most fulfilling work after-hours!

Actually, the activity itself can also provide fulfilling strokes. When we no longer look to others for encouragement or direction but find that our energy and excitement come from seeing the fruits of our own talents, the strokes are intrinsic rather than extrinsic. In fact, they feel the best when what we're doing draws out our true potential and challenges our skills and imaginations. Have you ever worked late in the night on a project without noticing the time because you were so excited about what you were doing? If so, you know how these fulfilling strokes feel. People who turn on to their jobs seldom watch the clock.

Activity strokes are not always positive. Sometimes we put our energy into *getting the wrong task done right*, or we get work done but it's boring, or we use our work to isolate ourselves from others.

Activity strokes also may not feel good if people are expecting other kinds of strokes. For example, suppose Pat, the office supervisor, strides out of her office and asks her secretary for the Bixby account. If her secretary, Alma, has just returned from a week's vacation and expected some pastime or ritual strokes, Alma may choose to feel put down even though Pat had no intention of slighting her.

APPLICATION ——————————————————

For each of the following situations, tell what kind of strokes are being exchanged (ritual, pastime, or activity).

1 Lorna: "Did you hear about Emma?"
   Donna: "No, I didn't. What's up?"
   Lorna: "Well, I'll tell you, she's pregnant."
   Donna: "Oh, really?! Will that interfere with her promotion?"
   Lorna: "I don't know yet. But it'll sure be interesting to see what happens!"

   What kinds of strokes are being exchanged?

   ___ (a) Ritual

   ___ (b) Pastime

   ___ (c) Activity

2 Joan: "Hey, Bob, what'd you think of the game last night?"
   Bob: "Man, we really romped those guys, didn't we?"
   Joan: "Yeah, but it was pretty rough going during the first half, don't you think?"
   Bob: "Yeah, it sure was, but Thompson really let them know who was boss when he started talking to the air!"
   Joan: "Yeah, did you see that fifty-yard pass?"

   What kinds of strokes are being exchanged?

   ___ (a) Ritual

   ___ (b) Pastime

   ___ (c) Activity

3 Mel: "Say, Jack, did we get the proposed cover designs for the new catalog from the art department?"
   Jack: "Yes, here they are. I'll spread them out on the table so we can compare them easily."
   Mel: "I like the one with the extra copy on the cover, don't you?"
   Jack: "Yes, I think it helps to clarify what we're doing."

   What kinds of strokes are being exchanged?

   ___ (a) Ritual

   ___ (b) Pastime

   ___ (c) Activity

4 Steve: "And now, Art, in recognition of your ten years of faithful service, I would like to present you with your ten-year pin."
   Art: "Thank you." (He reaches out to accept the pin, as other employees standing around applaud.)

What kinds of strokes are being exchanged here?

___ (a)   Ritual

___ (b)   Pastime

___ (c)   Activity

~ · ~ · ~ · ~ · ~ · ~ · ~ · ~ · ~ · ~ · ~ · ~ · ~ · ~ · ~ · ~ · ~ · ~

The first two examples illustrated pastime strokes; the third, an activity stroke; the fourth, a ritual stroke.

Games

As we have seen, game strokes are the negative payoffs—the cold pricklies—we get from ulterior transactions. They are powerful and intense: we "feel" a game stroke for a long time.

As a pastime Ain't It Awful is an exchange of gripes. As a game *Ain't It Awful* is an ulterior setup to compulsively collect feelings of frustration or helplessness in the face of problem situations. It becomes a way to act out a vested interest in the Rescuing role, a way to avoid facing problems, personal weaknesses, and social responsibilities.

Here's an interesting encounter with an *Ain't It Awful* game:

> I attended a luncheon meeting where individuals from the Heart Association, March of Dimes, Mental Health, Planned Parenthood, etc. were gathered together to share their particular achievements, questions, and happenings. The day before this meeting was held, the vaccine for polio was announced. This was surely a time for celebration. On my way to the meeting I fantasied what kind of a celebration we might have. Throw away the usual peanut butter and bologna sandwiches and have champagne and cold cuts!
>
> When I arrived at the meeting, the woman from the March of Dimes was not there. I was not the only one anticipating her entrance. Most of us expected something special, and an air of excitement filled the room.
>
> The woman finally arrived. She entered the room visibly slumped. Assuming a downcast physical posture, she walked over to her place and tossed her sack lunch on the table. Plopping herself down in her chair, she looked up dejectedly at the rest of us and complained, "It is certainly going to be hard to get people interested in another disease."
>
> This woman had a reputation of being a dedicated, hard worker and a dynamic fund raiser who was able to get volunteers to work. On the surface she was doing a great job helping the unfortunate. Underneath, she had no intention of solving problems, no intention of *really* rescuing anybody. Her energies went into her game of *Ain't It Awful.* [6]

People often go after game strokes because that's how they've learned to meet their stroke needs: they don't know how else to get them. A good way to give up games, then, is to structure our time so we get and give more of the kinds of strokes that are *good* for people: for example, rituals, pastimes, and activities. Better yet, we can risk a little more and learn to get more *intimacy strokes*—strokes that reflect honesty, authenticity, tenderness, and caring.

Intimacy

Intimacy strokes go much deeper than ritual, pastime, or activity strokes. Intimacy strokes are the kind of strokes we give when we are having a heart-to-heart talk and sharing feelings. We're coming on straight, being honest. We drop pretense and aren't afraid to be ourselves. Often the words "sex" and "intimate" are considered interchangeable. They are not. At best, sex does involve the depth of intimacy, but sex can certainly occur *without* intimacy. For example, sex can be a Friday night ritual, a pastime for an otherwise boring evening, an activity for making babies, or a game to hurt or be hurt. It's important to recognize that the real basis for intimacy is not sex, but rather an authentic encounter with another person—an encounter that is open, honest, and game-free.

Recall Ron and Greg, who experienced a moment of real closeness (pages 127–128). They weren't afraid to share feelings, to be authentic in relating to each other. Such encounters can result in the extraordinary sense of togetherness felt by people working cooperatively with a sensitive, caring attitude. More on intimacy strokes in Chapter 17 on "Transacting Authentically."

Strokes for Fun

Intimacy and most other kinds of strokes can involve an element of fun. Sometimes a hard task can be lightened because it's made fun. Some managers in the style of Huckleberry Finn are able to take an otherwise boring task and make it painless by encouraging workers to giggle, laugh, and have fun while they're "getting the fences painted." Although work *can* be satisfying and enjoyable, sometimes a job is just plain dull. Often we can add something to such a job or look at it in a new way so we're able to laugh and joke with our co-workers. If we can do that, we may be a lot more productive. A sense of humor often saves an otherwise tense or dreary situation. And nothing makes the world brighter than a good belly laugh.

Example

A half dozen people who worked for a major airline reluctantly gathered together to discuss ways to improve the timetable brochure that was being sent to travel agents and important accounts. The goal was to make the timetable a better selling tool. The group leader got everyone to agree that no criticism would be allowed during the brainstorming session so that highly unusual and creative ideas would be free to emerge. He did this to encourage them to use their Natural Child and Little Professor ego states and to avoid Adaptive Child behavior that would inhibit creativity. As the meeting progressed, all kinds of ideas appeared—including some outrageous yet really funny ones. Everyone got to laughing. They laughed so hard that they began to hurt.

Finally, each member of the committee had to leave and go into a separate room. But as soon as any two of them would come back to the meeting room, they would break out laughing again. Eventually, everyone settled down, but the meeting continued to be great fun. Ideas poured out because everyone was loosened up and not afraid of being criticized. Some really useful, creative ideas emerged. The brainstormers never forgot the experience. The next day, when a transcript of the meeting was typed out, a rather amused selection committee read over 152 ideas! Many of them were worthless: simply too far out to be practical. But a selection committee pruned the list down to 62 ideas that looked promising and even exciting. The airline put many of these ideas to work and significantly improved the timetable. It became more attractive, informative, and usable.

APPLICATION ———————————————————

Here's some more practice that will sharpen your ability to identify different ways of structuring time. For each item tell whether withdrawal, ritual, pastime, activity, game, or intimacy strokes are being exchanged. Also, indicate which examples involve the exchange of fun strokes.

1 Lyle's job is to check job requisitions and requests for cash advances. His routine work is boring and gives him little opportunity for interaction with other employees except when he rejects cash-advance requests. He studies each request meticulously and repeatedly rejects those that are not perfect in every detail. For example, he rejects any advance requests where the receipts for expenses are sloppily written or the signature does not include the requester's middle initial. A heated discussion then follows and the requester ends up feeling put down.

   Type of strokes exchanged: _____

2 Hilary, Sylvia, John, and Ron get together for a bridge game without fail every lunch hour. They laugh and have a good time.

   Type of strokes exchanged: _____

3 Before making a crucial management decision, Brian goes for a walk to clear his mind, center himself, and gain confidence.

   Type of strokes exchanged: _____

4 During a coffee break, Linda and Judy casually describe improvements they would like to see take place in their office. They do not commit themselves to any change but the conversation is relaxed. Neither person collects bad feelings.

   Type of strokes exchanged: _____

5 Ruth and Charlotte, two head supervisors, had just been told that a project that they had proposed had been accepted by upper management. They jumped up, hugged each other, and screamed, "Whoopie!" After a few minutes of this, they settled down and quietly expressed to each other how well they thought each had done and shared their excitement about carrying out the project.

   Type of strokes exchanged: _____

~·~·~·~·~·~·~·~·~·~·~·~·~·~·~·~·~·~·~

1 Game strokes.
2 Ritual strokes and fun strokes (you might also say pastime strokes).
3 Withdrawal strokes.
4 Pastime strokes.
5 Intimacy strokes and fun strokes.

Now that you're able to identify six different ways in which people struc-ture time in relating to others, take a few moments and think about how you spend your time during a typical workday. What percentage of the total time do you invest in each way?

APPLICATION: Awareness Exercise ────────────

How Do You Spend Your Time?

Think of your average workday as a pie. Let each piece of this pie stand for the portion of the day that you spend in a particular way.

Do you spend your time like this?

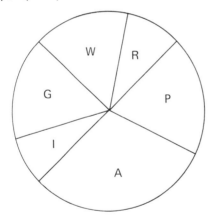

R = Ritual
P = Pastime
A = Activity
G = Game
I = Intimacy
W = Withdrawal

Or do you spend it like this?

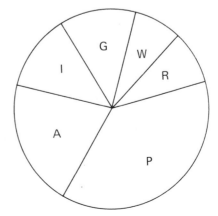

Now divide this pie into six pieces. Label each piece to show the amount of time you spend in each category.

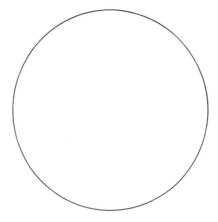

Study your diagram; if you're not satisfied with it, diagram how you would like to spend your time.

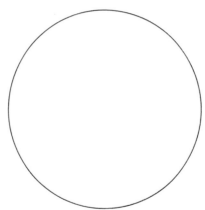

Your Stroking Pattern: Strokes You Give

In Chapter 5 you analyzed your stroking pattern in terms of stroking performance. In this exercise you'll analyze your stroking in terms of how you structure your time.

1 Think of *all* the strokes you *give* to yourself and to at least three others during a typical working day.

What percentage of them would you say are ritual strokes? _____

Pastime strokes? _____ Activity strokes? _____

Game strokes? _____ Intimacy strokes? _____

(Total should equal 100%—don't count withdrawal strokes here.)

2   Now make a bar graph so you can visualize the answers you gave in question 1.

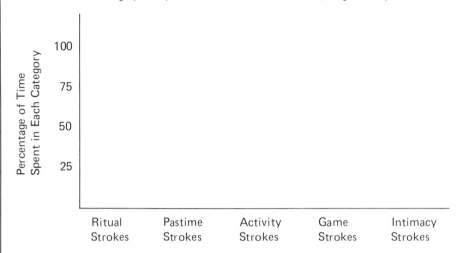

3   Of the different strokes that you give, what percentage are warm fuzzies as opposed to cold pricklies? Show this in the bar graph above by shading in the part of each bar that represents warm fuzzies.

4   If you're not satisfied with how you're giving strokes, draw a bar graph in the space below to show how you'd like to give them out. Once again, let the shaded portion of each bar represent warm fuzzies and the unshaded portion cold pricklies.

5   We left out withdrawal strokes in questions 1 through 4 because you give them only to yourself. Think now about the withdrawal strokes you give yourself.

What percentage are positive? _____ Negative? _____ Do you take time

out on the job to clear your mind? _____ Organize your thinking? _____

Relax? _____ Do you give yourself cold pricklies by scolding yourself with statements like, "You dummy!" or "How could you have been so stupid?" and

so on? _____ Do you praise yourself when you've done something especially

well? _____

Your Stroking Pattern: Strokes You Get

1 Now, in general, think of all the kinds of strokes you *get* from others during a typical day at work.

About what percentage would you say are ritual strokes? _____ Pastime strokes? _____ Activity strokes? _____ Game strokes? _____

Intimacy strokes? _____

(Again, the total should be 100%)

2 Make a bar graph to visualize the breakdown of strokes that you *get* on the job.

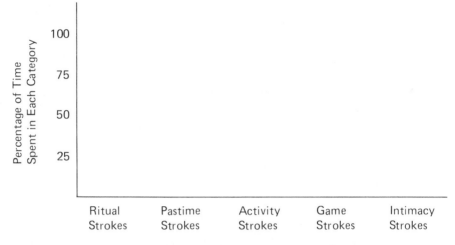

3 As before, shade in part of each bar that represents warm fuzzies.
4 If you'd like to be stroked differently, draw your ideal bar graph below.

(In Chapters 9–14 you will learn how to rearrange your environment to approach your ideal.)

Parent Tapes About Time

Most of us have Parent tapes about time. These tapes are often a part of our Unknown Self or Blind Self. They play and affect our choices without our being aware of them.

1   Which of these Parent tapes have you heard?

____ A stitch in time saves nine.

____ Time is money.

____ Work before pleasure.

____ Idle hands are the devil's workshop.

____ Whatever is worth doing is worth doing right.

____ Relax, take your time.

____ You can always do it tomorrow.

____ If you really want to do something, you can always find the time to do it.

2   Write out other Parent tapes you heard about time:

3   How do these tapes affect the way you use your time on the job? Do you see them as positive or negative?

(Note that in Chapter 12 we will discuss some specific ways to counter negative tapes. For now, though, let's concentrate on positive and negative tapes about *time*. This is important not only because we tend to follow our Parent tapes about time unthinkingly, but also these messages influence our expectations of the way others should use theirs!)

4   Think of yourself as a manager. Suppose you have the Parent tape "Work before pleasure." How might it affect your expectations of subordinates?

~ • ~ • ~ • ~ • ~ • ~ • ~ • ~ • ~ • ~ • ~ • ~ • ~ • ~ • ~

Usually "Work before pleasure" really means "No pleasure" since there's almost always work to be done. If you have a strong "Work before pleasure" tape, you might become tense if anyone seems to be having fun. Fun could always seem like goofing off. You could seem austere, rather like a slave driver or tyrant, to your subordinates. You might even be tempted to "punish" fast people with more work!

   Your answer is right if you pointed out that with such a tape you'd probably have a not-OK attitude about someone else's good times or more relaxed attitude.

EXPLORING YOUR SCRIPT

Parent tapes include not only directions, admonitions, and encouragements about how we should structure our time in relationships, but also how we should structure our *life's time.*

In turn, how we use our life's time depends largely on our script, the life plan we decided on when we were children. For most of us an important script element concerns what we do in our work. Whether we have decided to fail, to succeed, to go nowhere, to find pleasure, expression, and contentment or challenge, joy, and sorrow, is reflected in how we choose to earn our living.

Although we cannot deal with your total life script here, we can look at some of the factors that specifically relate to your job. In previous chapters, we have explored:

— your personal patterns, whether self-defeating or self-enhancing;
— your ego-state development;
— the kinds of transactions that you've learned to engage in;
— the games that you play;
— the kinds of stamps you give and get.

These explorations have given insights and clues into the pieces that fit together to form your psychological script. Let's continue that process.

APPLICATION: Script Exploration ——————————————

Parent Tapes Related to Work

Focus now on the Parent tapes that mold your stance about work.

1 What messages about success did you receive:

   From the significant man in your life?

   From the significant woman in your life?

   From your culture or subculture?

2 What messages did you get about earning money:

   From the significant man in your life?

   From the significant woman in your life?

   From your culture or subculture?

3 Did anyone ever tell you what you *should* do? If so, what?

4 Did anyone ever tell you what you would be good at? If so, what?

5   Did anyone ever tell you what you wouldn't be good at? If so, what?

6   How was work looked at by your family?

By your culture?

7   Did you learn that work was enjoyable or that it was a drudgery?

8   Who was the most important person in setting your life goals?

9   What did this person tell you about your life goals?

10   What messages did you receive about what was OK or not-OK for you to do because of your sex?

11   Did you hold a job as a child? If so, what were your feelings and thoughts about it?

12   How did other people appraise your work? What kinds of strokes did you get?

Reread the answers that you've given and reflect on the thoughts and images that came to mind as you answered these questions.

13   Now think about how your answers may relate to where you are on your job today. How do they relate to:

The kind of job you have?

The status you have on your job?

The feelings you have about your job?

Your expectations?

14   Think about the general impact of your script on your present working situation. Jot down some of your thoughts and feelings.

Your Work and Your Unique Qualities

1   Now begin to get in touch with your unique qualities as expressed through work. What kinds of things were you good at when you were young?

2   What subjects in school seemed to be the easiest for you?

3   What kinds of activities and subjects challenged you or turned you on?

4   Did you have any burning interests outside of school? If so, what?

5 Do you act on these interests today?

6 When you were in grade school, did any of your teachers think you had special talents? If so, what?

In high school?

In higher education?

7 Summarize in general some of the ways that your teachers looked at you. For example, what did they think about:

What you would be able to do?

How successful you would be able to be?

How creative you were?

Your potential for earning money?

8 Review your answers and get in touch with your feelings and attitudes about what happened to you in school. Then write down some general concepts about the kinds of strokes you got and the way you learned to think about yourself and your own possibilities.

9 Today are you in any way living up to the expectations—negative or positive—of your teachers?

10 Now begin to evaluate the messages you got, first from parental figures and then from your teachers. Is what they expected of you in line with what seemed to be your real potential or possibilities?

11 For just a moment project yourself ahead in time. Imagine you are retiring from work and getting a ritual stroke—a gold watch, the kind that has an inscription on it such as:

- We could always rely on you.
- A nice guy.
- She was always a hard worker.
- He was always on time.
- You gave your all to XYZ.

You never made waves

Now in the outline of this watch,
write *your* inscription.

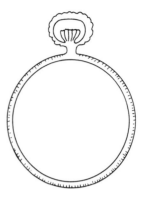

12 Consider whether you are satisfied with your inscription. Assess what you are doing right now that is living up to other people's expectations. Evaluate whether these expectations are good or bad for you to follow. If you want, rewrite your inscription.

13 If you followed messages that did not fit your potential or possibilities, write down some things that you think you would rather be doing now.

14 Each person's script is unique, so you must tailor these general exercises to your own particular needs. If you are not satisfied with your job, put together what you now know about your ego states, transactions, strokes, games, and begin to develop a plan to enrich your working life. These questions might guide your thinking:

- Do you have a talent or skill that you've never bothered to develop?
- How can you arrange to do more of the things that excite and challenge you?
- Do you need more or a different kind of education to do what you really want to do?
- What specific things about your ego states do you want to improve—to use more or less?
- Are you using your work now in any way to fulfill a self-defeating script?
- Are there some things that you need to straighten out with other people?
- Is there someone who might help you plan?
- What is the best place to get information?
- Who are the best people to get information from?

Now outline a tentative plan. Come up with at least three things that you might want to do differently.

You'll be working with this plan as the book develops and as you learn more techniques for choosing success.

SUMMARY

All of us structure our time in six basic ways. We:

— withdraw from other people;
— act out rituals;
— engage in pastimes;
— carry out activities;
— play psychological games;
— experience feelings of intimacy.

Each way has its positive and negative aspects and provides us with different kinds of strokes of different intensities. Withdrawal is negative when it results in depression or shirking of responsibility, but it can be positive when we use it to cope with stress, still our minds, or create new ideas.

Rituals can be positive when they give us roots and help us make contact with others. They are negative when they become outdated and no longer serve their original purpose.

Pastimes, if carried to excess, can hurt our productivity. But when used appropriately, pastiming can give us social skills and increase productivity. Pastiming can help us relate to the people that we work for and with, and pastime strokes can often lead to activity strokes.

Activity strokes are goal-oriented. When we're carrying out an activity, we're getting a job done, which can be very satisfying. But activity strokes can have a negative effect, especially if our energies are misdirected.

Game strokes are almost always negative, because they are ulterior. Game strokes are the bad feelings—the cold pricklies—that we get when we're not coming on straight with other people.

In contrast, intimacy strokes almost always feel good. They reflect our authenticity and go much deeper than ritual, pastime, or activity strokes. They can add enormous energy and vitality to our lives.

Most of us have Parent tapes that affect, positively or negatively, the way we use time on the job. To gain control over any negative tapes, we must first become aware of them and how they are affecting our thoughts, feelings, and actions.

In a sense, our life is time. We all have a script, a life plan to fill that time. In this chapter you have begun to explore your script and have started writing yourself a new one. In the following chapters, you will learn some specific self-management techniques that will help you make your new script an even more successful reality.

SOURCE NOTES

[1] Eric Berne, *Games People Play* (New York: Grove Press, 1967), p. 37.
[2] *Ibid.*, p. 41.
[3] John Dusay, speech at ITAA Conference, San Francisco, 1977.
[4] Personal communication with Val Zemitis, information transfer specialist, Davis, Calif., 1978.
[5] Assertiveness training, which is beyond the scope of this book, could give you a hand, or you could gain ideas from reading. See, for example, Gabriel Della-Piana, *How to Talk with Children (and Other People)* (New York: Wiley, 1973); and Eileen Gambrill and Cheryl Richey, *It's Up to You* (Millbrae, Calif.: Les Femmes, 1976).
[6] Dorothy Jongeward, *Everybody Wins: Transactional Analysis Applied to Organizations* (Reading, Mass.: Addison-Wesley, 1976), pp. 28-29.

Part **II**

THE SELF-CARE
PROGRAM

9

Autonomy and Self-Management

Do you:

☆ find yourself procrastinating when you have a deadline on a project?
☆ find that people complain you haven't heard them?

Would you like to:

☆ be more productive, assertive, self-confident?
☆ expand or shrink a particular aspect of an ego state?
☆ stop playing games?
☆ give and get more positive strokes?
☆ get rid of negative Parent tapes?
☆ stop collecting gray stamps?
☆ collect more gold stamps?
☆ do more of the things that excite and challenge you?

If you've answered *yes* to any of these questions, you'll find the next five chapters especially useful. They will give you some specific self-management techniques for improving the quality of your life on the job and off. You will learn more about using your Adult as the Executive of your personality to help you increase, decrease, or maintain the frequency of positive thoughts, feelings, and actions so you achieve a greater degree of personal autonomy.

AUTONOMY

Autonomy! That is the final goal of TA. Being autonomous means claiming yourself. It means owning yourself, deciding on your own destiny, and taking responsibility for your own thoughts, feelings, behaviors, and the creation of your own life. It means rejecting Parent tapes and learned Child feelings that are not useful to you now. According to Berne, an autonomous person has the ability to be:

— aware,
— spontaneous,
— authentic (intimate).[1]

Awareness

People who are aware can perceive what is happening *now*. They see other people as they *are* rather than as Parent figures or helpless children. They can look at a tree, a car, or a book and see it in their own way rather than as they were taught. Aware people ". . . can stand by a lake, study a buttercup, feel the wind in their faces, and experience a sense of awe. They can look at a sunset and say, 'Wow!' "[2]

Aware people not only are in touch with the environment but they also *listen* to other people and to their own inner selves. They surrender their attention to others and don't rehearse their response or carry on an internal dialogue. Instead, they listen and *respond* to what others are saying. By listening to their own bodies, aware people can tell when they are opening, closing, playing Parent tapes, tensing, relaxing. People who are aware synchronize their resources. They don't greet people at a meeting while mentally writing a proposal. Mind and body are in the same place at the same time.

Spontaneity

The spontaneous people are free to choose, from the many options available, those most appropriate for the situation. They move fluidly as situations change, being free to pick from a storehouse of feelings and behaviors— Parent, Adult, or Child.

Spontaneous people are not only free, however, but are also responsible for their choices. They keep their Adults in gear, consciously making decisions. They carry out these decisions, but not at the expense of others. They are no longer bound and mesmerized by their environmental influences.

Authenticity

Authentic people are free to be intimate, open, and honest, free to express feelings of warmth, tenderness, or closeness to others.

When we transact authentically, we drop our masks and avoid playing phony roles. We also do away with stamp collecting, putdowns, and games. We don't see ourselves and others as stuck but rather as capable of growth and productive self-management.

AUTONOMY THROUGH SELF-MANAGEMENT

Few people are totally autonomous—totally aware, spontaneous, and authentic. But most of us experience times of autonomy. Some of us even experience times when we feel so wonderfully free it's as if we're flowing like a river or soaring like a bird. If you choose to build an even greater sense of autonomy, you will want to follow the four-step process presented in Part II. The four steps of self-management involve:

— making a *commitment;*
— increasing your *awareness* of your current behavior, thoughts, feelings, and environment;

— *rearranging* your environment;
— *evaluating* your progress.

To remember these four steps, think of self-CARE (C for commitment, A for *a*wareness, R for *r*earrangement, and E for *e*valuation).[3]

Making a **C**ommitment
     A
     R
     E

Often we feel dissatisfied but don't succeed in changing our situation because we fail to clarify what we really want. We fail to make a commitment.

An important part of making a commitment is developing a clear mental picture of what you want. With a sharp mental picture you can become enthusiastic, energized, committed—you can focus your energy. It's hard to get excited if you have only a hazy idea of where you want to go, what you want to happen, what you want to do, and how you want to feel. If you don't know where you're going, you're not likely to get there.

In Chapter 8 you began the process of identifying some important goals for yourself. In Chapter 10 you will choose one of your major goals, develop a commitment to it, bring it into sharp focus, and break it down into manageable subgoals.

     C
Increasing *A*wareness
     R
     E

After making a commitment, the next step is to improve your awareness, not only of the world around you but also of your inner world: your Adult thoughts, Parent tapes, racket feelings, genuine feelings, Little Professor intuition, and so on. By increasing your awareness of your inner world, you open up your Blind Self and get in touch with part of your script. If you've tried in vain to change an aspect of your behavior, you may be scripted to spin your wheels and go nowhere or even to fail. Chapter 11 will offer you techniques that can help you identify and break out of some negative script patterns.

C
A
*R*earranging Your Worlds
E

The first two steps—making a commitment and developing awareness—are mainly preliminary. The real action starts when you begin to manage your world so that you *choose* success rather than failure. For better or worse, we each *create* much of our own reality—we make true what we believe about ourselves and our possibilities. There are many things you can do to create an even better world for yourself, a happier and more productive reality.

Each of us experiences two worlds—an outer world (everything outside us) and an inner world (everything that's inside). Your three ego states are part of your inner world. When you *act* from these ego states, you affect your outer world.

In rearranging your worlds, you will plan changes in events that trigger, block, or strengthen specific behaviors in your inner and outer worlds. Chapter 12 will give you some specific tools for managing your inner world; Chapter 13, your outer world.

C
A
R
Evaluating Your Progress

How many times have you heard, "I keep telling myself I ought to stop procrastinating, but I just seem to keep doing it." Sometimes it's hard to admit that our present system of self-management isn't working for our benefit and that we need to try something new. All too often we continue to use ineffective techniques. Consequently, one of the most important parts of a self-management program is the process of *evaluation.* Chapter 14 provides a troubleshooting flowchart that will enable you to diagnose any weakness in your self-management program and to develop improvements.

SUMMARY

The main goal of TA is autonomy. Autonomous people express awareness, spontaneity, and authenticity (intimacy). The next five chapters present a self-management plan to build autonomy: the self-CARE program (C for commitment, A for awareness, R for rearrangement, and E for evaluation).

SOURCE NOTES

[1] Eric Berne, *Games People Play* (New York: Grove Press, 1967), p. 178.
[2] Muriel James and Dorothy Jongeward, *Born to Win: Transactional Analysis with Gestalt Experiments* (Reading, Mass.: Addison-Wesley, 1977), p. 264.
[3] Thanks to Carl Thoresen at Stanford University for the acronym self-CARE.

10

Making a Commitment

In Chapter 8 you identified some goals that you'd like to work toward. In this chapter we will focus on the "C" in the self-CARE program: commitment. You'll learn some techniques for building a commitment to go after those goals.

OBJECTIVES

When you finish this chapter, you'll be able to:

- define your goals in measurable terms;
- make an approximation toward:
  - — gathering information about your goals, and
  - — treating yourself in some way to something related to your goal.

DEFINING GOALS

Our environment today is so crowded that we can become overloaded, especially if we don't have a sytem for filtering the many stimuli that come our way. But we can use a clear goal to help us evaluate our opportunities. By identifying goals and defining them clearly, we set a clear direction for ourselves and gain more control of our lives. Here's how Anne Morton puts it:

> When I was in graduate school, I knew that I wanted to be a *clinical* psychologist, that was my specific goal. I wanted to work with people; that was my general goal. At Stanford, whenever I had an opportunity to do something that was in line with my goal—that is, working with people—I took it. I had a chance to work at the VA hospital, I had a chance to work at the counseling center—all for nothing. But I took these jobs because I knew they would help me get the experience I needed to help me go in the direction I wanted to go. When I was offered research jobs that literally paid something, I would say *no*. I didn't want more research experience. That was the last thing I needed to move me in my direction.
>
> The interesting thing is that my goal helped me to evaluate my opportunities. It helped me to move in the direction I wanted to go. I didn't end up reaching my specific goal of becoming a clinical psychologist, but I did end up getting a job right after graduation in my field of counseling. I could never have gotten that job if I hadn't had the practical experience of working with people in those volunteer jobs.[1]

Often we have difficulty committing ourselves to our goals because we're not clear about what we want. We find it hard to be specific because we have only a *hazy* idea of what we'd like to accomplish. We can overcome this difficulty by defining our *hazy* (unclear goal) in specific terms. Let's look at an example.

Example

Tom was unhappy at work. He recognized that he played *Kick Me* and collected cold pricklies from his manager and other workers. To improve his situation, he did a little goal analysis. First he wrote this *hazy* at the top of a clean sheet of paper: "To be happier on the job and get fewer putdowns." He then asked himself, "What do I really mean by that goal? What changes would I like to see?" The result was this list:

Hazy: To Be Happier on the Job

— to have more friends at work
— to have less time being bored, hurt, (fewer gray stamps), depressed, fearful
— to have fewer guilt feelings
— to have more good feelings about a job well done (more gold stamps)
— to have more energy
— to have more productivity

Tom then put each item, in turn, at the top of a new piece of paper and wrote down more concrete goals beneath it. For example, he took the goal "to have more friends at work" and put it at the top of a clean sheet of paper. Here is what resulted:

Goal: To Have More Friends at Work

— eat lunch out with someone at work occasionally
— have more interactions with co-workers
— have more meaningful interactions
— feel more comfortable asking for what I want

— feel good about myself more of
the time
— do things for others without their
asking

(Notice that some of the items are still hazy.)

Tom's aim was to come up with a number of small *measurable* outcomes. To be measurable, an outcome should be so well defined that you can easily tell if you've attained it. To test if an outcome is measurable, imagine that you are describing it to another person. If the description is adequate, you and your imaginary friend should agree at least 70% of the time on whether the outcome has been attained.

To take his hazy goals measurable, Tom took each new item in turn and listed more specifics. Here's what he came up with for "more meaningful interactions":

Goal: More Meaningful Interactions
with Co-workers

— co-workers will be more friendly
when talking with me
— at least one person each day will
come to see me just to talk —not to
get something from me such as
information
— when making eye contact with
co-workers, I will more frequently
study their eyes carefully and try to
intuit what is going on inside them
— I'll exchange greetings with at least
four more people by name when
passing them

By continuing to analyze his *hazies*, Tom made progress: he was able to identify a number of measurable outcomes. (Note that this list still has some hazies.)

APPLICATION ———————————————————————

1   Let's look at three of Tom's goals. Which do you think are measurable out-
    comes? Hazies? Write MO beside each measurable outcome and H beside each
    hazy.

    _____ (a) Co-workers will be more friendly when talking with me.

    _____ (b) At least one person each day will come to see me just to talk—not to
                 get something from me such as information.

    _____ (c) I'll exchange greetings with at least four more people by name when
                 passing them.

    ~ • ~ • ~ • ~ • ~ • ~ • ~ • ~ • ~ • ~ • ~ • ~ • ~ • ~ • ~ • ~ • ~

    We would say that outcomes (b) and (c) are measurable; (a) is a hazy.
    What, specifically, will Tom's co-workers be doing when they are "being
    more friendly" when talking to him? Will they smile more? Pat him on
    the back? Will they ask about his parents? What he thinks about the
    weather? The latest movie or sporting event? What?

    ~ • ~ • ~ • ~ • ~ • ~ • ~ • ~ • ~ • ~ • ~ • ~ • ~ • ~ • ~ • ~ • ~

2   Think about Tom's hazy in item 1(a). Change "more friendly when talking with
    me" into a measurable outcome.

    ~ • ~ • ~ • ~ • ~ • ~ • ~ • ~ • ~ • ~ • ~ • ~ • ~ • ~ • ~ • ~ • ~

    Here's how Tom might have defined his hazy. Co-workers will be more
    friendly when talking with me—that is, they will discuss such things as:

        — my family,
        — what I'm doing this weekend,
        — a change in my hairstyle, clothing, appearance, and so on,

    as well as talking to me about job-related matters. When talking to me
    they'll:

        — use my name at least once during each conversation,
        — look me in the eye (at least 50% of the time),
        — laugh out loud with me at least once a week.

    Your answer is acceptable if it would allow you and another person to
    reach the same decision (at least 70% of the time) about whether Tom's
    co-workers were being "friendly" when talking to him.

    ~ • ~ • ~ • ~ • ~ • ~ • ~ • ~ • ~ • ~ • ~ • ~ • ~ • ~ • ~ • ~ • ~

3   Think of a long-range goal you have for *yourself.* (By "long-range" we
    mean a goal that will take you approximately a year or more to reach.) You
    may want to look back at pages 178–179 to review some of the things you plan
    to change. For now don't worry about whether it's a hazy or a measurable out-
    come. Just write it down.

(a) My personal goal is:

(b) If you're successful in reaching this goal, how will you know it?

(c) What measurable changes will take place?

(d) What changes will you see in the way you act?

(e) In the way you feel?

(f) In the way others react to you?

4 Probably some of your answers in item 3 came out as measurable outcomes, but some may still be hazies. If so, take one of those hazies and analyze it further into more specific terms.

(a) Hazy:

(b) More specific:

5 Now take one of the more specific items you just listed that *still* seems to be a hazy and break it down to even more concrete terms.

(a) Hazy:

(b) More specific:

The process you've just gone through was designed to help you clarify one of your long-range goals.[2] Another useful approach for analyzing a long-range goal involves what we call a rainbow-of-success pyramid.

Rainbow-of-Success Pyramid

The rainbow-of-success pyramid is a good technique for analyzing important long-range goals and breaking them down into manageable chunks, small steps that you can easily achieve. Here are the steps in our rainbow-of-success approach.[3]

— Gather materials. In developing a rainbow-of-success pyramid, you will find it useful to get a large sheet of paper from a graphics-art supply store (say about 2 feet by 3 feet), a stack of white index cards, some scotch tape, and a pencil.

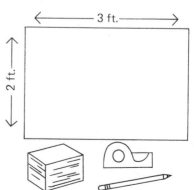

— Write your final long-range goal on an index card. Write your goal as clearly as possible, specifying such things as when you want to obtain it and how you will know when it will be accomplished. Tape this card at the top of your large sheet of paper.

— Ask yourself, "What other subgoals will I need to accomplish before I can accomplish my final long-range goal?" Write each subgoal on a card. Arrange the cards under your long-range goal as shown in the diagram at the right. With a pencil draw a light line down from your final goal to each of your subgoals. (Draw it lightly in case you want to erase it later.)

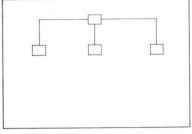

— Next, look at each subgoal and ask yourself, "What would I need to do to achieve this subgoal?" Write these subgoals on cards and put them in place as shown.

— Continue your analysis by listing sub-sub-subgoals for your sub-subgoals. Your pyramid should then look something like this. Actually it may be squashed or lopsided since some subgoals may break down easily into sub-subgoals and some may not. That doesn't matter.

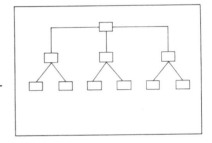

The important thing is that you identify all of the key subordinate goals you need to accomplish before you can reach your long-range goal. Not only will your rainbow-of-success pyramid help you do this, but it will give you a graphic picture of how each little thing you work on fits into the big picture.

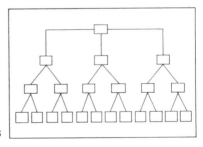

Why is it fun to have a rainbow of success? Because as time goes by, you may wish to color each index card with a magic marker as you accomplish it.* This excites and pleases your Natural Child. It's great to see the pyramid filling in with a rainbow of colors! It is also fun to write the date of accomplishment on each card as you accomplish each goal. Doing this will help you build your commitment!

*Instead of using white cards and coloring them in, you may want to get different-colored cards for goals and subgoals.

Here is a rainbow-of-success pyramid developed by Doug, who wanted to learn to be more patient and to avoid raising his voice unnecessarily.

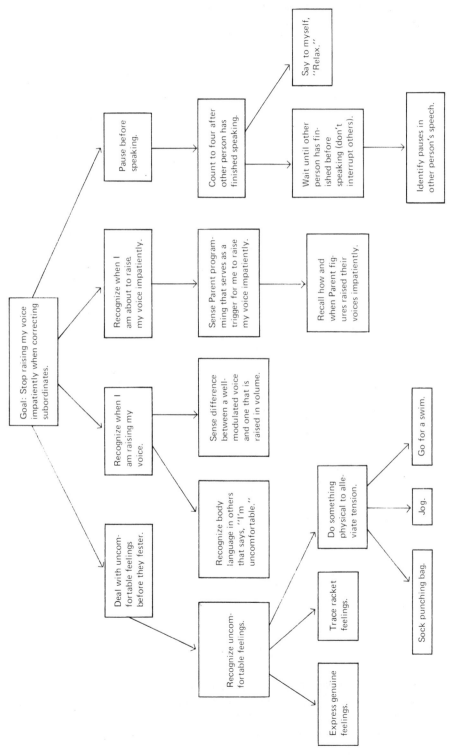

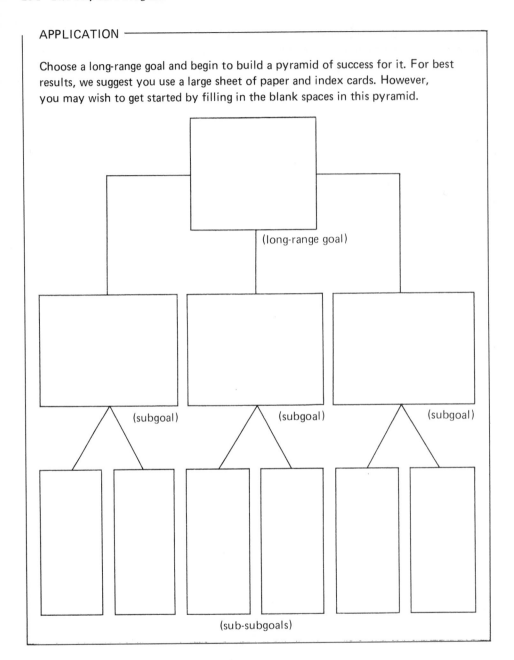

APPLICATION —————————

Choose a long-range goal and begin to build a pyramid of success for it. For best results, we suggest you use a large sheet of paper and index cards. However, you may wish to get started by filling in the blank spaces in this pyramid.

(long-range goal)

(subgoal)   (subgoal)   (subgoal)

(sub-subgoals)

MAKING A DECISION

You've seen how you can start with a hazy and define it in measurable terms. You've also seen how you can break a long-term goal into subgoals. But there's more to making a commitment than this! For one thing, if you want to be an effective self-manager, you will want to make a clear-cut Adult decision about whether or not you really want to achieve the goals and sub-goals you have listed.

Sometimes we talk about wanting to change and start out with a strong effort to do so only to fail. If this happens repeatedly, it *could* be because we are acting out a circular, going-no-where script rather than making an Adult decision to choose success, to take responsibility for writing and directing our own life dramas.

In the rest of the chapter you'll learn how to analyze your goals and make Adult decisions to either scrap them or move forward toward accomplishing them. We'll discuss these techniques:

— Gathering information (outer world and inner world)
— Rewarding yourself
— Making approximations

Gathering Information

To help yourself make a firm decision to change, gather information related to your goal. There are two kinds of information you can gather: outer-world information and inner-world information.

Outer-world information is information you gather outside yourself, from other people (friends, family members, experts, professional people such as doctors, psychologists, teachers, therapists, counselors) as well as from books, newspapers, magazines, classes, seminars, and so on. For example, if you want to increase your ability to concentrate on high-priority tasks, you might gather outer-world information by reading about successful people who had great concentration powers. Or suppose you want to stop playing *Harried* and start taking more time for swimming, tennis, or jogging. Then you might look for a book or magazine on one of these topics. You might also talk to other people who get a lot of exercise and ask them what *they* think about its value. Do they think it gives them more energy? Do they miss it if they can't do it for some reason? You might also talk to your doctor about the dangers of excessive stress and lack of proper exercise.

APPLICATION

Look back at the goal you described on page 191. What kind of outer-world information can you gather that would help you build a commitment to that goal?

Inner-world information is information about your Blind or Unknown Self that you bring to your awareness by self-examination. For example, when you become more aware of your different ego states, the skull games you play, your Parent tapes, and the feelings you collect, you are gathering inner-world information. Sometimes you may use your Parent or Child to sabotage your efforts. That is, you may unwittingly play Parent tapes that will discourage you from what you want to do. Or you may avoid what your

Adult wants because it doesn't feel good—predictable and comfortable—to your Child. A self-exploratory study may help you minimize this problem.

APPLICATION ———————————————————————

What kind of inner-world information can you gather about your goal? Explore these questions as a start.

1 Think of a parent figure. What would this person say about the goal you have chosen?

2 What would this parent figure want you to do?

3 Would this be helpful, harmful, or not make any difference?

4 Now, consider how you *feel* deep *inside* about working toward your goal. For example, do you feel anxious, uncomfortable, happy, angry, excited, what?

5 As a child were you ever in a situation parallel to this one? If so, how did you react?

6 Does this sound familiar now?

7 Do you really *want* to pursue your goal or are you just making an empty resolution?

8 In what ways might you sabotage yourself?

9 Do you feel you deserve to reach your goal?

10 How can you use your Adult to manage and mobilize all your ego states to work toward this goal?

Based on what you have learned here, you may wish to review and add to your script exercises beginning on page 175.

The purpose of the exercise you just finished was to get all three of your ego states in on your goals. When people experience difficulty in achieving a goal, it's often because their ego states are not working together. For example, based on information that your Adult has collected, you may make a rational decision to pursue a given goal. But, for some reason, your Child ego state may not feel like doing so or a Parent tape may be playing in your head, running counter to your objective. You may not even be aware of the Parent tape. By sitting down and having a friendly chat, as it were, with your various ego states, you may be more successful in developing a firm commitment. Let's look at two examples.

Example

Ruth wanted to be better organized. Usually her desk looked as though someone had emptied a wastebasket on it. She had a specific objective of keeping all her high-priority paper work in a neat stack on her desk and all lower-priority items out of sight in her desk drawer. She had a friendly conversation with her Child: "How do you feel about keeping your desk neat? Why do you feel that way?" Similarly, she explored her Parent ego state by asking, "What would my parents say about how I should organize my desk? What would their desk look like if they had my job?"

In asking these questions, Ruth discovered that she felt very uncomfortable about keeping her desk neat. She became aware of a distinct, painful sensation in her gut. She realized that in keeping her desk messy, her Child was rebelling against Parent tapes like, "A place for everything and everything in its place," "Always be neat," and "Messy is as messy does." She also realized that the only reason she wanted to keep her desk neat was to please other people. When Ruth had these Parent and Child responses figured out, she raised the question, "What is it that really is best for me and my work?" Once she realized what she was doing, she found it much easier to keep her desk in order, for Adult reasons.

Example

John had a similar problem with his desk. When he chatted with his ego states, he discovered something different. He realized that he did not keep his desk in order because that behavior was missing in his Adapted Child. His parents had *not* tried to teach him to be neat, but had laughingly stroked him for being disorderly. His parents would grin at him in the midst of his messy room, "Now look at this. You're just a chip off the old block all right." He also became aware that his father had had a very messy office, often misplacing or losing important papers, and that he had incorporated his father's bad habits into his own personality. Knowing this helped him to understand his problem and feel less frustrated. He was then able to focus his energy on ways to develop the skills that were missing in his Parent and Adapted Child.

Notice that although Ruth and John had the same problem, the answers they got by exploring their ego states were different. This points out an important fact that is often overlooked: no two ego states are alike. Everyone has a unique Parent, Child, and Adult. Notice that Ruth and John were each able to become more successful by getting in touch with their Child ego states.

Remember that if we have distorted our self-image because of our early life experiences and childhood decisions, then our Child needs to make a fresh decision, a re-decision, with the help of our Adult.[4] We must see ourselves and our true potential clearly, perhaps for the first time.

But we need to be serious about our goals. If we make frequent New Year's-style resolutions that we have no intention of keeping, we only add to our negative feelings about ourselves.[5]

Rewarding Yourself

You've seen how defining your goals in writing and gathering information can help to build a commitment. Another useful approach toward building a commitment is to treat yourself to something *related to your goal.* Reward yourself with something you might enjoy doing or having that would expand your interest in your goal. For example, if you want to jog more than you do now, you might buy some new jogging shoes, jogging clothes, a device for measuring how far you jog, or a subscription to a jogging magazine. Or you might spend time talking with a friend who likes jogging. Stimulate your interest and also cash in a few gold stamps for a prize that feels good.

Similarly, if your goal is to increase the amount of time you spend in your Adult while supervising a particular person, you might enroll in an inter-personal-communications class offered by your company, or check out a book you've heard good things about that would feed your Adult new ideas. If you want to increase the amount of time you spend in your work location, you might make it more attractive: rearrange the space, add a painting, a new bulletin board, or a plant. If you're playing *Kick Me* by consistently missing important appointments, you might treat yourself to an attractive calendar or appointment book.

APPLICATION

Think about *your* goal. What little something might you treat yourself to that would help you build a commitment to work toward this goal?

Making Approximations

When you set out to develop a commitment toward a goal, it often helps to give yourself a deadline for doing a *little* something toward defining your goal, gathering information, or treating yourself. Start with an approximation. For example, if you decide you want more information about a subject, don't try to read every book published on it by next Monday. Start small. Just get your feet wet. Make a list of people you might talk to, read a magazine article by bedtime, or perhaps simply pick out an item you want to read and lay it out where you'll see it.

Or suppose your goal is to increase your time-management skills and you plan to buy something to help you build a commitment. Don't start off by buying a $130 electronic memo timer. Start small. Get something like a notebook for recording your "to do" list and your decisions about priorities, or get a special "in" basket to help you physically separate high-priority tasks from tasks of less importance. Or start by simply looking through a catalog of office products.

Even thinking about something is an approximation of doing it! An approximation, remember, is anything that moves you closer toward a goal.

If you doubt that thinking is an approximation of doing, close your eyes (after reading this sentence) and imagine yourself eating and enjoying your favorite healthful snack. If you're like most of us, you have just increased the probability that you'll soon be munching on your favorite food.

One reason for starting small is that you won't be stuck feeling guilty with an expensive white elephant if you change your mind about pursuing a particular goal. But a more important reason is that it's easy to get started on a project if your first step is small. Once you take even a tiny step, your chances of being more successful zoom! You are on your way!

APPLICATION

"Fred, would you step into my office for just a moment?" said Joyce, Fred's supervisor. "Sure," said Fred, following Joyce into her office. Fred's eyes widened as he felt his teeth clench. He knew Joyce was upset, but wasn't sure why. She turned to Fred and said crisply, "Fred, I've been pleased with the quality of your work, but I . . . am very unhappy that you usually turn it in late. It raises cain with our production schedule and then morale goes to pot." "I'm sorry, Joyce. I seem to have a real problem with meeting deadlines these days." Fred appeared to be concerned about improving his ability to get things done on time. But he had been concerned about this nearly all his life and hadn't done anything about it.

Write down some things that Fred might do to help himself develop a commitment to do a better job of meeting deadlines. In answering this question, use the suggestions mentioned in this chapter. If you'd like some hints, answer the questions that follow.

1 One way to develop a commitment is to state your goal in measurable terms so that two independent observers could agree on whether the goal had been achieved. How might Fred apply this idea to his situation? What specific measurable goal might he write for himself?

2 Another technique for developing a commitment is to gather internal and external information. How might Fred apply this idea?

3 Sometimes it helps to treat yourself to a *little* something. What might Fred treat himself to that would help him develop a commitment to get his work done on time?

4   How might Fred apply the idea of building a commitment through a series of successive approximations?

~ • ~ • ~ • ~ • ~ • ~ • ~ • ~ • ~ • ~ • ~ • ~ • ~ • ~ • ~ • ~ • ~

Fred could do many things to help himself make a commitment in this situation. Here are some of our ideas. You may wish to compare your answers with ours.

1   Fred could break down his larger goal of improving his ability to meet deadlines to something more specific such as:
    — Turn in four out of the next five projects on or before deadlines.
2   To gather *external information* about "late behavior," Fred might do things such as:
    — Ask himself, "What happens to other people when I'm late? How are they likely to feel and what are they likely to do?"
    — Talk to Joyce or others about what the consequences are when his reports are turned in late.
    — Find others who do a good job of getting their reports in on time and interview them to find out what techniques they use to be so successful.
    To gather *internal information,* Fred could:
    — Examine Parent tapes that might relate to getting work done on time.
    — Think of how various Parent figures would tend to perform in his situation, what they would say about his problem, what they would advise him to do.
    — Examine his feelings about work he has to do and the deadlines.
    — Examine the reasons or excuses that he usually gives for not getting the work done on time to see if they are valid or merely rationalizations. For example, he might ask himself, "What's my payoff for this *Sorry About That* game? How do I feel when other people are unhappy with me? Did I have this feeling as a child? How often do I collect it now?"
3   Fred might treat himself to many different things to help him build a commitment, such as:
    — Materials for noting deadlines or reminders about deadlines:
    A special wall calendar
    Blackboard
    A large graph (for charting progress)
    A diary or journal
    — Instructional materials:
    A book on time management
    A cassette tape on time management

> — Tools, supplies, or equipment that might encourage him to get to work on his projects:
> A new pen or automatic pencil
> New stationery
> Automatic pencil sharpener, and so on
>
> 4 Fred might apply the idea of successive approximations by buying himself some inexpensive item that would be useful for whatever project he is working on. He might just decide to go to a stationery store to *look at* items for noting deadlines. (This is an approximation of buying such items.) Similarly, he might decide to go to the library or a bookstore and just *look at* books on time management.

If you've not yet made a commitment to work toward a specific goal, here's another opportunity.

APPLICATION ———————————————————

1 What's your general goal?

2 Describe it in measurable terms:

3 What external information will you gather to help build a commitment?

4 What approximation toward gathering this information could you make starting this week?

5 What internal information will you gather to help build a commitment?

6 What approximation toward gathering this information could you make within the next twenty-four hours?

7 What might you treat yourself with?

8 What approximation could you make within the next twenty-four hours to bring yourself closer to getting that treat?

SUMMARY

In this chapter we have discussed the first step in the self-CARE program: *commitment.* When building a commitment toward a goal, it's crucial to define that goal in measurable terms. If we are satisfied with hazies, we may never be able to tell whether we're moving toward our goals or what we might do to get what we want.

Gathering information often can help us build a commitment. We can gather two kinds of information: outer-world information is gathered by talking to people, reading books, observing our environment, and so on; inner-world information is gathered by self-examination. Once we become more aware of our ego states, we are better able to make a fresh decision about the direction of our lives.

Sometimes it helps if we treat ourselves to a little something that is related to our goal. This little something may make our work toward that goal more pleasing to our Child ego state.

When defining our goals, gathering information, or treating ourselves, it helps to make approximations. Inch by inch, everything is a cinch!

Having read this summary, you may be asking, "Now that I've made a commitment, what's next? How do I get started on my self-management project?" If you've made a definite commitment, after examining how each of your ego states is involved, then you've already taken a very important first step toward being more successful. After making your commitment the next step is to increase your awareness. That's the main focus of our next chapter.

SOURCE NOTES

[1] Anne Morton, in tape-recorded talk on effective self-motivation given for University of California extension class, San Francisco, October 1977.

[2] For information about the audio cassette *Imagery for Change*, write Success Dynamics, 1840 Lambeth Lane, Concord, CA 94518.

[3] Our rainbow-of-success concept synthesizes work from Peter Pipe, *Objectives—Tools for Change* (Belmont, Calif.: Fearon, 1975), p. 25; Robert M. Gagné, *Conditions of Learning* (New York: Holt, Rinehart and Winston, 1965), p. 181; and Morton, *op. cit.*, who coined the phrase "rainbow of success."

[4] Robert Goulding and Mary Edwards Goulding, "Injunctions, Decisions, and Redecisions," *Transactional Analysis Journal,* 1976, 6(1):41–48.

[5] A cassette tape designed to help you clarify your goals by gathering inner-world information is available from Success Dynamics (see Appendix B).

11

Increasing Awareness

You've explored the process of making a commitment to your goals. Now we will focus on the next step in the self-CARE program: *awareness.* Even after you make a commitment, it is important to increase your awareness. By gathering more information about your current environment—your inner and outer worlds—you enlighten your Blind Self and expand your Open Self.

OBJECTIVES

When you finish this chapter, you'll be able to:

- increase your awareness by identifying, recording, and analyzing:
  — the frequency of your target behavior;
  — critical events that may affect your target behavior.

COUNTING AND RECORDING YOUR TARGET BEHAVIOR

The goal you have set for yourself probably involves increasing or decreasing the frequency of an outward behavior, a feeling, or a thought. For simplicity, we use the term "target behavior" to refer to any outward behavior, feeling, or thought that you'd like to work on. (*Note:* Thoughts and feelings are behaviors, too, even though they are not *outwardly* observable.)

Top business people have long used various counting and recording techniques to increase their awareness of their organization's performance. For example, often they record net-profit data on a chart. The chart helps them to get an overall picture and see trends. When the chart gives them good news, they note what seems to be giving them such good results. When the chart reveals a negative trend, they can try corrective measures and watch their chart to see how well they work. As individuals we can use the same technique to increase our awareness of our target behaviors.

Example

Jeff, a salesperson in an exclusive clothing store, felt that he could improve his job performance by knocking off ten pounds or so. To increase his awareness of how well he was sticking to his diet, he decided to count the number

"Gentlemen, I've got good news and
bad news. . . ."

of bites he took of nondiet food. Jeff used a hand counter (like those used
to add up grocery bills) to keep an accurate record. Whenever he took an
"unauthorized bite," he pushed a button on his counter. At the end of the
day, he recorded the number of "unauthorized bites" on a graph. Here's what
the graph looked like after five days:

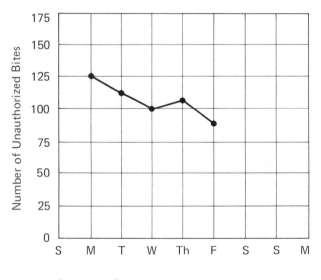

When Jeff first became aware of how many times he was actually going
off his diet, he was shocked. He never imagined he was doing it 125 times a
day! But notice the trend. Although he fluctuated from day to day, Jeff
tended to take fewer "illegal" bites as time went by.

Other patterns that he helped himself conquer by counting were eating in a big rush while on his feet and eating absentmindedly while he was doing something else. Both of these patterns robbed him of positive strokes from proper dieting. Knowing the number of times he actually did this was a real surprise and a motivator in itself. Pinpointing these problem areas helped Jeff to focus his energy on his goal and clarify his commitment to it.

Example

Dean made a commitment to use his Adult ego state more when meeting with Louis, his immediate supervisor. Typically, he met with Louis once or twice a day for fifteen or twenty minutes and took notes on the discussion. During these meetings he tended to get into his Adapted Child. He felt inadequate and had butterflies in his stomach. When this happened, he became argumentative and defensive. After the meetings, he would regret the way he had acted. To increase his awareness of how often he acted this way, he decided to monitor and record his ego states. Here's how he did it: four different times during the meeting with Louis, at five-minute intervals, he made some quick notes about the ego states he had been in. To make this easier to do, he made up a chart like this (each box representing a five-minute period):

	Time Period in Minutes			
Date	5	10	15	20

At the end of each five-minute period, Dean evaluated his ego states and decided which one had predominated. If he found it hard to decide between two ego states, he recorded both of them. Here's what Dean's chart looked like after the first five meetings:

	Time Period in Minutes			
Date	5	10	15	20
3/6	a	ac	ac	ac
3/7	a	aAP	ac	ac
3/8	a	a	ac	ac
3/9	a	a	a	ac
3/10	a	a	a	ac

APPLICATION ──────────────────────────────

Keeping track of his ego states in this careful way took some concentration, but it was worth the effort! Dean became more aware of where he was putting his psychic energy. He had thought that he was using his Adapted Child at times when working with Louis, but he had no idea that his Adapted Child was so much in control. But Dean also discovered a desirable pattern in his behavior from looking over his ego-state charts. Can you see the pattern or trend? Describe it.

~ · ~ · ~ · ~ · ~ · ~ · ~ · ~ · ~ · ~ · ~ · ~ · ~ · ~ · ~ · ~ · ~ · ~ · ~

Notice that at the beginning of each meeting, Dean started out in his Adult ego state. In the first meeting, he moved into his Adapted Child during the second five-minute period and stayed there for the rest of the meeting. By the fourth meeting, he managed to stay in his Adult for three full time periods. The trend, then is that Dean is tending to use his Adult more and more.

Techniques for Counting Your Target Behavior

Dean was able to increase his awareness by keeping track of his ego states. But it's not always that easy to keep track of target behavior unless you have a plan or technique for doing it. Let's look at some possible techniques.

Keeping a Tally

One simple way to keep track of your target behavior is to make tally marks on a piece of paper or index card. If you are keeping track of more than one kind of behavior at the same time, you can draw a box on a sheet of paper for each kind of behavior and label each box. Then when a behavior occurs you just put a mark in the appropriate box.

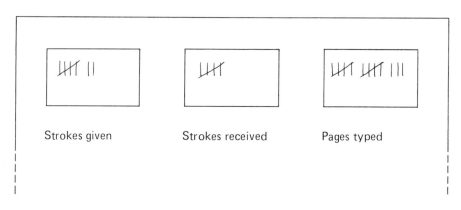

Strokes given   Strokes received   Pages typed

Using a Counter

Another way to keep track of your target behavior is to use a special counter. You can buy a number of counters to help you keep track of things that are important to you. For example, the inexpensive grocery counter that we mentioned earlier was originally designed to help people keep track of their grocery bills. Since it goes from 1¢ to $20, it has an effective counting range of 1 to 2,000. Another handy device is a golf counter, first made to help golfers keep track of their swings. Most well-equipped sporting-goods stores stock it. You can wear the golf counter on your wrist (it makes an interesting conversation piece), or keep it in your pocket if you don't want others to know what you're up to. You can also buy counters especially designed for counting target behaviors. For example, a company called Success Dynamics (see Appendix B) offers a fancy, color-coded bead wrist counter. The advantage of a color-coded bead counter is that you can use it to keep track of a number of different target behaviors, assigning a separate color for each behavior.

Counting with Coins

If you wear clothes with pockets, another handy technique is to fill your right pocket with coins each morning. Then, whenever you wish to count a target behavior, you simply transfer one of your coins from your right pocket to your left pocket. (To make this work, be sure you spend money only from your right pocket!)

Time Sampling

Sometimes you may be less interested in the frequency of a target behavior than in the percentage of time that a target behavior is occurring. For example, every half-hour you might at that instant decide whether you are feeling good, bad, or so-so. This is called a *time-sampling procedure*. The accompanying chart shows how Susan, a dispatcher, kept track of her feelings from 8 A.M. to 12 noon (G = good, B = bad, SS = so-so):

	Time Period								
Day	8:00	8:30	9:00	9:30	10:00	10:30	11:00	11:30	12:00
Monday	SS	SS	G	G	B	B	SS	SS	G
Tuesday	B	SS	G	SS	SS	B	SS	SS	G
Wednesday	(late)	B	SS	SS	SS	B	G	SS	SS
Thursday	SS	SS	SS	SS	SS	SS	G	SS	G
Friday	SS	SS	G	SS	SS	B	G	SS	SS

After you have a clear picture of your target behavior, options begin to open up to you. By recording her feelings in the chart, Susan became aware that she felt bad around 10:30 A.M. almost every day. This helped her to realize that she was collecting gray stamps when she saw Anita, who arrived at work every day at that time. Once she was aware that she was collecting these racket feelings, she was able to deal with them. Note that it is possible to count feelings. Janet chose the classification of "good," "bad," and "so-so" because they made sense to her and she was able to distinguish these feelings in herself quite clearly. You don't always need to describe the target behaviors in such a way that they are observable by others; the important thing is that you be able to detect the presence or absence of the target behavior *yourself.*

Using a Stopwatch

Sometimes you may be interested in the duration of a target behavior. For example, Gerald found that about once each day he used a negative aspect of his Controlling Parent for a certain period of time. It was more meaningful to measure the amount of time that his Controlling Parent was activated than to try to count the number of different times that it was activated. Whenever Gerald became aware that he was transacting from his Controlling Parent, he clicked on a stopwatch that he carried in his pocket. When he felt that he had moved into another ego state, he turned off the stopwatch. Since this only happened once a day or so, it was easy for him to do. He recorded his data by simply writing the number of minutes shown on the stopwatch on his calendar at a certain time each day.

Pick any method of counting that works best for you. Perhaps you can come up with some new method that will be especially suited to your situation. The important thing, however, is that you *care enough to count.* This business of actually counting target behaviors may be difficult for you to accept. Does it seem too cold and calculating to you? Too mechanical? Too much of a bother? We know you might feel that way, but we also know that many people have had great success by keeping track of their behavior. We strongly urge you to try out this useful technique. Remember that even though it may seem cold and calculating, the technique is good because it gives your Adult important information. It can help you structure more of your time the way you really want to.

APPLICATION

For each of the following situations indicate what technique would be most appropriate for keeping track of the target behavior.

___1 Doug is concerned about stroking others positively. He would like to keep track of the number of subordinates that he strokes positively at least once during the day. He'd also like to keep track of how many times he gives strokes for being as opposed to strokes for doing.

___2 Doris is not as productive as she'd like to be. She expects that it may be because she's spending too much time pastiming.

___3 Carolyn frequently meets with coworkers to discuss the projects she is working on. She would like to keep track of the number of times she strokes others for making positive suggestions. During her meetings it is usual for her to make notes on a clipboard.

___4 Cliff would like to find out roughly how much time he devotes to each of the basic ways of structuring time. He has a wrist alarm that he can set to go off automatically every twenty minutes.

(a) Count frequency of target response by keeping a tally.

(b) Count frequency with a color-coded bead counter.

(c) Estimate the percentage of time that a target behavior is occurring by deciding at predetermined times whether or not a target behavior is occurring.

(d) Measure the duration of the target behavior with a stopwatch.

~ • ~ • ~ • ~ • ~ • ~ • ~ • ~ • ~ • ~ • ~ • ~ • ~ • ~ • ~ • ~ • ~ • ~

1 (b) The color-coded wrist bead counter is probably best for Doug since he wants to keep track of several different target behaviors. He can use a different color of bead for each.

2 (d) The stopwatch is best for Doris because she is concerned about the length of time she engages in just one target behavior. Each time she begins a pastiming transaction, she can click on her stopwatch. When she ends that transaction, she can click it off. She can do that for each pastiming transaction; then at the end of the day she can check her stopwatch and record the total time.

3 (a) A simple paper-and-pencil tally is probably best for Carolyn since she can do it unobtrusively by marking on a sheet of paper on her clipboard.

4 (c) For Cliff a time-sampling procedure would probably be most appropriate since he has several categories of target behavior that he is concerned about.

Techniques for Recording Your Target Behavior

There are two main ways to record numerical data. You can record the data
in a table like this:

Date	Number of Warm Fuzzies Received
1–2	2
1–3	3
1–4	1
1–5	4
1–6	4
1–10	3
1–11	4
1–12	5
1–13	5

or you can record your data on a graph like this:

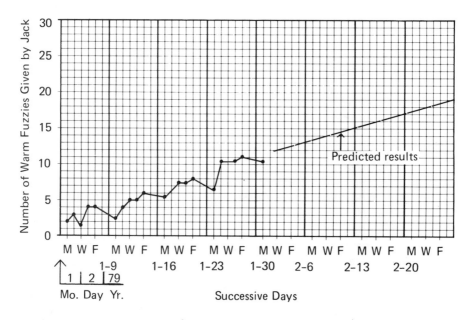

The advantage of a graph is that it gives you a picture of your behavior. You
can see patterns and tendencies developing, and can predict where you are

headed. (See the broken line in the preceding graph.) Behavior patterns, Parent tapes, and scripts usually develop over many years, so when you try a self-management project, change may come very slowly and gradually. But with a chart, you'll be able to see the slow but steady progress that you *are* making. If you don't chart your behavior, you may *not* realize that you're winning the race!

APPLICATION ────────────────────

Look back at the previous chart showing the number of warm fuzzies that Jack gave each day.

1 How many warm fuzzies will Jack probably be giving by February 20 if he keeps improving at the same rate?

2 What weekly pattern seems to be occurring?

~ · ~ · ~ · ~ · ~ · ~ · ~ · ~ · ~ · ~ · ~ · ~ · ~ · ~ · ~ · ~ · ~

1 By February 20, Jack will probably be giving out about fifteen warm fuzzies per day.
2 One definite pattern is that every Monday Jack gives out fewer warm fuzzies than he did on the previous Friday. Becoming aware of this pattern, Jack might want to study more closely what is going on in his outer and inner worlds on Mondays, to find out why this pattern exists.

An effective way to record your data is to put it on a large chart, one that you can't miss seeing when you come to work in the morning. You can make such a chart yourself or buy commercially prepared blank charts.*

Here is a chart that Dean made in his Adapted Child management program:

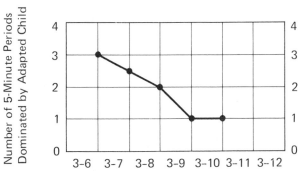

---

*You can pick up a single large chart for less than a dollar at a schoolteacher's supply store. (Originally designed to help teachers chart students' performance, it's equally useful for charting personal goals as well as the teacher's performance.) If no teacher's store is near you, you can order these large charts from Success Dynamics (see Appendix B). Write for current prices.

This chart shows the number of five-minute periods during which his Adapted Child was the dominating ego state. During this time, Dean was intent on increasing his awareness of his ego states. He had not yet set up a self-management program to change his behavior. But note that merely by becoming *aware* of his ego states, he improved. That is, Dean began to spend less and less time in his Adapted Child ego state and more and more time in his Adult. Research in behavioral self-management shows that when people become more aware of a troublesome behavior, the behavior tends to change in a desirable direction. Undesirable behaviors decrease in intensity or frequency and desirable behaviors tend to increase in intensity or frequency. So, in many cases, merely becoming aware of what we are doing tends to improve the situation.[1,2,3] That improvement tends to stop after a while and our target behavior levels off at what is called our *baseline performance.*

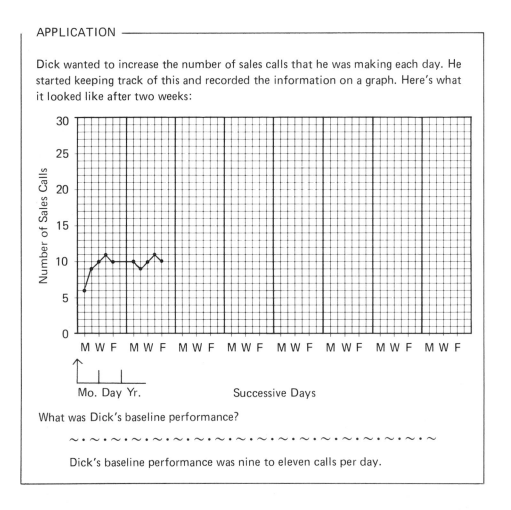

APPLICATION

Dick wanted to increase the number of sales calls that he was making each day. He started keeping track of this and recorded the information on a graph. Here's what it looked like after two weeks:

What was Dick's baseline performance?

~ · ~ · ~ · ~ · ~ · ~ · ~ · ~ · ~ · ~ · ~ · ~ · ~ · ~ · ~ · ~

Dick's baseline performance was nine to eleven calls per day.

Only if you chart your baseline performance can you tell if any new techniques are working. Knowing your baseline is also valuable for making self-contracts. For example, since Dick knows that he typically makes nine to eleven calls per day, he might decide to reward himself for making twelve or thirteen calls, a slight improvement. (More on this in Chapter 13.)

WATCHING YOUR ENVIRONMENT

It's also important to open your eyes to your environment, particularly the environment that exists just before and just after your target behavior occurs.

Example

Brian found that he was often trapped into the game of *Yes, But*. Whenever Brian would light his pipe and put his feet up on his desk, Scott would begin the *Yes, But* game by asking him for advice. (It was almost as if these behaviors served as a trigger for Scott to start the game.) After the game would grind to a conclusion, Brian would feel put down, get angry, and usually take an extended trip to the water cooler.

In this case, the event that occurs just before the target behavior is Brian's act of lighting his pipe and putting his feet on his desk. The events that occur just after are the bad feelings and the extended trip to the water cooler.

Notice that we're talking about events in your inner world as well as your outer world. By outer-world events, we mean things in your environment that you see, hear, feel, smell, taste, and so on. By inner-world events, we mean thoughts and feelings. When watching these critical events in your environment, ask yourself: "What was I thinking? What did I feel just before (or after) I did that? What did I see? What sounds did I hear? What did I hear inside my head? What were other people doing nearby?" By becoming aware of these critical events in our environment, we can begin to identify:

— *Triggers*—events that signal or trigger your target behavior. For example, Brian's lighting his pipe seemed to trigger Scott's *Yes, But* game.
— *Payoffs*—events that maintain or increase the frequency of your target behavior. These need not be positive. For example, you may unwittingly be punishing yourself with negative payoffs.
— *Roadblocks*—events that are somehow blocking your target behavior. For example, if an important project is buried in a pile of papers on your desk, that pile of papers is a roadblock, barring your target behavior of getting to work on the project.

You may also discover events that are triggering behaviors incompatible with your target behavior. For example, a particular picture may stimulate a person to daydream. Because it's usually difficult to daydream and concentrate on a work project at the same time, daydreaming is incompatible with the target behavior of working. The picture, then, triggers a behavior that is incompatible with the target behavior. In the next two chapters, we'll explore more thoroughly these critical events in your inner and outer worlds, as we focus on how you can rearrange those worlds.

Keeping a Journal

To help increase your awareness of your environment, we suggest that you keep a journal in which you regularly write down your observations about what happens in your inner and outer worlds just *before* and just *after* the target responses occur. Keep the journal handy so that you can make appropriate notes of such things as conversations and actions of others as they occur. If you wait until the end of the day, you may forget important details. But do set aside a certain time each day to review and comment on the observations that you've made. A fun place to record your observations is in a blank book, the kind that looks like a regular hard-cover book, but has blank pages. Besides making notes of conversations, you may wish to diagram them. For example:

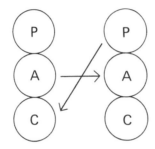

Norma:
"May I see
the memo I
gave you
yesterday
on X?"

Tina:
"What's the
matter with
you anyway?
Don't you
keep a car-
bon copy?"

By diagramming conversations in this way, you can capture the nature of the transaction concisely without a lot of unnecessary words. The diagrams also prompt you to focus on important issues such as:

— What ego state was I transacting from?
— Which ego state was activated in the other person?
— Was anyone sending an ulterior message?
— Was the transaction open or blocked?

APPLICATION

Suppose Norma in the previous example knew that she was supposed to keep a carbon copy of the memo. Suppose she seemed to be transacting from her Adult but was actually sending an ulterior message from her Child designed to activate Tina's Parent. How might an enlightened Norma diagram this transaction? (Put in the proper arrows, including a dotted arrow to show the hidden transaction.)

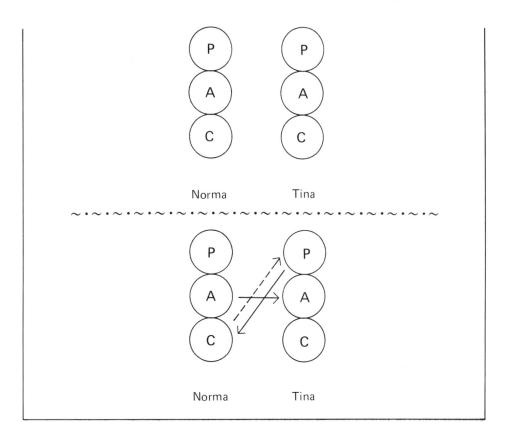

Drawing a diagram like this may help Norma to see the *Kick Me* game she is playing with Tina. The first step in stopping a game is recognizing it. Recording transactions that baffle *you* may *also* prove useful. In fact, it might clear away some haze if you begin to see patterns.

Now think about your own self-management project.

APPLICATION

1 What target behavior are you going to count?

2 How will you keep track of your target behavior? Tally with paper and pencil? Coins? Special counter?

3 When will you count? All day at work? 9 to 12? 12 to 1? When does it suit you?

4 Will you:

____ Count the frequency of your target behavior?

____ Measure the exact duration of your target behavior?

____ Estimate the percentage of time that your target behavior is occurring with a time-sampling procedure?

5   What events occur just before your target behavior begins?

6   What events occur just after your target behavior ends?

Note: You can do this application by just trying to remember what usually happens. However, you will learn much more if you actually watch and record what happens the next time your target behavior occurs.

7   Using the following chart, keep a daily record of your target behavior. As the graph develops, study it for patterns and tendencies.

Important: Be sure to try this! You will enjoy the feeling of seeing yourself making progress as the line zigzags across the page. When your performance starts to level off, you know you have reached your baseline performance. Then you can start the next part of your self-management program and see how it affects your performance.

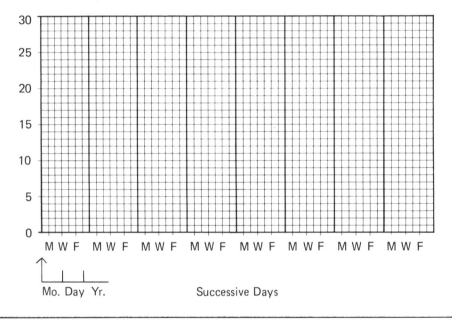

SUMMARY

Awareness paves the way to change. The feedback we give ourselves from just counting our target behavior often in itself stimulates us in a more successful direction. Watching our environment allows us to identify the critical events that occur just before and after our target behavior. Recording our data on a chart lets us find our baseline performance. This awareness lets us monitor the change in our behavior as we put into effect the next step in our self-CARE program: *rearranging* our inner and outer worlds.

SOURCE NOTES

[1] S. M. Johnston and G. White, "Self-Observation as an Agent of Behavior Change," mimeo, University of Oregon, 1969.

[2] R. M. McFall, "Effects of Self-Monitoring on Normal Smoking Behavior," *Journal of Consulting and Clinical Psychology*, 1970, 35:135–142.

[3] Adam Smith, *Powers of Mind* (New York: Ballantine, 1975), p. 107.

12

Rearranging Your Inner World

Now let's focus on the third step of the self-CARE program: *rearranging* our worlds. So far you've identified a hazy goal that you'd like to achieve. You've turned that hazy into specific measurable outcomes that, if all accomplished, would result in successful attainment of your goals. You've learned to increase your awareness of your inner and outer worlds as a first step toward attaining your personal goal.

In this and the next chapter, you'll learn some useful techniques for rearranging your worlds to increase even more your chances for success on the job. This chapter focuses on rearranging your inner world and Chapter 13 focuses on your outer world.

OBJECTIVES

When you finish this chapter, you'll be able to arrange your inner world by:

- making positive changes in inner-world events that are triggers, roadblocks, or payoffs for target behaviors;
- strengthening positive thoughts;
- strengthening positive aspects of your Child.

REMOVING INNER TRIGGERS AND ROADBLOCKS

In Chapter 11, we focused on increasing awareness of events that occur just before and just after a target behavior. Once we recognize these critical events, we can begin to rearrange our world. Here we're particularly interested in two types of events: triggers and roadblocks. A *trigger* is an event that for some reason signals you to think, feel, or act in a certain way. A *roadblock*, on the other hand, is something that gets in the way of a target behavior.

Negative, unduly oppressive, or outdated Parent tapes can trigger undesirable behaviors. They can also act as roadblocks for desirable behaviors.

Example

Jean needs to write a proposal and deliver it orally to upper management. Whenever she thinks of writing it, a number of related Parent tapes start to play:

— Anything worth doing at all is worth doing right.
— If you can't do it right, don't do it.
— Always do it right the first time.

These Parent tapes trigger undesirable Child feelings. Both the tapes and the feelings block Jean from writing her speech. To get rid of these triggers and roadblocks, she needs to rearrange her inner world. If she can do that, her fear and anxiety about writing the report will diminish and she can get on with it.

We all talk to ourselves—positively and negatively—inside our heads. If we strengthen negative tapes by allowing them to play repeatedly, we may put energy behind those thoughts and bring them to life. We need to listen to how we speak to ourselves and make sure we're not putting ourselves down but rather affirming ourselves. Remember, thoughts have power to influence our chances for success.

We can use a number of different techniques to get rid of undesirable Parent tapes and Child feelings. Here are three important ones:

— countering,
— internal screaming, and
— adult intervention.

We'll discuss these one by one.

Countering

Using countering, described by Rian McMullin and Bill Casey, you counter irrational thoughts with sensible self-talk.[1] In TA terms, whenever an undesirable Parent tape starts to play, you accept that it is part of your Parent and then counter it with a rational message from your Adult. A counter, then, is a rational statement from your Adult that takes command and firmly challenges your Parent tape. For example, when Jean hears a Parent tape that says, "Be perfect so I can be proud of you," she might consciously counter it with a thought like: "Nobody's perfect," or "That's asking too much," or "That tape seems to cause me to become more nervous, not more perfect. It's not helping me to be at ease with myself. The most important issue is to please myself . . . ." Other counters might be questions such as, "If I'm not perfect, what will the consequences be?" or "Is it really important that I invest the energy doing this job perfectly?" Just making such statements and raising these questions focuses energy in the Adult rather than in the Parent.

Sometimes it helps to let your Child in on the countering, too. For example, you might counter "Be perfect" with "Oh, wow! How silly! Will the sky fall on me if I'm not perfect?" or "Phooey on that! This needs to be good, not perfect." or exaggerate with "Ah, yes, that's me. Just call me Superperson!" or "See how great I am at sharpening these pencils. They look absolutely perfect!" A little power to the Child can also diminish the impact of our Parent. Just make sure your Adult is still the Executive.

APPLICATION ──

1 Here's some practice in countering. Assume that each of the following statements is an undesirable Parent tape. For each statement, write one or more counters. Remember, you're not really talking to your parent figures; you're talking to something inside of you that *you* are responsible for. You're talking sense to yourself!

Undesirable Parent Tapes	Counters
1. Don't start anything if you can't finish it.	
2. Don't get yourself dirty.	
3. Never talk to strangers.	

~ • ~ • ~ • ~ • ~ • ~ • ~ • ~ • ~ • ~ • ~ • ~ • ~ • ~ • ~ • ~

There's no one right way to counter these Parent tapes. You may find it helpful, however, to compare your counters with the ones others have come up with.

Undesirable Parent Tapes	Counters
1. Don't start anything if you can't finish it.	I'll never know if I can finish something if I don't start it. What's so terrible about occasionally not finishing something, anyway? This tape could be hurting me: it could hold me back from trying out new things.
2. Don't get yourself dirty.	To do certain kinds of jobs well, it's necessary to get dirty. There is nothing wrong with getting dirty. I can always clean up.
3. Never talk to strangers.	I want to meet new people and be friendly with them. If I *never* talk to strangers, I sure won't make many new friends!

~ • ~ • ~ • ~ • ~ • ~ • ~ • ~ • ~ • ~ • ~ • ~ • ~ • ~ • ~ • ~

2 Here's some more practice. Write a counter for each of these undesirable Parent tapes. (You may wish to use your Child as well as your Adult.)

Undesirable Parent Tapes	Counters
1. Never throw anything away.	
2. You don't have what it takes to be successful.	
3. You can do things only when you're in the mood.	
4. Strong people don't ask for help.	

~ • ~ • ~ • ~ • ~ • ~ • ~ • ~ • ~ • ~ • ~ • ~ • ~ • ~ • ~ • ~ • ~

Compare your counters with these possibilities. Remember, you're the best judge of what counters are best for your own Parent tapes. Any counter is correct if it helps you handle an undesirable Parent tape more productively.

Undesirable Parent Tapes	Counters
1. Never throw anything away.	Phooey! I don't have to keep a junk-yard!
2. You don't have what it takes to be successful.	But I have been successful on a number of occasions.*
3. You can do things only when you're in the mood.	Sometimes it's really important to do a task regardless of how you feel about it. I have managed to do things before that I didn't feel like doing.
4. Strong people don't ask for help.	Most strong people are strong because they've been smart enough to ask for help when they needed it.

*Your gold-stamp collection can be extremely helpful as you counter Parent tapes like these.

Internal Screaming

Another technique for dealing with Parent tapes is *internal screaming.* Using this technique, suggested by Joseph Wolpe,[2] you simply shout silently to yourself with all your might: "STOP!" or "GET OUT!" or "GET OFF MY BACK!" or "CUT!" (as in the movies) whenever an undesirable Parent tape starts to play. This is a very intense counter and often gives relief to the Child. Repeat this scream until the Parent tape stops playing. If it's all right (give yourself Adult protection), you might scream the words out loud—as loud as you can. It may even help to slam a book on the table as you scream "STOP!" or similar counters. The sudden loud sound often energizes the Child and jolts you out of your Parent ego state. This may give your Adult a chance to gain the upper hand. Remember these four important points about internal screaming:

— When you are using internal screaming or countering a Parent tape, understand that you are not talking to your actual parent figures. The tapes you continue to hold in your head represent how you chose to remember and to emulate your parental figures. These tapes are now *your* responsibility. Most parents, for better or for worse, do the very best they know how. Remember, they also have Parent, Adult, and Child ego states, along with certain cultural sets.

   Generally, Parent tapes encourage us to survive, but as times change rapidly, some of them become outdated or even defeating. To be your own person more fully, take full responsibility for your Parent ego state. You can now decide what part is setting up a roadblock. Thinking autonomously, you can choose what is best for you now. Holding a grudge against a parent figure won't help you—in fact, it diverts your energy and may hurt your chances of living as rich a life as you can choose.

— You might think of this screaming as coming from your Child—it probably is. But note that your Adult is also involved because you very deliberately plan this screaming. You also use your Adult to protect yourself from embarrassment or harm.

— Beware of any negative dialogue between your Parent and Child. Such dialogue is usually unproductive and drains your energy. You also may allow it to upset you or use it to stay stuck in old patterns. But with your Adult in control, internal screaming may release you, possibly clarifying what's been happening inside you for years.

— By using internal screaming fervently and consistently, *you can be successful* in dealing with persistent Parent tapes. Sometimes this technique takes a little practice to reap the benefits. So give yourself some time and space to do it.

APPLICATION

1 Write down one of your Parent tapes that you have discovered is self-defeating.

2 In what situation does this tape tend to play?

3 Imagine yourself in this situation right now. Hear the Parent tape start to play. Then mentally shout, "STOP! STOP! STOP! STOP! STOP!" (Say it as many times as necessary until the tape stops playing.)

Adult Intervention

As you've seen, countering and internal screaming are useful for stopping Parent tapes. A related technique is *Adult intervention*, which is useful for stopping unproductive inner *dialogue* between Parent and Child.

The first step in Adult intervention is to use your Adult to listen to how your Parent and Child talk inside your head. Then you step in with your Adult and speak to both your Parent and Child. Finally, you think through the problem at hand and make a new decision. Here's an example of this taken from *Women as Winners:*[3]

Amanda became aware of a strong "Be Perfect" message as a driving force in her script.

It is the afternoon before Amanda's committee meeting. The chairperson calls with an urgent request: "We need an update on the fund-raising campaign. Since Lee's sick, I'm counting on you to give the report. Now, I know you like to do everything perfectly, but we're very short on time." Amanda's inner dialogue looks like this:

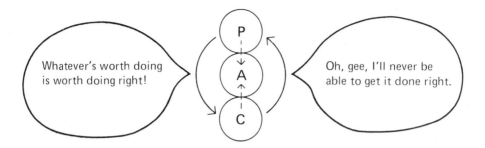

Awareness of Parent and Child

After she became aware of this inner dialogue, Amanda's Adult took over.

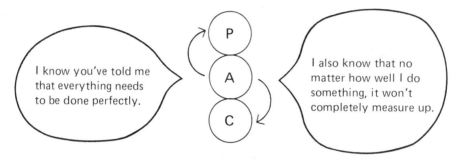

Adult Intervention

Amanda's Adult intervention enabled her to think through a new decision which eventually changed what she did.

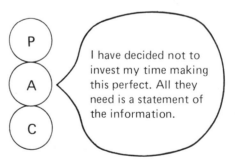

Decision Based on Awareness

APPLICATION ———————————————————————

Sheldon needed to make an important phone call to a Mr. Turner to clarify the specifications in a contract he was working on. But he kept putting it off and he didn't know why. Then he became aware of his inner dialogue.

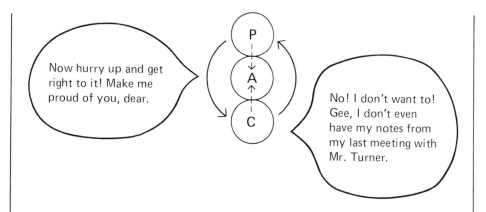

1 What might Sheldon's Adult say to the Parent and Child? (Write your answer in the balloons.)

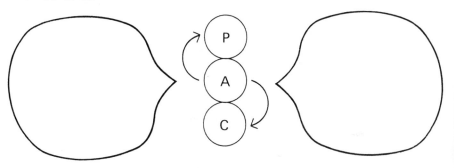

~•~•~•~•~•~•~•~•~•~•~•~•~•~•~•~•~•~•~•~

Here's one possibility:

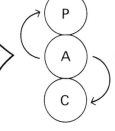

I hear you saying that you want me to hurry up and make the call and do a good job so you can be proud.

You're afraid you won't be able to make P proud of you. You feel upset because you don't have the notes you need to do a good job.

~•~•~•~•~•~•~•~•~•~•~•~•~•~•~•~•~•~•~•~

2   What decision might Sheldon make using his Adult?

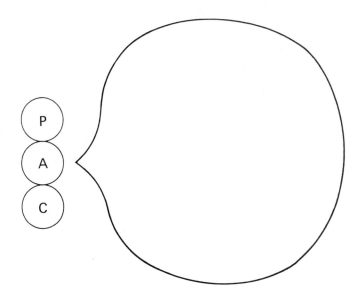

~.~.~.~.~.~.~.~.~.~.~.~.~.~.~.~.~.~.~

Here's one possibility:

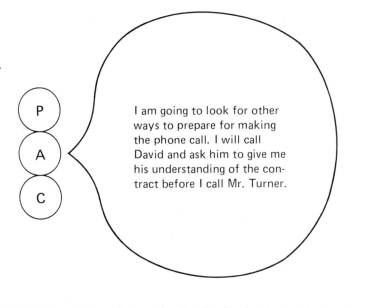

I am going to look for other ways to prepare for making the phone call. I will call David and ask him to give me his understanding of the contract before I call Mr. Turner.

~.~.~.~.~.~.~.~.~.~.~.~.~.~.~.~.~.~.~

3 Think again about your target behavior. Listen to what your Parent and Child are saying to each other about that behavior. To help yourself hear the dialogue, you may wish to role-play a conversation as a little child might. Loosely close one fist and let that fist represent your Child. Hold your other hand like a pointing finger or a bear claw (or whatever best symbolizes *your* Parent). Then as you look at each hand, listen to what each is saying to the other.

Continue the dialogue until your Adult is ready to intervene and help you reach a new decision. Remember that the pointing finger and bear claw don't represent your parents. Rather, they represent imagery you carry inside and can change as you choose. (As you continue the dialogue you may wish to change the bear claw into a softer, more supporting and nurturing image such as a swan.)

   Write the important points from your inner dialogue here:

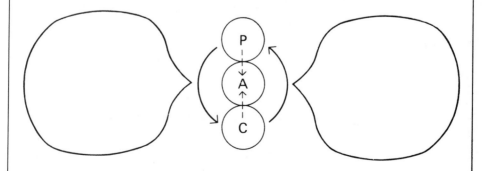

Summarize your decision:

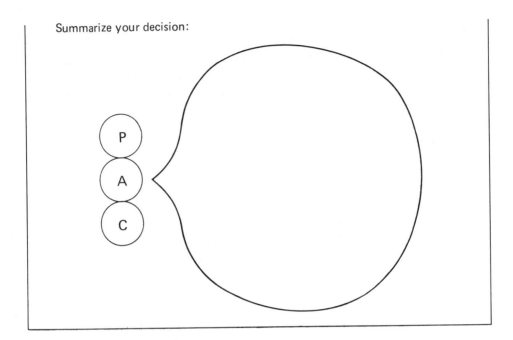

As you've seen, it's helpful to:

— stop Parent tapes with countering and internal screaming;
— reach new positive decisions with Adult intervention.

With Adult intervention you can consciously decide what positive tapes you want to put in place of your negative Parent tapes. These new tapes can come to function much as Parent tapes: eventually they play automatically and are triggered by certain kinds of environmental events. So pick your new tapes with care. Be sure they help you and won't get in your way as some of your old Parent tapes did. New tapes need to be updated occasionally, too!

Letting Thoughts Go

You may choose to take a more passive approach to dealing with negative thoughts. If so, when you are aware that a negative tape is playing, quiet yourself, let the thought drift through your mind, listen to it, and say passively to yourself, "I'm preoccupied with the past. This thought is meaningless to me now." Don't fight it but let it go by. Let go of the negative and make way for the positive.

STRENGTHENING POSITIVE THOUGHTS

Once you reach new decisions and begin to think constructively, it is important to maintain and strengthen your new positive thoughts. Let's look at two techniques for doing just that.

Frequency Modification

One ingenious technique for thought control, called *frequency modification,* was suggested by Homme and Tosti.[4] They emphasize the *frequency* of thinking certain positive thoughts rather than the intensity. That is, you don't concern yourself about, "Am I really concentrating hard enough on this thought?" You simply focus on increasing your *frequency* of thinking the positive thoughts. This technique has been used by a number of people to pull themselves out of depression or to change undesirable personal behaviors. Here is what Homme and Tosti suggest:

— Identify positive thoughts you'd like to think more frequently.
— Identify a specific situation that regularly happens early in the morning and occurs frequently throughout the day. That situation should involve a unique stimulus and a high-probability response to that stimulus. By unique stimulus we mean something that gives you a sensation that you can easily distinguish from other sensations—for example, cold water running over your hands or the sound of a telephone ringing. A high-probability behavior is something that you're very likely to do soon after you encounter the stimulus, such as answering the phone.
— Make a contract with yourself that each time you sense the unique stimulus, you will think the positive thought that you'd like to strengthen.
— After thinking the positive thought, carry out the high-probability behavior that is associated with the unique stimulus.

This procedure may sound complicated, but it really isn't.

Example

Paul felt depressed about his mediocre performance as a salesperson. In fact, he felt depressed most of the time. Whenever some little thing would go wrong (such as his forgetting a pencil or missing a turn when driving to a client's place), these heavy Parent tapes would play:

"Why do you always make things go wrong?"
"You should never show any weaknesses."
"You'll never amount to anything."

Paul had learned a pattern to depress himself. These thoughts served as an inner trigger for Paul's not-OK Child to feel like it was being squashed by a huge elephant. The more depressed he got, the worse his sales record got and the more mistakes he made. As his performance slumped and his mistakes increased, his depression increased. In fact, being a salesperson was a "perfect" job to experience his sense of not-OKness because his performance was constantly quantified.

Paul seemed to be trapped in a never-ending downward spiral, but he was able to pull out of it by using countering combined with frequency modification. First he developed a good counter for each of the Parent tapes that were haunting him:

Parent Tape	*Counter*
Why do you always make things go wrong?	I don't *always* make things go wrong. After all, mistakes can point the way to success—especially if I become aware of them and make adjustments in what I'm doing so mistakes aren't continually repeated. A winner learns from mistakes and doesn't repeat them.
You should never show any weaknesses.	It's better to level with people than to put on a show. It's all right to express my feelings. To err is human.
You'll never amount to anything.	I have something worthwhile to contribute to: — my family, — my friends, — my employer, — my community, — myself.

After Paul developed his list of counters, he picked a unique stimulus to serve as a trigger for his counter. Since Paul often used the phone in his work, he picked the sound of the dial tone as the unique stimulus. He made a contract with himself to think one positive thought (counter against his negative Parent tapes) as soon as he heard the dial tone *and before* he started to place a call. The first day he tried this, Paul made ten phone calls and thought one of his counters before each call. Almost immediately Paul noticed that his feelings of depression were diminishing. He had replaced his negative thoughts with positive, helpful ones. He was taking charge of how he thought about himself. He, indeed, had a choice.

APPLICATION ———————————————

1 Write down another self-defeating Parent tape.

2 Give at least three counters for this Parent tape.

3 Name a unique stimulus that might serve as a trigger for your counters. (Remember: if possible, pick a unique stimulus that occurs early in the morning and frequently throughout the day.)

4 Name the high-probability response associated with that unique stimulus.

5 Make a contract with yourself to think of one of the counters each time the unique stimulus occurs. Agree that you will not engage in the high-probability response until after you have thought of at least one of the three counters that you wrote in item 2.

6 Write down the details of your self-contract.

7 When will you start?

8 What will you expect in:

3 weeks?

2 months?

1 year?

Deliberately Changing Perceptions

Another way to strengthen positive thoughts is to deliberately change your perceptions. Remember that a roadblock is something that keeps you from carrying out a target behavior. It's important to realize that you are often blocked by your *perception* of some external object rather than by the object itself. For example, suppose you are being supervised by Mr. X, who comes on like a not-OK boss. Perhaps he is overcritical, or doesn't make sound decisions, or is too wishy-washy. Whatever his problem, let's assume that you can't get rid of him (short of quitting) and there seems to be nothing you can do to change him. You're stuck, right?

Wrong! Remember, part of what is blocking you in a situation like this is your boss. But another important roadblock is your *perception* of your boss. You hold a bad attitude toward him—perhaps with good reason! But remember that when you have a bad attitude toward a person, *your* performance is going to be hurt and *that* affects *you* as well as other people.

The technique, then, is to get rid of the inner-world roadblock that you have created. Here's one way to tackle it. Visualize a hypothetical boss: let's call him Mr. Q. Mr. Q is happy, friendly, free with his strokes, creative, intelligent, a good manager, able to delegate effectively and fairly, firm when necessary, and so on. The next time you're about to walk into Mr. X's office, visualize him as Mr. Q and respond to him as if he *were* that ideal boss. Greet him cheerfully. Smile. Be open with him. Don't collect any stamps while you're with him. Avoid playing any games. And when you have a chance, give him a few warm fuzzies.

"Oh, I couldn't do that!" you may be thinking. Well, don't knock it if you haven't tried it. Remember, you'll be responding to an ideal boss (the one *you* have fantasized) rather than your former perception of your not-OK boss.

"OK, suppose I am able to pull this off and do it spontaneously without looking like I'm putting on an act. What good will it do, anyway?" For one thing, you'll feel a lot better, knowing that you are taking a positive attitude toward your boss in spite of his shortcomings. And because you're happier, and have a positive outlook, you'll be able to perform your own job better.

It's too easy to allow other people's problems to spill over on us. Too often, we take their bad vibes and use them to crunch our stomachs, restrict our vascular system, and give ourselves pains in the chest (and a few other places). Instead we can choose to let the bad vibes slide right by us. That way we don't take "ownership" of someone else's problem. After all, most of us have enough of our own!

If you realize that someone else has a problem, protect yourself from becoming like that person or responding in the complementary role. Sometimes it's helpful to think of such a person as having a very scared Child deep inside, a Child that is fearful of reaching out and touching others in a warm, loving way. As a consequence, that person may be very negative. Think of their negative vibes going right past you and not penetrating your good energy field.

The truth is that people who act not-OK probably hurt inside. Changing your perception—being more sensitive to what is really happening inside them rather than taking their external behavior at face value—just could help you all to feel better. Remember, by doing so you are removing a roadblock that may release the hidden energy you need to choose success more often.

APPLICATION ───────────────────────────────

1 Suppose Vernon, Kirby's boss, frequently discounts Kirby's ideas: he not only fails to take them seriously, but often puts Kirby down with caustic remarks. As we look in on this scene, Kirby is suggesting another idea (which he is convinced is a good one).

Kirby: "So I don't think it would be a good idea to install the elevators as planned. We would have to cut a hole in each ceiling and install doors. It would be a big mess. There would be plaster in the hallways for weeks. I have an idea that will save us both time and money. Why don't we put the elevator on the outside of the building?"

Vernon: (He jumps up from his desk, throws his hands in the air, and shouts): "Now I've heard everything! Why, it's impossible. I'm sorry, it just won't work. Now is there anything else? I've got *important* work to do."

Which response would be most in line with our guidelines?

___(a) Think: "He makes me mad; he never listens to me; he's just not a good manager."

___(b) Say: "I'm not leaving until you explain what you are so angry about or until you let me clarify my idea."

___(c) Think: "Vernon very likely feels not-OK inside. Poor guy. I'll collect some information and approach him later with the facts."

~ • ~ • ~ • ~ • ~ • ~ • ~ • ~ • ~ • ~ • ~ • ~ • ~ • ~ • ~ • ~

We like choice (c). Kirby needs to realize that Vernon has a problem; he also needs to protect himself from becoming a big bear like Vernon.

~ • ~ • ~ • ~ • ~ • ~ • ~ • ~ • ~ • ~ • ~ • ~ • ~ • ~ • ~ • ~

2 Think of a person who appears to be acting as a roadblock for your target behavior. How would you like this person to be different? Describe in detail:

3 Imagine as vividly as possible that this person is—SHAZAM!—suddenly transformed into the ideal person you have just visualized. How would you respond differently to this transformed person?

4 Now see yourself actually responding this way. Describe yourself. How does your voice sound? What is your face and body posture saying?

Next time you meet this person, respond as if she or he were eminently reasonable, wise, warm, and so on. At best, you may be surprised to find this person will actually become eminently reasonable, wise, and warm! In any case, you'll feel better and consequently be more effective.

STRENGTHENING POSITIVE ASPECTS OF YOUR CHILD

So far we've discussed how you can remove inner-world roadblocks by countering harmful Parent tapes and replacing them with helpful positive thoughts and Adult decisions. Just as you can change your Parent ego state, you can also change your Child. The Child in all of us has certain beautiful qualities and helpful abilities. For example, the Natural Child can:

— relax,
— tune in to the surroundings,
— enjoy ordinary experiences,
— see visions,
— be imaginative,
— create new things and ideas,
— be aware of internal feelings and happenings,
— relish what feels good,
— be charming.

Many times we don't experience these qualities because tension in our Adapted Child *blocks* them out. We can strengthen the positive aspects of our Child and remove those roadblocks, bringing out these qualities in many different ways. Some of those ways we'll discuss now.

Relaxation

Unnecessary tension saps your strength. If you learn to be more relaxed, you'll feel better and have more energy. You'll also feel more confident. Confident people are relaxed people. If you're tense about something you must do, such as reorganizing your subordinates' work stations, your tension is likely to slow you down, making it difficult for you to do your best. By learning to relax, you put aside anxious feelings and unblock your energy so that you can move effortlessly when you:

- present a proposal,
- talk with a VIP,
- speak up at important meetings,
- say "no,"
- give people your opinion,
- learn a new system,
- ask for help,
- express feelings,
- refuse to collect stamps,
- face a deadline,
- make a decision,
- create a new system.

Relaxation also helps you to clear your mind and think creatively. Most of us use our Controlling Parent to edit our thoughts. Unconsciously we say to ourselves: "It's always been done this way . . . it won't work . . . you tried that before . . . what will other people think? . . . that's naughty . . . DON'T YOU DARE THINK THAT!" When we relax deeply, however, we seem to turn our Natural Child loose and allow it to communicate with our Adult. In fact, experimental studies have shown that people can actually see subliminal or hidden messages in visual material better when deeply relaxed.[5] They seem to be better able to turn their Natural Child loose, without their Controlling Parent editing everything rigidly.

The ability to relax is more important to health and positive energy than many of us think. Recent research indicates that people's health and performance (in many areas) may dramatically improve if they learn to relax and focus their minds on positive self-affirmations.[6-10]

One simple way to become more relaxed is to use frequency modification: make a contract with yourself to relax and let go temporarily when a unique stimulus occurs. For example, Paul (see page 229) chose the dial tone as the unique stimulus. Whenever he heard the dial tone, he took a deep breath and then let his muscles go limp as he exhaled. He spoke to himself in an easy way, saying "Relax." This way the dial tone became a trigger for two desirable behaviors: relaxing and thinking positive thoughts.

Another approach to relaxation is to take more time and learn to become very *deeply* relaxed. The brain generates a rhythmical electrical energy that can be measured by a device called an *electroencephalograph*. The rhythm of the brain's energy is measured in cycles per second (cps). The different rhythms are:[11]

14 or more cps	beta waves
7–13 cps	alpha waves
4–7 cps	theta waves
below 4 cps	delta waves

When we are wide awake, we are in beta. When asleep we fluctuate among alpha, theta, and delta. By learning to relax deeply, we can put ourselves into alpha or theta while staying awake. There is some evidence that while we are in alpha or theta our thoughts may have a greater impact on target behaviors.[12] We are able to think more creatively and productively and we are more receptive to positive suggestions.

Now, how do you go about getting deeply relaxed? Before beginning any deep-relaxation session, find a quiet place where you can be alone for twenty to thirty minutes. Sit or lie in a relaxed position. Do whatever you need to do to be comfortable: loosen tight clothing, uncross your arms and legs, take off your shoes, glasses, or contact lenses, and so on. When you are in a comfortable position, follow these relaxation instructions. (For the moment, just read the instructions.)

Instructions for Deep Relaxation

Raise your eyebrows up as high as you can, as if you were startled or frightened by something. As you tighten these muscles, hold your breath and think thoughts like: "These muscles are becoming very tense, very tight . . . , tighter . . . , tighter, tense." Hold this position for five seconds. Then exhale slowly and let your muscles go limp as you repeat to yourself several times, "Relax." For the next twenty seconds, think thoughts like: "I'm focusing my attention on the feelings connected with relaxation . . . I'm enjoying the nice feeling . . . My upper facial muscles are relaxed . . . There's nothing for me to do right now but to focus my attention on the beautiful feeling of relaxation flowing into the upper part of my face. I'm thinking about nothing but just letting those muscles go, letting them relax, letting them be *completely* relaxed. I'm noticing how different those muscles feel now. Before they were tense and now I'm letting them become limp and relaxed. I'm relaxed, I'm relaxed, I'm relaxed."

After about twenty seconds of such relaxation thoughts, if you still notice any tension in your facial muscles, tighten them again for five seconds and then let everything go and think relaxation thoughts for another twenty seconds.

Once your upper facial muscles are completely relaxed, go on to relax each of the main muscle groups in your body in the same way. To make this easy to do, we have listed muscle groups below with suggestions on how to tense the muscles. Tensing the muscles is an important part of this exercise. It gives you a sort of "running start" for deep relaxation. When you release your muscles after holding them tight, you're able to let them go more completely. As you tense your muscles, pay particular attention to what they feel like, so you'll be better able to recognize when you are allowing your job to cause muscle tension. Move your tension from your Blind Self so that you can deal with it more openly.

Here are the muscle groups to relax one at a time:

Muscle Group	Tensing Instructions

Face:
  1. Upper face
  2. Middle face
  3. Lower face
	1. Lift eyebrows as if surprised . . . relax.
	2. Squint eyes and wrinkle nose . . . relax.
	3. Exaggerate a big smile . . . relax.

Neck	Clench teeth and tense neck muscles while pulling shoulders toward your ears . . . relax.

Shoulders and arms:
  1. Shoulders
 	
  2. Biceps (upper arm)
  3. Lower arms
	1. Extend your arms straight out in front of you. Put your left hand on top of your right hand. Push down with your left hand, up with your right hand . . . relax.
	2. Tense biceps . . . relax.
	3. Make a tight fist . . . relax.

Chest and upper back	Thrust chest forward; try to touch shoulder blades together . . . relax.
Abdomen and lower back	1. Make your belly hard . . . relax. 2. Arch your lower back . . . relax.
Buttocks and pelvis area	Tense muscles in buttocks and pelvis area . . . relax.

Legs and feet:
  1. Thighs
  2. Lower legs
  3. Feet
	1. Lock knees and tense muscles in upper legs . . . relax.
	2. Pull toes toward head . . . relax.
	3. Curl toes and move foot forward . . . relax.

Entire body	Arch back and suspend body so only your heels and the back of your head are touching the surface supporting you . . . relax.

It's best to carry out the deep-relaxation exercises without referring to a book. You may wish to simply memorize the muscle groups and the tensing instructions. Or you may wish to tape-record the instructions and then relax as you play back the tape.[13] To make the muscle groups easier to memorize, we've listed them in a logical order, starting with the top of your head and progressing down your body. You may wish to start with your toes and move up to your head. Whether you use a tape recorder or memorize the relaxation procedure, remember these important points:

— Tense each muscle for five seconds. (Exception: If your muscles cramp easily, you may wish to curl your toes for only three seconds rather than five.)
— As you tense your muscles, think about how they are becoming tighter and tighter. Think TENSE!
— As you tense each muscle group, take a deep breath and hold it. After five seconds exhale and let your muscles go limp.
— After letting go, think relaxation thoughts for about twenty seconds.

— If a muscle group seems completely relaxed after the tension and relaxation procedure, go on to the next muscle group. If it doesn't, repeat the tension and relaxation as many times as necessary until the muscle group feels *deeply* relaxed.

— For best results, practice relaxation daily for twenty to thirty minutes.

After you are accomplished at deep relaxation and your muscles have the feel of it, you will find benefit in just telling your muscle groups to relax. "My feet are warm and relaxed." "My legs are warm and relaxed." You can do this a few times throughout the day for "relaxation breaks."

Deep relaxation by itself is beneficial. But you can maximize the benefits of deep relaxation if you combine it with vivid visualization.

Vivid Visualization

Vivid visualization is a process of deliberately creating positive mental images while your brain is in alpha or theta. Here's how to do it:

— Go through the deep-relaxation procedure just outlined.
— Visualize yourself executing your target behavior. For example, see yourself:
   walking briskly with good posture;
   breathing freely and easily with no tension;
   smiling warmly and making eye contact easily;
   transacting effectively, opening up blocked transactions;
   expressing feelings easily and appropriately;
   accepting constructive criticism;
   giving and receiving warm fuzzies;
   speaking up easily;
   being the icebreaker, the first one to make contact;
   thinking positive thoughts;
   solving problems;
   looking for opportunities;
   converting worry time into study time;
   dealing confidently with important people.
— After visualizing yourself thinking the way you'd like to think, feeling the way you'd like to feel, performing the way you'd like to perform, open your eyes and make a number of reaffirming "I am" statements that relate to your goals, such as:
   I am confident.
   I am friendly.
   I am outgoing.
   I meet people well.
   I'm on time.
   I'm productive.
   I pay attention to important details.
   I am relaxed.
   I am without unnecessary fear.
   I am important.

I am valuable.
I am able to turn today's impossibilities into tomorrow's possibilities.
I am creative.
I am inventive.
I am helpful.
I am a first-class performer.
I am enthusiastic.
I am persistent.

These are just a few of the possibilities. List some "I am" statements that fit your particular needs and interests. Then use them in a vivid visualization session!

Lloyd Homme[14] has pointed out that when we imagine ourselves doing something, that act of imagining is in itself an approximation of doing it. If we imagine our target behavior often enough or vividly enough, we greatly increase the probability that we will actually carry out the target behavior. For example, experiments have shown that basketball players who practice shooting free throws with vivid visualization make as much improvement as those who practice physically.[15]

When practicing vivid visualization, keep this important point in mind: visualize only *positive* target behavior. What you visualize may happen! As a wise sage puts it, "What you foresee is what you get."

Notice that while deep relaxation helps you to get rid of a roadblock (unnecessary tension), with vivid visualization you also give yourself inner-world triggers for desirable behaviors, positive thoughts, feelings, or actions.[16]

Meditation

Another technique for ridding yourself of roadblocks is meditation. The objective in most meditation techniques is to clear the mind and quiet the body. Meditation releases more of our energy and creativity, and heightens our inner wisdom. In this fast-paced world we too seldom take time to get in touch with our innermost thoughts and feelings. Meditation can help us explore our Unknown Selves and bring more of them into our Open Selves.

Meditation can benefit us in other ways. Julius Fast, author of *The Pleasure Book*, reports what his friend Chuck says about his experience with meditation:

> . . . At this point in my development I'm able to feel pleasure constantly. Other people's craziness doesn't bother me. I breathe and rise above them. Eventually I hope to be my own man completely, responsible for myself for good or bad.
>
> He straightens up, closes his eyes, and takes a deep breath, his face peaceful.
> "I still haven't made it. I'm still afraid to risk rejection or failure, but I'm learning. Now I know that unless I take risks, I can't prove myself. I know it in my mind, but the next step is to know it with my body—"[17]

Alex, another friend of Fast's, says:

> "What you get out of it is a sense of euphoria. You feel good. It's a very pleasant procedure. It's as if something inside you begins to unwind the moment you start. Now I use it to relax during a business day, especially if I'm very tense. I sit down in

my office chair, ask my secretary not to disturb me, turn off my desk lamp, and simply meditate. I find my whole body relaxing and I'm flooded with a deep, pleasurable feeling. The sense of relaxation is tremendous, as if someone were caressing me gently. I come out of it as relaxed as if I'd taken a tranquilizer . . . . It's helped me," he confesses. "I enjoy it, and now I get more pleasure than I used to out of life. I don't know about the subtle states of thoughts that people talk about—I figure that's all gobbledygook. For my part meditation is really a pleasant experience. . . ."[18]

Patricia Carrington's report from her research and personal experience implies that an overly Critical Parent ego state may be mellowed by meditation. She writes:

Many people conduct an inner dialogue in which they criticize themselves for not behaving "properly" or doing things "well." . . . An important change frequently brought about by meditation is the altering of the superego so that it becomes more flexible—the meditator will begin to be more patient and understanding with him- or herself: ". . . In meditation I float rhythmically, effortlessly, almost totally divorced from the nagging of commands and 'shoulds' . . . ." (from Meditation Journal of Harmon S. Ephron—personal communication.)

If this newfound self-acceptance begins to affect their everyday lives and it often does, then the meditators may find themselves becoming more tolerant of their own weaknesses, life may be seen in better perspective, and they may become more efficient since their actions are no longer hampered by unproductive self-criticism. Easing of self-blame also makes it easier for the meditator to accept certain thoughts that otherwise might be difficult to face without guilt or anxiety.

. . .

Resolution of an uncomfortable emotional reaction during meditation is not unusual. When this occurs, the person may feel more emotionally alive outside of meditation too. This can mark the beginning of a new era in the meditator's life, a deeper awareness of who he or she really is.[19]

In his book, *The Relaxation Response*, Herbert Benson has developed a simple technique for meditating.[20] This technique fits nicely with deep relaxation. Here are the main steps in Dr. Benson's technique:

— Get comfortable.
— Shut your eyes.
— Relax deeply. (We suggest you use a shortened version of the deep-relaxation procedure described earlier. Simply tell yourself to relax.)
— Breathe normally.
— Continue to breathe normally as you become aware of your breathing.
— Each time you exhale, silently say the word "one" to yourself.
— Keep this up for ten to twenty minutes. To keep track of the time, place a clock or watch in a position where you can see it easily merely by opening your eyes. Avoid using an alarm to signal the end of your meditation—it may have a jarring effect and spoil the sense of calm that you bring to yourself through meditation.

When your meditating time is up, sit quietly for about five more minutes. Keep your eyes closed for approximately two minutes and open them for the last three minutes. Avoid standing up suddenly.

— Don't worry. Allow yourself time to learn to reach a deep level of relaxation. If you catch yourself thinking various thoughts instead of clearing your mind, simply stop thinking them and go back to repeating "one." Don't make a special effort to concentrate on "one." Simply let your mind return to "one" whenever you catch yourself thinking distracting thoughts. Meditate in this way once or twice a day. Wait two hours after any meal before doing so.

Benson's method is based on his research and is easy to do. However, other easy methods of meditation may suit you even better. You'll find *Freedom in Meditation* by Patricia Carrington a useful guide. Experiment. You may come to treasure this time with yourself.[21]

Caution: In the process of clearing your mind you may find yourself getting in touch with some racket feelings or Parent tapes that aren't too pleasant. John Norton sums up this idea in his poem "Meditation":

Meditation

Empty the mind, say the handbooks.
Drain away the chatter
and when the level behind the dam drops,
wade into the black ooze, thigh-deep,
and approach the still intact,
long buried stumps of your past
preserved in that reservoir of inattention.
Rub your palms along the slick sides;
thrust your whole hand back into once hidden places
and grope there for evidence of life.

You passed word to begin
          earthmovers move out

scraping away the topsoil
          a town levelled

your family
          sent somewhere else

stone fences
          marked certain limits

no halt to the rising waters
          streams merge

one field with the others
          through the fences

flooding the farms
          streams now ponds

then one flat wide lake
          checked behind the new dam

Empty the mind, the handbooks say.[22]

So when you meditate you may discover "long buried stumps of your past." This can be frightening but it is worthwhile because by meditating you release and expand energy in your Natural Child—energy that previously had been locked up by clutching stamps and racket feelings.

Grounding

Yet another technique for rearranging your inner world and expanding and releasing the power in your Natural Child is called *grounding*. Ever come rushing into an afternoon meeting and find that your body was present but your mind was still out to lunch? If so, you've experienced fragmentation of mind and body. Perhaps you've even said to yourself something like, "I'm not all here!" or "I don't have my head together yet!" As you probably found out from your own experience, you're usually not very productive when you're in this state. One way to avoid this is to practice a grounding exercise in which you bring yourself fully to where you are. This technique combines aspects of vivid visualization and relaxation.

Here's one way to do it. If you're seated, sit erect. If you are standing, feel the floor supporting your feet. Put both feet flat on the floor and imagine that your feet are part of the earth, that you are connected directly to the ground. When you have this mental picture in sharp focus, pay attention to your breathing. Feel your lower back and sides expand as you inhale. Think "relax" as you exhale. Stay aware of your breathing. *Be* your breathing for a few moments. Now imagine rods coming from your hips and running down through your legs. See these rods going deep into the earth. (You might prefer roots like tree roots spreading and sinking into the earth.) Feel the energy flowing through you and attaching you to the ground. See yourself feeling a part of everything, feeling great! Stay with this feeling of being part of the earth for a few moments. Then open your eyes and look around you. Experience your surroundings as if you were seeing them for the first time. Focus on specific objects in the room—a table, a chair, a person—and really see them. Think: "His hair is red, that table top is smooth, the wall paneling is dark brown, this room is a large room, she's wearing a long skirt, and so on." When the meeting starts, focus on the speaker and enjoy the feeling of having your mind and body united harmoniously rather than fragmented. It's like bringing peace to yourself.

APPLICATION

Think of a meeting or other situation in which you might plan to use grounding. Imagine that the time for the meeting has come. Picture yourself walking into the meeting room, sitting down, and going through the grounding procedure. Wait for a few moments, then repeat this event in your mind, adding more details. Later, repeat this a third time.

We call this kind of mental practice *covert rehearsal*. Covert rehearsal is valuable here because it will increase the probability that you will actually practice grounding when the time for the meeting arrives.[23] Whether we know it or not, we rehearse in our heads all the time. The key is to take charge of what we are rehearsing!

REARRANGING PAYOFFS

We've seen how to remove roadblocks and how to strengthen positive aspects of the Natural Child. Another effective way to rearrange our inner world is to remove payoffs for undesirable behavior and replace them with payoffs for desirable behavior. Remember that a payoff is something that occurs *after* a behavior that serves to increase the probability that the behavior will recur. Although payoffs are often pleasurable, unpleasant racket feelings can be payoffs, too (as we noted in Chapter 7).

If you find that you are into a racket—that you are using some feeling as a payoff for an undesirable behavior—you can get rid of the undesirable behavior by getting rid of that inner-world payoff and substituting a payoff for desirable behavior. Here's an example that combines several of the things you've learned.

Example

Bob usually arranged things so he was late to meetings, late in turning in reports, late to appointments, and so on. Afterward he would feel guilty and then would "bask" in the guilty feelings. Even though it hurt, his world was predictable and it was what he knew. Once Bob became aware of this racket, he decided to give up his inner-world payoff: the guilt feelings. He recognized that he set himself up for being late and that his guilt feelings were self-imposed.

So whenever he was late and the guilt feelings came upon him, he simply rejected them, using internal screaming. He would silently scream to himself, "Stop feeling guilty! Stop feeling guilty!" and the feelings would diminish. But patterns don't change overnight. (His Adapted Child and Little Professor would certainly start looking for other ways to indulge in the old guilt feelings!) Realizing this, Bob put energy into his Adult and began planning a program designed to bring on a new kind of feeling: confidence.

Bob started coming ten minutes early to meetings and going through a grounding procedure to get himself mentally and physically prepared. He then savored a warm feeling of accomplishment when he was able to participate in the meeting with increased effectiveness. He had never consciously done this before. This warm feeling became his new payoff. Bob learned to seek warm fuzzies instead of cold pricklies. In the same way, he began to figure out ways to accomplish his projects on or before his deadlines. He also made it a point to arrive for his appointments early. Whenever he was successful in doing this, he treated himself to eating lunch out in his favorite little spot. Bob grew comfortable with the idea that success was really for him.

Removing the payoff for undesirable behavior opens the way for new, more desirable behaviors and more positive payoffs. *Caution:* When you remove a negative payoff, be sure you substitute positive behaviors and feelings. Otherwise, you may compulsively start performing other kinds of undesirable behaviors to get those accustomed negative payoffs.

APPLICATION ───

1 Recall an undesirable target behavior you'd like to get rid of. (This may be the behavior you described on page 179 or a different one.) Think for a moment. Describe how you usually feel after you do this target behavior.

2 When did you first have this feeling as a child?

3 How often did this happen?

4 Even though this feeling may be uncomfortable to you on one level, is it some-how satisfying to you to continue to feel it?

_____ Yes _____ No _____ Maybe _____ Unsure

(If so, consider using internal screaming to get rid of this feeling following an undesirable target behavior.)

5 What good feeling will you substitute for the undesirable target behavior?

6 What can you do to rearrange your world so that you'll get more of this *good* feeling?

Just as feelings can serve as payoffs, so can thoughts. Think of the thoughts that run through your head right after you've performed an unde-sirable behavior. Do you kick yourself with "Boy, am I stupid!" or "Why do I keep doing this?" or "I'll just never learn, will I?"? These thoughts may really be payoffs for you. If so, you may unwittingly *want* to think these thoughts that trigger the bad feelings. If you're playing any of these games with yourself, try this. Make a one-week contract with yourself in which you agree that you *won't:*

— call yourself stupid or use any language that might suggest this NO MATTER WHAT YOU DO;
— make excuses or rationalize;
— feel sorry for yourself;
— talk to anyone about how bad you're doing.

Also, agree to give yourself a positive internal payoff when you do things right. When you carry out a positive target behavior (or avoid a negative behavior), say to yourself: "All right!" "That's the way to go!" "Great, genius!" or "Good thinking."

When rewarding yourself in this way, don't wait until you have reached your long-range goal. Instead, reward yourself for approximations. Remember Dick on page 212 who wanted to make twenty sales calls a day? His baseline performance was nine to eleven calls. He made a contract with himself like the one just described. After each call he made, he would say to himself, "All right!—another call—I'm on my way!" At the end of the day, when he did better than his baseline performance, he congratulated himself: "Dick, you're great! You're really improving!" When Dick didn't make enough calls on a particular day, he didn't bawl himself out for it, rationalize, make excuses, or tell anyone about it. Instead, he looked forward to the next day as another chance to do better. We'll focus even more on positive payoffs in the next chapter.

APPLICATION ————————————————————————

1 Name a thought that frequently occurs after you perform an undesirable target behavior.

2 Are you willing to agree to give up this thought?

_____ Yes _____ No

3 What positive thought might you substitute for this irrational thought?

4 When will you start strengthening the positive thought?

5 When will you start giving up the irrational thought?

6 For how long will you agree to give it up? (We suggest three weeks.)

7 Jot down some notes about your experience in trying this:

SUMMARY

In this chapter you've learned some techniques for rearranging your inner world: countering, internal screaming, making Adult interventions, replacing undesirable Parent tapes with new ones, and strengthening the positive aspects of your Child by relaxing, visualizing, meditating, grounding, and giving yourself positive payoffs. All of these techniques require that you assume responsibility more fully for your inner self. Many ask you to get in touch with your body and its tensions as well as with your thoughts and feelings and how you use them. Taking responsibility for your inner world lets you rearrange things to suit yourself better. In the next chapter you'll learn some ideas about rearranging your outer world.

SOURCE NOTES

[1] Rian McMullin and Bill Casey, *Talk Sense to Yourself* (Lakewood, Colo.: Jefferson County Mental Health Center, 1975), p. 46.

[2] Joseph Wolpe, *The Practice of Behavioral Therapy*, 2nd ed. (New York: Pergamon Press, 1973).

[3] Reprinted with permission of Addison-Wesley Publishing Company, from Dorothy Jongeward and Dru Scott, *Women as Winners* (Reading, Mass.: Addison-Wesley, 1976), pp. 211-212.

[4] Lloyd Homme and Donald Tosti, *Behavior Technology: Motivation and Contingency Management* (San Rafael, Calif.: Individual Learning Systems, 1971), pp. 4-10.

[5] Wilson Bryan Key, *Subliminal Seduction* (New York: New American Library, 1973), p. 27.

[6] Jonathan Kirsch, "Can Your Mind Cure Cancer?" *New West*, Jan. 3, 1977, pp. 40-45.

[7] Laurence E. Morehouse and Leonard Gross, *Maximum Performance* (New York: Simon and Schuster, 1977), p. 35.

[8] Mike Samuels and Hal Z. Bennett, *Be Well* (co-published by Random House, New York, and The Bookworks, Berkeley, Calif., 1974), p. 123.

[9] Jose Silva and Philip Miele, *The Silva Mind Control Method* (New York: Simon and Schuster, 1977), p. 46.

[10] Anthony and Mary Zaffuto, *Alphagenics* (New York: Warner Books, 1974).

[11] Silva and Miele, *op. cit.*, p. 26.

[12] *Ibid.*, p. 61.

[13] Cassette tapes to help you relax deeply are available from Success Dynamics (see Appendix B).

[14] Personal communication with Lloyd Homme, San Rafael, Calif.

[15] Maxwell Maltz, *Psycho-Cybernetics* (Englewood Cliffs, N.J.: Prentice-Hall, 1960), p. 32.

[16] A cassette tape designed to help you practice vivid visualization is available from Success Dynamics (see Appendix B).

[17] Julius Fast, *The Pleasure Book* (New York: Stein and Day, 1975), p. 106.

[18] *Ibid.*, p. 176.

[19] Patricia Carrington, *Freedom in Meditation* (Garden City, N.Y.: Anchor Press/Doubleday, 1977), pp. 211-212.

[20] Herbert Benson, *The Relaxation Response* (New York: Morrow, 1975), p. 162. (First Avon printing, August 1976.)

[21] A cassette tape designed to help you meditate is available from Success Dynamics (see Appendix B).

[22] John Norton, "Meditation," © 1977, all rights reserved, used with permission of the author.

[23] Maltz, *op. cit.*

13

Rearranging Your Outer World

So far you've identified a hazy goal that you'd like to achieve. You've turned that hazy into specific, measurable outcomes that, if all accomplished, would result in successful attainment of your goal. You've learned a number of techniques for rearranging your inner world.

OBJECTIVES

When you finish this chapter, you'll be able to:

- move closer to your goal by rearranging your outer world;
- make appropriate changes in three kinds of outer-world events that trigger, block, or strengthen target behaviors.

OUTER-WORLD TRIGGERS

As we have seen, an outer-world trigger is a person, place, thing, or happening that for some reason signals you to engage in a positive or negative target behavior.

Example

Roger, the editor of his company's newsletter, often took his editorials home but failed to work on them. He repeatedly disappointed himself by doing this even though he had decided that forty-five minutes to an hour at home was all he needed while at the office, with interruptions, it took two hours of his time.

One evening he wanted to spend some time perfecting an especially important editorial. After dinner he planned to sit on the sofa and read the paper. Then, after relaxing for a while, he'd start his work. But directly opposite the sofa sat a beautiful 21-inch color television—and right beside him on an end table was a remote-control switch. As usual, before Roger was even aware of what he was doing, he had picked up the remote control and turned on the television. Once he was hooked into watching it, he found it difficult to get to work on the editorial. His good intentions went by the wayside.

In this situation a number of triggers were operating. The presence of the newspaper was a trigger to read it. The soft, cozy sofa was a trigger to sit down and relax. The presence of the TV set directly opposite the sofa and the remote-control switch on the end table triggered TV watching. Notice that by reading the newspaper and watching television, Roger engaged in behaviors that were incompatible with his goal.

With a little environmental engineering, Roger was able to solve his problem and fulfill the commitment to himself to work on his editorials in the evening. Here's how he did it: Following through on an earlier decision, he stopped getting the evening paper and subscribed to the morning paper. He put the remote control out of sight so he'd have to *consciously* get it to turn on the TV set. He also bought an attractive desk organizer. Now when he looked across the room after dinner, the sight of his desk organizer triggered the target behavior of working on the editorial. It really worked! Roger became much more productive. Then when he did watch television after finishing an editorial, he enjoyed it much more than before because he didn't feel guilty about failing to meet his personal commitment.

Example

David wanted to increase the amount of time he spent concentrating on creative ways to advertise a new product. In watching his outer-world behavior, he discovered that he often interrupted his creative work session to jump up and scold his subordinates about their poor job performance. He suppressed his Child and put energy into his Parent. He also became aware that just before jumping up to lecture his people, he would often glance at the pile of reports on his desk. He realized that the pile of reports was a trigger for his Parent to leap into action!

As a result he decided to do some environmental planning. With his Adult in gear, he cleared out a drawer in his desk and kept his pile there. Thus he removed the undesirable trigger. Then, whenever he wanted to concentrate on his creative projects, he cleaned up his surroundings first. It worked! With the trigger out of sight, David was able to concentrate and avoid slipping into his Controlling Parent. The graph on the following page shows his progress.

APPLICATION ───────────────────────────────────

1   Thus, one effective environmental-planning technique is to take away anything that stimulates *un*desirable responses. A flip side to this technique is also effective. Instead of *taking away* a trigger for a negative behavior, what might you do?

~ · ~ · ~ · ~ · ~ · ~ · ~ · ~ · ~ · ~ · ~ · ~ · ~ · ~ · ~ · ~ · ~

You might *add* a trigger for a positive one.

~ · ~ · ~ · ~ · ~ · ~ · ~ · ~ · ~ · ~ · ~ · ~ · ~ · ~ · ~ · ~ · ~

2   In the last example, David managed to increase his concentration span and his productivity. Before removing the trigger, he was able to come up with only one or two new creative ideas per week. After removing the trigger, he was able to

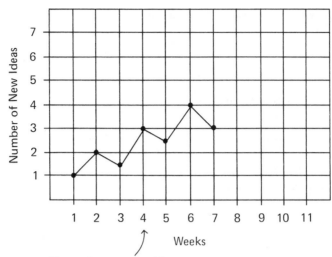

Change in outer world:
used clean desk for
creative sessions

increase his output to four or five ideas per week. He still wasn't satisfied, however. He wanted to loosen himself up, to use more of his Little Professor and his
uninhibited Natural Child. He felt that if he could do this, he could come up with
more original and dynamic advertising ideas. Can you suggest any changes David
might make in his environment to get this result?

~ • ~ • ~ • ~ • ~ • ~ • ~ • ~ • ~ • ~ • ~ • ~ • ~ • ~ • ~ • ~

David could come up with many different solutions. He could:
—Put things around him to stimulate creative thinking:
    advertising displays that turn on his Child;
    the product or a mockup of the product;
    competitive products or mockups that are especially novel;
    fun pictures or cartoons that caused him to chuckle;
    plants that helped him feel "up";
    brightly colored paper on the wall.
— Talk creatively to himself by putting up signs or posters with phrases
  like:
    Let your Child have fun!
    Hitchhike on ideas.
    Turn on your Little Professor.
    Relax and let loose!
    Turn the problem upside down.
— Invite others to brainstorm the advertising problem with him.

~ • ~ • ~ • ~ • ~ • ~ • ~ • ~ • ~ • ~ • ~ • ~ • ~ • ~ • ~ • ~

3 Describe two ways to change your outer world by dealing with triggers.

You can change your outer world by removing triggers for undesirable target behaviors and adding triggers for desirable target behaviors.

If you have not been arranging your environment to encourage desirable behavior, you may be missing out on a simple but effective self-management technique. (Notice that if we arrange our outer world to trigger negative behavior, we are choosing failure over success!)

Now, let's look at another example of how outer-world triggers can work.

Example

Debbie's goal was to increase her productivity. She wanted to be able to type at least twenty letters a day. A pile of about sixty letters (three days' work) was an unpleasant reminder for her to type. A coffee machine was located on a table nearby, where co-workers would frequently come to get coffee and stop to chat with her briefly—and sometimes not so briefly. Now and then she would engage in an "Ain't It Awful" session or a game of *Yes, But*. Debbie used some of the techniques we've been discussing to improve her productivity. She arranged to have the coffeepot moved, so that co-workers would not come by her desk so frequently. She got an extra "in" box, and put five letters in it. When she finished those five letters, she put five more in the "in" box. In this way she felt a sense of accomplishment as she finished each set of five letters. Before, with a pile of sixty letters on her desk, she hadn't felt she could make a dent in the seemingly overwhelming task of typing them. With her new system, she kept track of how much time it took her to type each batch of five letters. She even made a game of trying to beat her previous performance.

Debbie also put a chart on the bulletin board above her desk on which she recorded the number of letters she typed each hour. Whenever she looked up at the chart, it prompted her to concentrate on her work and try to beat her previous record.

APPLICATION

1 What was Debbie's target behavior?

2 Name a behavior that was just the opposite of her target behavior.

3 What was triggering the behavior that was incompatible with Debbie's positive target behavior?

4 What did Debbie do to get rid of that trigger?

5 What was triggering Debbie's positive behavior?

6 What did she do to make better use of that trigger?

7 What other triggers did she add to her environment?

~ • ~ • ~ • ~ • ~ • ~ • ~ • ~ • ~ • ~ • ~ • ~ • ~ • ~ • ~ • ~

1 Debbie's target behavior was to type at least twenty letters per day.
2 Engaging in pastimes and games with co-workers was incompatible with her target behavior.
3 The presence of the people near her desk was a signal to pastime and play games with them.
4 She removed the trigger by having the coffeepot moved.
5 The pile of letters on her desk served as a trigger for her to type.
6 She made better use of this trigger by putting groups of five letters in an "in" box.
7 The chart that she put on the bulletin board above her desk served as an additional trigger for her to be productive in her typing.

Now, let's analyze the outer-world triggers related to your personal goal.

APPLICATION

1 Name a target behavior that you'd like to increase the frequency of.

2 Now name a behavior that is incompatible with your target behavior. (For example, laughing is incompatible with crying; feeling happy is incompatible with feeling sad; and so on.)

3 Name a trigger that signals you to engage in that incompatible behavior. (For example, the messy desk to David and the TV remote control for Roger triggered a response that was contrary to their goals.)

4   What might you do to get rid of that trigger?

5   What seems to be your positive target behavior?

6   How can you make better use of the triggers for your positive target behavior?

7   What other triggers might you add to your environment that would cause you to do more of what you'd like to do?

FRANK AND ERNEST   **by Bob Thaves**

OPPORTUNITY KNOCKED BUT I DIDN'T HEAR IT -- I HAD THE TELEVISION ON.

THAVES 12-22

© 1976 by NEA Inc. TM Reg US Pat Off

Reprinted by permission of Newspaper Enterprise Association.

OUTER-WORLD ROADBLOCKS

Getting Rid of Roadblocks

An outer-world roadblock is simply some physical thing that gets in your way—something that makes it difficult for you to do what you'd like to do. It might also be the lack of something that you need to carry out a target behavior.

Example

XYZ Corporation was having a quality-control problem. Peggy, a performance analyst, was called in to find a solution. She discovered that a piece of the complex machinery that was essential to turning out the corporation's television tubes was frequently out of adjustment. She traced the problem to a particular adjustment screw on a master-control machine. Nathan, a normally competent technician, had been failing to make the adjustment regularly as he should have, according to the normal maintenance schedule. To assess the problem, Peggy asked Nathan to show her how to make the adjustment. She quickly learned why Nathan had not been performing as expected. To make the adjustment he had to turn himself into a human pancake and crawl into a tight, greasy area. Nathan had a "Be perfect" Parent tape. He was embarrassed to say he couldn't do it easily. Peggy was able to solve the quality-control problem by arranging a comfortable access route to the crucial adjustment screw.

APPLICATION ————————————————————————

What was the outer-world roadblock to Nathan's performance?

~ • ~ • ~ • ~ • ~ • ~ • ~ • ~ • ~ • ~ • ~ • ~ • ~ • ~ • ~ • ~ • ~

The uncomfortable work location.

In the preceding example the roadblock to Nathan's performance was clear. Most roadblocks *are* clear if we take the time to look for them with our Adults. But too often we don't take the time. As a result, we may not accomplish what we'd like to because of some seemingly small obstacle that we haven't noticed. Notice that in Nathan's case, an inner-world roadblock kept him from dealing with the outer-world roadblock. We can avoid this problem by first recognizing our inner-world roadblocks (Child feelings and Parent tapes) and then removing them with the techniques we've discussed in the previous chapter. Once the inner-world roadblocks are gone, we can begin to see our outer-world roadblocks and remove them, too.

Debbie (page 250) discovered some outer-world roadblocks that hindered her performance. She did a lot of technical typing for a variety of people. Sometimes she had to transcribe cassette tapes that came marked only with the name of the person who did the dictation. She did not always know when each tape was given to her or how much dictation it contained—one minute or as much as thirty. She also had no way of knowing what was on each tape (whether it was a letter or a memo) or whether the typing was to be final copy or rough draft. In addition, every so often she would need to check the spelling of a technical term. Frequently the word was not in her desk dictionary. A special dictionary of technical terms was available, but not nearby. She and her supervisor agreed that her productivity was less than it could be.

APPLICATION ————————————————————————

1 What roadblocks can you see in this example?

2 What might Debbie do to get rid of them?

254 The Self-Care Program

~·~·~·~·~·~·~·~·~·~·~·~·~·~·~·~·~·~

1 Debbie has these roadblocks:
   — The cassette tapes are difficult to deal with: date not indicated,
     no caption indicating the nature and length of the material on the
     tape.
   — Her dictionary is inadequate.
2 To get rid of these roadblocks, Debbie might do several things:
   — She might send a memo to each of the people giving her cassette
     tapes and ask them to list on each cassette:
       the date,
       the length of the tape,
       a caption indicating its content,
       the form desired—final or rough,
       a deadline for completion of the transcription.
   — She could ask for a special technical dictionary for her own use.

If you're in your work location right now, stop for a moment and first
do a grounding exercise to remove any inner roadblocks. (If you're some-
where else, imagine your work location.) Then look for physical things that
might be blocking a positive target behavior you'd like to make more frequently. Next, answer the following questions.

APPLICATION ────────────────────────────────

1 Name a target behavior that is being slowed down by a roadblock in your outer
   world.

2 What is the roadblock?

3 List some things you might do to get rid of that roadblock, or at least change it
   so it's not so much of a hindrance. (Make sure doing the things you list here
   won't create new blocks.)

In answering item 3 above, your first thought might have been, "There's
nothing I can do. I'm just stuck with this ugly situation." Although that's
possible, you might want to reconsider. Ask yourself again, "What can I do
to remove this roadblock without creating a new one?" While you think
about this, close your eyes and relax. If an answer doesn't come to your
mind right away, don't assume that it will *never* come. Remember, "What
your mind can believe, you can achieve."

Now look around your room again. As you focus on different objects, describe your reaction or opinion of each. Be aware of the intensity of your reactions and the amount of your energy that's invested in each item. Sometimes we've learned to react so intensely even to inanimate objects that we continually drain ourselves. If you discover that you do this, you might want to examine whether investing your energy this way is what you chose to do.

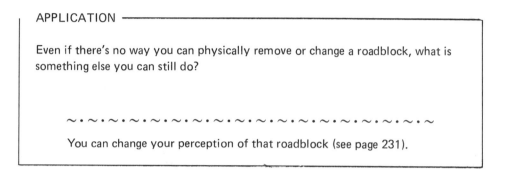

APPLICATION ————————————————————————

Even if there's no way you can physically remove or change a roadblock, what is something else you can still do?

~ • ~ • ~ • ~ • ~ • ~ • ~ • ~ • ~ • ~ • ~ • ~ • ~ • ~ • ~ • ~ • ~ • ~

You can change your perception of that roadblock (see page 231).

REARRANGING PAYOFFS

In Chapter 12 we discussed eliminating payoffs for negative behavior and substituting payoffs for desirable behavior. Let's look more closely at how these principles apply to our outer world. When we choose to change an undesirable behavior, an important step is to become aware of the payoff we get for that behavior.

Example

Carl had a problem with his Controlling Parent: he criticized every wrong move his subordinates made. Carl noticed that after he made a cutting critical remark, a heated argument usually developed, and since he was supervisor, he always had the last word. Carl's game (called *Uproar*) earned him isolation. As a consequence, he was lonely at work. He rarely got more than just a few ritual strokes. When his stroke bucket felt too empty, he provoked arguments. This way he was able to fill his stroke bucket with cold pricklies, if nothing else. After analyzing the situation, Carl realized that the arguments led to a payoff that eventually made him so uncomfortable that he repeated the cycle.

So Carl decided to change his outer world by refusing to collect that kind of payoff. Whenever he caught himself being overly critical of a subordinate and starting to argue, he checked his impulse and simply said, "Bill, let me give this some thought and get back to you on it." He then walked away, thus buying a little time to consider the actual problem with his Adult. This way he got rid of much of the payoff for being overly critical.

Just doing this wasn't enough, however. Carl was hungry for strokes. By merely cutting off his source of cold pricklies, he could have made matters worse. A person hungry for strokes may do all sorts of things to get them, especially if his usual source runs dry. Carl, however, avoided this problem. By using his Adult, he figured out a way to get *positive* strokes. First, he made a special effort to find something good to say to at least one subordinate each day about his or her performance. As he gave more and more warm fuzzies, he started to get a few back. While he felt awkward at first, he was determined to continue, so he wrote out this contract with himself: "When I give at least four good strokes during the day, I'll allow myself to take a stroll in the park after work." (He loved to stroll in the park.) In this way Carl arranged for a positive payoff for a positive behavior.

Notice these key elements of Carl's *first* contract:

— He was easy on himself. (He asked himself for an approximation.)
— The terms of the contract were clear. (Carl specified what he expected of himself and what his payoff would be in clear language.)
— The contract was positive.
— The payoff was available to him relatively soon (the same day).
— The contract was written down. Doing this helps to ensure that it won't end up in never-never land.

Here's a graph showing how Carl's contract worked. It shows how many strokes Carl gave each day.

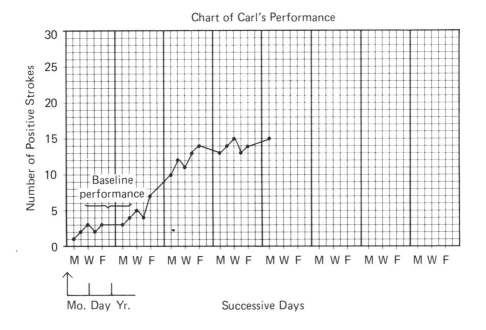

Chart of Carl's Performance

A good way to reward yourself for an approximation is to first find your baseline performance and then make a contract to do slightly better than that. Be sure that your contract is clear, complete, positive, possible, pays off in gold stamps, and is written down. (See page 212 to review "baseline performance"; to review "approximation," see page 198.)

APPLICATION ────────────────────────────────

According to the preceding chart, what was Carl's baseline performance in giving positive strokes?

~ • ~ • ~ • ~ • ~ • ~ • ~ • ~ • ~ • ~ • ~ • ~ • ~ • ~ • ~ • ~ • ~

Carl's baseline performance was about two or three positive strokes per day.

In view of his baseline performance, Carl required himself to give only four positive strokes in his first contract. Making an approximation like this in your first contract is vital to success.

Returning to our earlier example, Debbie might benefit from analyzing the payoffs associated with her work. Typically, it did not seem to matter to anyone how many letters she typed, unless her productivity dipped significantly. When she didn't get an important letter typed, her supervisor would call her into her office and talk to her for fifteen minutes about why she needed to be more productive. When Debbie did increase her productivity slightly, her supervisor said nothing about it.

APPLICATION ────────────────────────────────

Write a positive-payoff contract that Debbie might make with herself. Be sure to design the contract so:

— Debbie is easy on herself at first.
— The terms of the contract are clear. (Specify what Debbie needs to do and what her payoff might be.)
— Make the contract positive.
— Select a payoff that Debbie can deliver to herself within a reasonably short time.

~ • ~ • ~ • ~ • ~ • ~ • ~ • ~ • ~ • ~ • ~ • ~ • ~ • ~ • ~ • ~

Answers will vary. Here is a possible contract:

I will type the equivalent of ten 250-word letters in one day for the next three weeks. Each time I accomplish this, I will allow myself to buy one of my favorite magazines (costing under $2).

Check your answer against these guidelines:

— Will it be relatively easy for Debbie to meet her contract?
— If you specified in the contract that Debbie needs to type twenty letters before she can get a payoff, you need to reconsider your answer. We don't know her baseline performance, but since twenty is her goal, a contract to type nine or ten letters might be more appropriate. As a rule of thumb, set your performance requirement just slightly above what you typically do.
— Did you write a contract in which Debbie is rewarded?
— Is the payoff that you specified one that Debbie can have soon after she performs the required behavior? (If she has to wait more than a day or two, the reward will probably be less effective.)
— Are the terms of your contract clear? Notice that our contract included the number and length of the letters, as well as the range of cost of the magazine. Sometimes a contract breaks down simply because it isn't clear. For example, if Debbie did not specify the length of the letters, she might be confused if she suddenly finds herself with a number of short letters. Similarly, if she earns a reward and finds a magazine costing, say, $1.50, she might feel guilty buying that as a payoff unless she's specified ahead of time whether she can afford such a payoff.

Sometimes we don't give ourselves positive payoffs because we can't think of appropriate ones at the moment. Lloyd Homme[1] suggests one solution to this problem: develop a positive-payoff menu. In developing this menu, you simply list several payoffs you could use to boost your motivation. Using this technique, make your list before you need to boost any particular target behavior. Then when the need arises, you can pick an appropriate payoff.

The good feelings that come with positive payoffs increase our gold-stamp supply. Remember, more gold stamps usually mean fewer gray stamps.

APPLICATION ──────────────────────────────

Here is a list of payoffs that may give you some ideas. (Your own menu should list payoffs that work for *you* so don't rely on this list — use it only as a guide.) Check each item that appeals to you:

___ Reading a favorite book, newspaper, or magazine.

_____ Listening to a favorite record or cassette tape.

_____ Soaking in a hot tub.

_____ Daydreaming for a specified time.

_____ Going for a walk.

_____ Sitting in a garden.

_____ Going shopping.

_____ Riding horseback.

_____ Enjoying a favorite beverage.

_____ Writing a poem.

_____ Eating lunch out.

_____ Doing part of your job you really enjoy.

_____ Meditating.

_____ Doing a yoga exercise or other relaxation activity.

_____ Going to a friend's office to chat.

_____ Calling a friend on the phone.

_____ Buying some new clothes.

_____ Playing bridge at lunch.

_____ Taking a long break without guilt.

_____ Going to a favorite place.

Perhaps you got some ideas for your own positive-payoff menu by reading over our list of suggested items. Another way to develop your positive-payoff menu is to interview yourself. Ask yourself: "What sort of things would I like to do? Like to have?" The following questions have been designed to help you develop your personal positive-payoff menu. Take a few moments now and answer each question.

1 List some things that you enjoy doing that won't take longer than about five minutes.

2 What do you like to do that typically takes about thirty minutes?

   An hour?

   Several hours?

3 List the names of people you enjoy being with.

4 What do you like to do with these people?

5 If you had an extra dollar in your hand right now and felt like spending it, what might you buy?

An extra $5?

An extra $10?

An extra $50?

6 If you could have anything you wanted for your birthday, what would it be?

7 Pause for a moment and get in touch with your Natural Child. What would make this part of you happy?

8 Close your eyes and imagine a parent figure. What kinds of things would this parent figure want you to have? (In other words, what would satisfy your Parent ego state?)

9 Get into your Adult ego state and write down the wants of your Parent and Child.

Collect any other facts you need to help you make a decision about what *you* would like to have as a positive payoff.

If you want to satisfy a particular aspect of your Parent or Child, and your Adult decides it's OK, go ahead and do it. The important thing is to make an objective decision from your Adult ego state. For instance, if you reject a Parent behavior because you still feel resentful toward a parent figure, your Child may be rebelling against your Parent and interfering with your Adult's ability to think clearly. For example, one woman enjoyed doing volunteer work in a hospital but wouldn't let herself do so because she held so much resentment against her mother who had spent many years helping out in a local hospital.

Also, when you pick a Child-pleasing payoff, make sure that the payoff is OK—protect your inner Child just as a good parent would.

Based on the information you've gathered on the last few pages, make yourself a payoff menu. Put it up where you'll be sure to see it. Make a new payoff menu from time to time, say, once a month. Refer to your payoff menu whenever you want to make a contract with yourself.[2]

A payoff menu can also give us some ideas when we just want to have some fun and don't know what to do. We all need to do something good for our Inner Child—at least once a day—to stroke it for being.

APPLICATION

Getting Rid of Undesirable Target Behaviors

So far we've discussed mainly projects in which you do *more* of what you want to do. Now here's an exercise for helping you get rid of undesirable target behaviors.

1   Name a negative target behavior that you'd like to *weaken* or *get rid of.*

2 Name an external event that seems to be triggering this target behavior.

3 What might you do to remove this trigger?

4 What would be a good roadblock for the undesirable target behavior?

5 How could you arrange for this roadblock to be present at an appropriate time?

6 What external events seem to be acting as payoffs after this undesirable target behavior occurs?

7 What might you do to get rid of this payoff?

8 Name a positive behavior that is incompatible with the undesirable target behavior you'd like to get rid of.

9 What would be a good trigger for this positive behavior?

10 How could you arrange for this trigger to be present at an appropriate time?

Strengthening Desirable Target Behaviors

1 Name a target behavior you'd like to strengthen. (It may be one you've listed before.)

2 Now, describe a behavior that would be an approximation of your target behavior.

3 Go one step further and describe an approximation of your answer to question 2. (You'll be identifying an approximation of an approximation!)

4 What would be a good reward for each approximation? (The size of a reward should suit the size of a response.) Refer to your positive-payoff menu.

5 Write a contract involving one (or both) of the approximations and the payoff you've listed. Be sure your contract has the key features we discussed earlier (see page 256).

SUMMARY

In this chapter you've learned some useful techniques for rearranging your outer world. You've learned how to make changes in outer-world events that trigger, block, or strengthen target behavior, especially by making contracts to rearrange payoffs.

Sometimes you're highly successful the first time you make an effort to rearrange your world: all of a sudden your problem seems to vanish. Other times, however, it isn't that simple. When your target behavior continues to be a problem, you need to *evaluate* your techniques and change them where necessary. In the next chapter you'll learn a systematic approach for evaluating your techniques and revising them (when necessary) to increase even more your chances of success.

SOURCE NOTES

[1] Lloyd Homme, *How to Use Contingency Contracting in the Classroom* (Champaign, Ill.: Research Press, 1970); and Roger Addison and Lloyd Homme, "The Reinforcing Event (RE) Menu," *NSPI Journal,* January 1966.

[2] For more ideas on payoffs, you may wish to read Julius Fast, *The Pleasure Book* (New York: Stein and Day, 1975).

14

Evaluating Your Progress

So far you've identified a hazy goal that you'd like to achieve. You've turned that hazy into a series of specific, measurable outcomes that, if all accomplished, would result in what you have determined will bring you more success. You've learned to increase your *awareness* of your inner and outer worlds as a first step toward choosing success more often. And you've learned some ways to *rearrange* your inner and outer worlds as you choose. The last step of the self-CARE program is *evaluation*.

OBJECTIVES

When you finish this chapter, you'll be able to:

- evaluate the progress you're making toward your goal;
- revise your self-management strategies if they aren't working;
- savor your successes and then move on to even greater heights if you choose.

On some pages in this chapter you may be asked to carry out certain projects and then return to those pages to continue reading. We suggest you use a bookmark to keep your place. Ready?

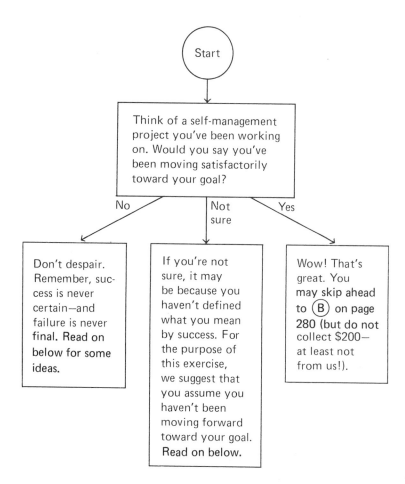

Start

Think of a self-management project you've been working on. Would you say you've been moving satisfactorily toward your goal?

No — Not sure — Yes

Don't despair. Remember, success is never certain—and failure is never final. **Read on below for some ideas.**

If you're not sure, it may be because you haven't defined what you mean by success. For the purpose of this exercise, we suggest that you assume you haven't been moving forward toward your goal. **Read on below.**

Wow! That's great. You **may skip ahead to (B) on page 280 (but do not collect $200—** at least not from us!).

WHEN YOU AREN'T MOVING FORWARD . . .

If you're not improving, perhaps you're failing to carry out one of the key steps in the self-management process. Let's review these steps.

Have You Written Down Your Goal?

Many of us carry hazy goals in our heads. When we have hazy goals, we're often unsure how to achieve those goals. Also, if we don't write them down, we're likely to push them to the back of our minds. When that happens, the chance that we'll do anything to achieve them is slim, indeed. So if you're having trouble reaching a goal, stop and ask yourself whether you've written it down.

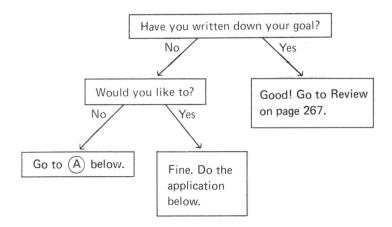

APPLICATION

1 My goal is to:

2 Now make it measurable. If you reach your goal, how will you and others be able to tell?

3 What will you be doing differently? How will you feel? What will have happened?

After you've finished writing down your goal and pinpointing your objective, turn to the Review of Your Evaluation on page 267.

So You Haven't Written Down Your Goal

Ⓐ You might consider asking yourself why you haven't taken this important step. We would guess it's because part of you wants to work toward your goal and part of you doesn't. In other words, your Parent and Child are probably in conflict. We suggest that you review pages 196–197 and also page 223. Use a bookmark so that you can return to the box on this page *after* you've done that.

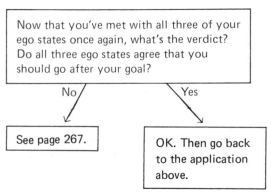

So Your Ego States Are Not in Agreement

When this happens, it's time to reevaluate your goal.

```
                  ┌─────────────────────────────────┐
                  │ Is your goal something you      │
                  │ really want?                    │
                  └─────────────────────────────────┘
                   No                          Yes
```

If your goal is really *not* for you (at least not at this time), you may wish to revise it or give it up and pick a new goal that is meaningful to you right now. This finishes your evaluation. When you're ready to evaluate your progress toward a new goal, turn again to **page 265.**	You've decided to pursue a goal that conflicts with either your Parent tapes or Child feelings. Two approaches are possible: 1. You can continue to go after your goal, using the various strategies we've discussed previously to overcome your stubborn Parent tapes or Child feelings: — countering (see page 219 — internal screaming (see page 221) — frequency modification (see page 229) — positive payoffs (see pages 243 and 255) 2. If your Child is the culprit, try to convince your Child to support your goal. Use role-playing and developing a conversation between your Adult and your Child; you may just discover some new answers to old problems. (See Adult Intervention, **page 223.**) If your Child ego state comes to agree with your new goal, you'll be well on your way to achieving it.

When you're ready to write down your goal, go to page **266 and do it!**

We suggest that you combine both approaches. Listen to your Child and your Parent. Consider making a decision from your Child or Parent to embrace your goal. Meanwhile, use the self-management strategies we've described to keep your Child or Parent from sabotaging your efforts.

Review of Your Evaluation

Where you are:

- You're not satisfied with your progress.
- You've written down your goal.

If that's not the case, please return to page 265 and start your evaluation again.

If you've written down your goal, but you're not moving forward toward it, the next question is:

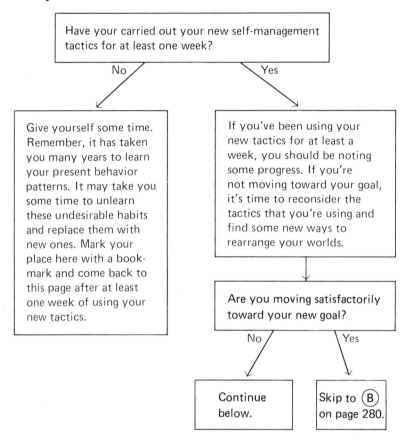

Have your carried out your new self-management tactics for at least one week?

No — Give yourself some time. Remember, it has taken you many years to learn your present behavior patterns. It may take you some time to unlearn these undesirable habits and replace them with new ones. Mark your place here with a bookmark and come back to this page after at least one week of using your new tactics.

Yes — If you've been using your new tactics for at least a week, you should be noting some progress. If you're not moving toward your goal, it's time to reconsider the tactics that you're using and find some new ways to rearrange your worlds.

Are you moving satisfactorily toward your new goal?

No — Continue below.

Yes — Skip to (B) on page 280.

Have You Made Molehills of Your Mountains?
Have You Made Them Measurable?

Often we choose goals that seem overwhelming, like a huge mountain that seems impossible to climb. If you're faced with a mountain, turn it into molehills: break the overwhelming goal into a number of small, easily achievable outcomes. And be sure to describe your objectives so that they can be measured; only then will you be able to tell when you've reached your goal. Remember, you can't measure progress toward goals such as: "I will improve my human relations skills," but you can count such things as the number of strokes you give per day. To review this idea, see pages 188–194.

Are You Recording Your Target Behavior?

If not, we urge you to do so. Just keeping a daily record can result in a dramatic change in your performance. It can raise your consciousness to new heights. However, if you continue to neglect this important step in self-management, perhaps your Parent and Child are in conflict. If you suspect that's the case, put a bookmark here, read page 267, and then continue reading below.

Are You Charting Your Performance on a Graph?

Just recording your performance each day in a notebook may not accomplish what you want unless you examine the data and note your progress. If you plot your data on a graph, you automatically get a picture of your present and past performance, so you can see how you're doing. If you haven't yet tried graphing specific response data, give it a try. It could be the one thing you need to do to be more successful!

Now how do you feel about making a daily record of your performance and plotting it on a graph? Choose the answer that best expresses your feeling.

____ (a) I'm doing that now, but I'm still not making progress. (See Ⓐ on page 271.)

____ (b) I think that would be good for me to do, but I just can't seem to get myself to do it. (See Ⓒ on page 270.)

____ (c) I don't like the idea of doing that. (See Ⓐ below.)

____ (d) I think it's a great idea, I'm going to try it. (See Ⓐ on page 271.)

Ⓐ Your response: You don't like the idea of keeping track of your performance and plotting it on a daily graph. If you feel this way, it could be because you're not yet really committed to your goal. If you suspect this is the case, we suggest you reread Chapter 10.

If you feel that you are committed but that it's not worth the time and effort to keep such careful records, remember that by doing it you're giving yourself *feedback.* Feedback is a powerful tool. With it you can learn to control your brain waves, muscle tension, headaches, feelings, and actions. With it you can move psychic and physical energy from your Blind Self to your Open Self. It *can* make a difference: the difference between success and failure! In fact, only feedback can help you *recognize* success.

Now how do you feel?

____ (a) I'm willing to give it a try, but I think it will be difficult for me. (See Ⓒ on page 270.)

____ (b) You've convinced me. Show me a graph. (See page 216. Then go on to Ⓐ on page 271.)

____ (c) Why bother to go to all the trouble of counting and graphing? It's easier for me just to *do* what I want to do rather than fool around making graphs. (Continue with Ⓑ below.)

Ⓑ Your response: It's easier for me just to do what I want to do rather than fool around making graphs.

Well, perhaps graphs just aren't your style. That's OK. But before you reject this idea entirely, why not give it a try? After all, you have defined something you want to do either more frequently or less often. And you know better than anyone else what you need to do to be more successful.

On the other hand, if it's easy for you to simply do what you want to do, then you don't *need* special self-management tools like counting and graphing.

Now, what's your response?

___ (a) I'm willing to give it a try, but I think it would be difficult for me. (See Ⓒ on this page.)

___ (b) You've convinced me. Show me a graph. (See page 216. Then continue with Ⓐ on page 271.)

___ (c) I'm getting upset. I feel kind of put down by what you've been saying to me. See Ⓐ on this page.

___ (d) I'm tired of this discussion. Let's get on with something else. See Ⓑ on this page.

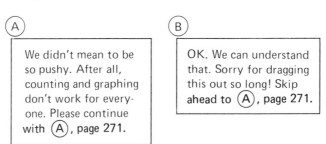

Ⓐ
We didn't mean to be so pushy. After all, counting and graphing don't work for every-one. Please continue with Ⓐ, page 271.

Ⓑ
OK. We can understand that. Sorry for dragging this out so long! Skip ahead to Ⓐ, page 271.

Ⓒ Your response:

— From page 269: "I think that would be good for me to do, but I just can't seem to get myself to do it."
— From pages 269 and 270: "I'm willing to give it a try, but I think it will be difficult for me."

If this is your problem, we suggest that you treat counting and graphing your performance as a separate goal. That is, use a four-phase approach to the problem (self-CARE):

C — Develop a *commitment* toward counting and graphing. Review Chapter 10 with that in mind.
A — Increase your *awareness* of how frequently you *are* counting and graphing. Become aware of what happens inside and outside you before and after you graph your data or fail to graph your data. You just could be in the business of collecting bad feelings about yourself. See Chapter 11.
R — *Rearrange* your worlds so it's easier for you to count and graph infor-mation. Do such things as these:
    Reward yourself for graphing data or ask a friend to reward you.

Surround yourself with triggers that will remind you to count and graph. Make it fun. Use color, coins, marbles, tally sheets, wall charts, whatever helps you stir your energy.

Remove roadblocks that may be making it difficult for you to count and graph your performance.

E — *Evaluate.* Decide whether you're making progress in your efforts to keep track of and graph your performance. If you're not, keep trying different strategies until one works for you.

Are You Keeping a Journal?

(A) As noted on page 214, it's also helpful to keep a journal in which you record your thoughts, feelings, impressions, and other observations about your activities and your worlds. If you're still not moving forward toward your goals and you haven't tried keeping a journal, we urge you to do so, especially if you have not been able to pinpoint, count, and graph your performance data. By keeping a journal, you can refine your thinking about your goal to the point where you will be able to count and record your progress toward it.

Keeping a journal can be a lot of fun. It's fun to write down your thoughts and it can be even more fun to read them later. Doing this also helps you to keep track of decisions you've made. Many famous people who have made significant contributions to society kept journals. Leonardo da Vinci, Thomas Edison, and Albert Einstein are three you'll recognize. So if you decide to keep a journal, you'll be in good company!

— Try keeping a journal. Then, if you're still not improving, continue reading below.

— If you find you are improving, turn to (B) on page 280.

Have You Tried Giving Yourself a Payoff for Desirable Performance?

___ (a) No, but I'd like to. (Review pages 243 and 255. Then, if you find that you are improving satisfactorily, go on to (B) on page 280. If you try it and you don't improve, then come back to (B) on this page.

___ (b) No, I don't like the whole idea of motivating myself with payoffs. (See page 273.)

___ (c) I've tried this, but it hasn't worked so well. (Go to (B) below.)

(B) So you've tried payoffs and they haven't worked. Let us ask you this. Are you having a hard time withholding the payoff from yourself until after you've performed?

___ Yes. (Go to page 272.)

___ No. (Go to (A) on page 275.)

Hmmmm! So you're cheating, eh? Letting yourself take an unearned payoff? Breaking your contracts? Well, don't feel bad, you're not alone. But you do need to understand what's happening. Perhaps your Child ego state wants the payoff so badly that you're letting your Child overpower your Adult. Repeating old behaviors often seems easier and safer than taking a step toward change. One way to solve this problem is to break your target behavior down into even smaller *approximations.* To review the idea of approximations, see pages 191 and 198. Then continue reading at Ⓒ on page 274.

Your response: "I don't like the whole idea of motivating myself with payoffs."

If you feel that way, perhaps this particular self-management strategy won't work for you. Different things work for different people. But before you give up on this idea entirely, let's ask you a few questions.

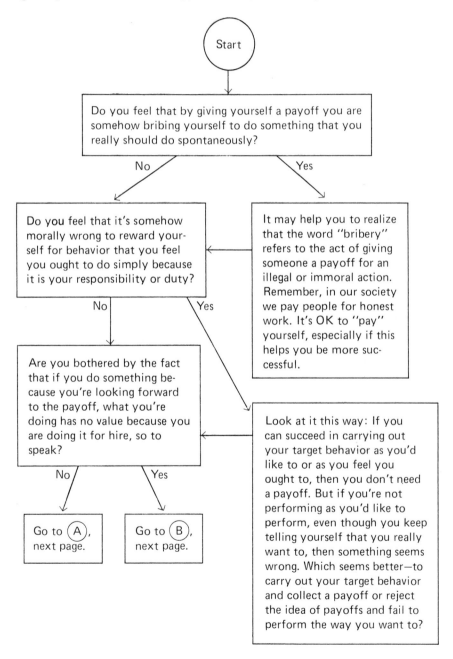

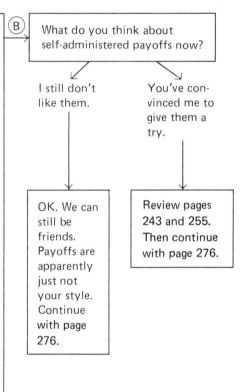

(A)

Yes, it would be nice if you could spontaneously do more of what you'd like to do without having to resort to payoffs. Unfortunately, there are many things that are good for us that we find hard to do. In such cases, we believe there's nothing wrong with offering ourselves a payoff. What we're doing is setting up a positive reward system that can take the place of the undesirable reward system that we're already using.

As for the idea that all behaviors, thoughts, and feelings must be spontaneous before they're worth anything—well, that's simply not true. Few people have learned to type or to play the piano that way. The groundwork of practice can offer the freedom to "do our own thing." We're sure you can think of many situations in which a well-rehearsed behavior, thought, or feeling is highly useful.

(B) What do you think about self-administered payoffs now?

I still don't like them.

You've convinced me to give them a try.

OK. We can still be friends. Payoffs are apparently just not your style. Continue with page 276.

Review pages 243 and 255. Then continue with page 276.

(C) Another way to keep your contracts better is to ask a friend to be a contract checker for you. If you decide to do this, a good approach is to make a written contract in which you spell out exactly what you must do to earn your payoff. Then ask your friend to check up on you so that you don't take the payoff without actually having earned it. Just knowing that another person is aware of your contract may help you to stick to it.

Another approach is to ask a friend to be the trustee for the payoff. For example, suppose the payoff is a new suit. You might purchase the suit and then ask your friend to keep it for you and not let you have it until after you have reached your goal.

Sometimes a buddy contracting system works. Using this method you act as a contract checker for your friend's self-management project and he or she does the same for you. In choosing a contract checker, look for someone who will be able to deal with you with Adult objectivity and straightforwardness as well as Parent caring. If you decide to work out an arrangement like this, be sure that when you are a contract checker, you avoid using the negative part of your Controlling Parent. Otherwise, you may energize your friend's not-OK Child.

If your partner experiences a setback, don't emphasize the failure but simply ask questions like, "Do you still want to fulfill your commitment?" If the answer is "yes," help your partner draw up a new contract.

Another important point: excuses are taboo, for you *or* your partner. If your partner starts to make them, simply say, "You don't have to make excuses." Similarly, if your partner indulges in verbal self-abuse, say gently, maybe from your Nurturing Parent, "You don't have to call yourself 'stupid' or put yourself down." It is not helpful to encourage the collection of bad feelings.

After trying out these ideas:

— if you're improving, go to (B) on page 280.
— if you're not improving, go to (A) below.

(A) If you've been arranging for a payoff to occur after a desirable performance and you've been faithfully maintaining your contract, but you're still not moving ahead, then the payoff is apparently not powerful enough. Pick a payoff that is more attractive to you. If you don't already have a positive payoff menu, have a solo brainstorming session. That is, sit down and try to think of things you'd like to do or have. Write down whatever comes to your mind, no matter how silly or ridiculous it sounds. You may also add your answers to the checklist of questions on page 259. After you've done this, go back and pick out the best payoffs. Make a menu and keep it handy. Don't fall into the trap of thinking that just because you've tried paying yourself and it hasn't worked, that it *can't* work. It could be that you simply haven't found the right payoff yet.

You might also consider arranging for a joint payoff, something that both you and a friend or spouse would enjoy. A joint payoff is different from a buddy contracting system in that each buddy usually has his or her own payoff. A joint payoff is one shared by one or more people. If you decide to use it, write out a new contract, including your new payoff arrangements. Try it out.

— If you've started to improve satisfactorily, turn to (B) on page 280.
— If you're still not satisfied with your improvement, turn to page 276.

Are Roadblocks Making It Difficult for You to Perform as You'd Like To?

____ Yes. (Go to (A) below.)

____ No. (Go to page 277.)

(A)

Take a fresh look at yourself. Is it possible that you are somehow unconsciously arranging roadblocks to be present?

— Hmmmm, now that you mention it, perhaps that's so. Go to (B) below.

— No. Go to (C) below.

(B)

How do you feel when you're confronted with these roadblocks?

Is this a feeling that you frequently have? ___ Yes ___ No

Can you remember having this feeling as a child? ___ Yes ___ No

If you're compulsively bringing on these roadblocks, it could very well be that you're into a racket feeling. If this seems to be the case, review pages 135–158 and 219–228 to see how you might solve this problem. Then if you start to improve satisfactorily, go to (B) on page 280. If you still aren't improving satisfactorily, go to page 277.

(C)

Consider once again what you might do to remove these roadblocks. If you can't remove them physically, consider fantasizing that the roadblocks have been removed. Recall that often our problem is *not* an actual physical situation but our interpretation of that situation.

     If after trying this, you start to improve satisfactorily, go to (B) on page 280. If you're still stuck, go to page 277.

Have you tried frequency modification?

No / Yes

No branch:

If you haven't yet tried frequency modification and you're not making progress toward your goal, we urge you to try it. Perhaps you have resisted trying this technique because it seems rather strange and unusual to you. Or perhaps you just don't think it will work. The best way to find out is to try it. One response that most of us could benefit from making more often is a relaxation response. So we suggest you set up a project to increase the frequency with which you stretch or tighten your muscles and then relax them. Imagine how good you will feel when you train yourself to do it 20 times a day. (No, you won't fall asleep. You'll just be more relaxed, more confident, more able to carry out your work energetically!)

Yes branch:

Have you reached a frequency of at least 15 per day?

No / Yes

No:

Try this: Identify several unique stimulus situations (triggers). Use each one to trigger your positive behavior. Example: If you're using the dial tone as a trigger to relax, use something else as a trigger too—like washing your hands.

Yes:

With this high frequency rate, you should be experiencing success in your self-management project. If you're not progressing toward your goal, perhaps you are repeating the responses automatically without being aware of what you're doing. To avoid this problem, have five different responses and alternate them throughout the day. For example, if you want to increase your self-esteem, write down five positive self-statements and memorize them. Then, as you engage in your high-probability behavior, think one of the positive thoughts.

If you're already making 15 varied responses, and you're still not moving ahead, take another look at the responses that you're using. Are these responses really helping you or would others be more appropriate?

(Continue with page 278.)

Have you tried vividly visualizing your goal daily?

No / Yes

If you haven't yet tried vivid visualization, you're missing something. It's easy to do and can be quite effective in helping you be more success-ful. Note: If you'd like to make more use of visualization, but simply don't remember to do it, consider making a contract to do visualization on a regular basis. Then use all of the various self-CARE techniques you've learned so far—Commit-ment, Awareness, Rearranging your worlds, and Evaluation.

If you're visualizing your goal daily and still show no improve-ment, consider these points:

1. You may need to increase the vividness and intensity of your visualizing. With this in mind, reread page 238.
2. You may also benefit from increasing the frequency of your visualizing. Try doing it once upon rising and once before going to bed.
3. You may need to increase the time you spend visualizing at each session. We suggest five to ten minutes.
4. Don't forget to end each visualization session by saying some positive self-statements aloud.
5. Then again you may be trying too hard. Visualize for ten minutes three times a day, then relax. Do this for at least three weeks.

(Continue with page 279.)

Do you feel that others are punishing you for doing what you'd like to do?

No / Yes

Go to (A), page 280.

As strange as it may seem, sometimes a situation develops in which an employee *is* punished for doing exactly what she or he should be doing. Often a supervisor or employer does this unwittingly, not realizing the game that is being played. If this is happening to you, realize that you *do* have control of your world and that you can do something to change this situation. What can you do?

Well, one simple thing you can do is to explain to the people who seem to be punishing you how you feel. For example, suppose that every time you suggest an idea in a meeting several people criticize it. You might solve this problem by arranging to have a brainstorming meeting in which all criticism is ruled out. Or you might meet with individuals who are criticizing your ideas and explain that it is difficult for you to speak up at the meetings if you are criticized frequently. Criticism seems to affect you by causing you to hold back. Before you do this we suggest you read Chapters 7, 15, and 17 for some tips on how to deal with your feelings and level with your co-workers.

Still another approach is to make a contract with yourself not to respond emotionally to the criticism. It is *not* their criticism that is making you feel uncomfortable but rather what you are saying to yourself in response to what they say. You are in charge of how you choose to feel.

Continue with (A), page 280.

A Give yourself some time (say another week), then ask yourself:
Are you showing improvement now?

No / Yes

If after trying all the techniques we've described, you're still not moving ahead toward your goal, you may wish to consider getting help from a counselor. In looking for such a counselor, you might find it helpful to seek out someone who uses the self-management techniques described here.

You may wish to write to the address below for a list of trained TA therapists:

International Transactional
  Analysis Association
1772 Vallejo Street
San Francisco, CA 94123

Great! Go to **B** below.

B So, you're moving toward your goal! Congratulations. Have you reached the main goal that you were working toward with your self-management program?

No / Yes

Keep on truckin'. As long as you're moving ahead, you're on the right track (or should we say road?) When you have reached your goal, follow the "yes" arrow on the right.

Great! Make a note of your success. Set aside an hour or so and write down some of the things that enabled you to be successful. What worked for you? Describe any special skills or techniques that you used to reach your goal. List any factors that you think contributed to your success. Add these to your gold-stamp collection.

Then, someday when you're feeling a bit down, you can pull out your gold-stamp collection and review your accomplishments. This will lift your spirits and perhaps give you some ideas for attacking the new problem that you are facing.

(Continue with page 281.)

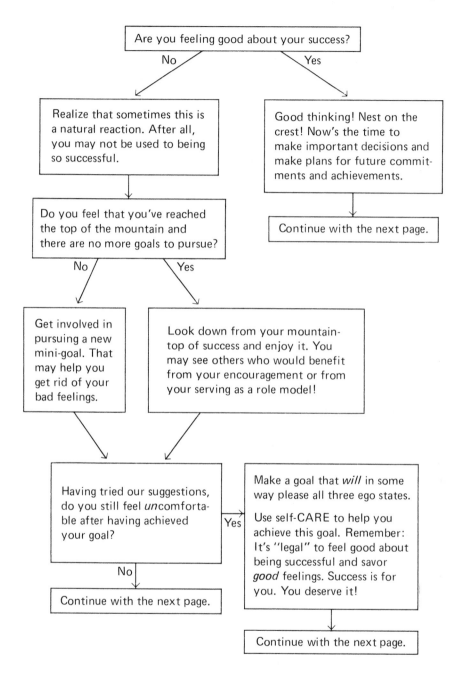

```
┌─────────────────────────────────────────────────────────────┐
│  Have you consciously stopped using the special self-management│
│  techniques that have helped you achieve success?             │
└─────────────────────────────────────────────────────────────┘
          No  ╱                              ╲  Yes
```

Consider tapering off, rather than stopping. That is, gradually phase out some of the special techniques that you've been using, such as payoffs, countering, and internal screaming. For example, if you've been paying yourself off daily, you might decrease that to every other day, then every third day, then once a week, and so on.

About once a month, do a follow-up study. That is, count the frequency of your target response for a short time to see if you are still performing as desired. If you're starting to backslide, you may wish to reinstate your self-management techniques.

SUMMARY

In this chapter we've presented a troubleshooting guide you can use to evaluate your self-management projects. Any time you run into a snag in a self-management project, we suggest that you work through this chapter again. Also use it whenever you reach a goal, to help guard against the possibility of a setback.

In these chapters you've focused on yourself and managing your own worlds. In Part III you'll be focusing on ways of interacting with others. These will include:

— tips on transacting with individuals;
— promoting autonomy;
— transacting authentically.

The more confident you are and the more you appreciate yourself, the more open you will be to appreciating and encouraging autonomy in others.

Part **III**

PUTTING IT ALL
TOGETHER

15

Tips on Transactions

You'll find many of the tips in this chapter useful in your successful dealings with other people.

OBJECTIVES

When you finish this chapter, you'll be able to:

- move from your Adapted Child into your Little Professor, Natural Child, or Adult when you are afraid to start a transaction;
- avoid transacting under undesirable conditions;
- keep transactions open more often by:
  - stroking the activated ego state in the other person;
  - using active listening and fogging for stroking an activated ego state;
  - activating another person's Adult by asking Adult questions;
  - criticizing others constructively so that you elicit Adult responses more frequently;
  - disagreeing assertively and arguing nonproductively less often;
- end transactions courteously without drawing them out unnecessarily;
- consider ego states in written transactions.

These skills are extremely useful for breaking up games and stopping rackets. Our discussion focuses on three topics:

- starting transactions,
- keeping transactions open, and
- ending transactions.

STARTING TRANSACTIONS

Preliminary Nonverbal Messages

Our body language often sets the mood of the transaction and is a preliminary ego-state contact. We tend to pick up one another's "vibes" in these moments. Before speaking to a person, it's helpful to give a few body-language strokes. For example, you might establish relaxed eye contact, smile, move closer, and so on. This step is especially important if you are beginning a transaction with someone you haven't met before. Without positive preliminary nonverbal messages, a person may be reluctant to transact with you.

Sometimes, however, the messages we send don't suit the situation. For example, with the aid of our Adapted Child and Little Professor we may send negative nonverbal messages to engage others in rackets, games, and stamp collecting. We call these messages *sweatshirt messages* because they are as clear as if we were wearing a message imprinted on a sweatshirt.

APPLICATION

1 The people illustrated here are each sending a definite sweatshirt message. Match each person with the message being sent.

 (a)

Sweatshirt Messages

(i) "I'm not going to tell you anything."

(ii) "I'm a better man than you are."

(iii) "You'd better do what I say or else."

 (b)

___ (c)

2 Now try matching these people with their sweatshirt messages.

___ (a)

Sweatshirt Messages

(i) "You can tell me all your troubles."

(ii) "You'd better listen to me. I have something important to say."

(iii) "Please don't kick me. I'm a victim."

_____(b)

_____(c)

~ . ~ . ~ . ~ . ~ . ~ . ~ . ~ . ~ . ~ . ~ . ~ . ~ . ~ . ~ . ~

1 (a) iii, (b) i; (c) ii.
2 (a) ii; (b) iii; (c) i.

Practice identifying sweatshirt messages so that you will:

— be more aware of your body language when you are approaching
  another person to begin a transaction;
— make sure that any nonverbal messages you're sending are appropriate
  for the situation.

Fear of Beginning a Transaction

Sometimes we want to transact with a person and the situation seems right, but we can't bring ourselves to start. We feel uneasy or fearful. If this happens to you, you might try tracking your feelings. Perhaps your feelings of fear or uneasiness are racket feelings. The situation may arouse old experiences or the person may remind you of something in your past.

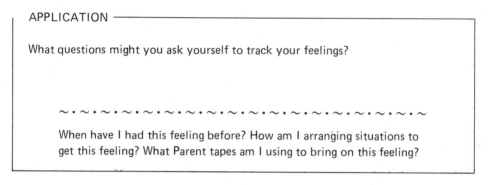

APPLICATION

What questions might you ask yourself to track your feelings?

~ . ~ . ~ . ~ . ~ . ~ . ~ . ~ . ~ . ~ . ~ . ~ . ~ . ~ . ~ . ~ . ~ . ~

When have I had this feeling before? How am I arranging situations to get this feeling? What Parent tapes am I using to bring on this feeling?

When you're fearful of starting a transaction, you can also ask yourself, "What's the worst possible thing that could happen?" In answering this question, you're likely to activate your Adult ego state and turn off the not-OK part of your Adapted Child. Remember, the Adapted Child ego state is at work when you are *unreasonably* fearful. The trick, then, is to move energy away from the not-OK part of your Adapted Child and into a more productive ego state such as your Adult, Little Professor, or Natural Child.

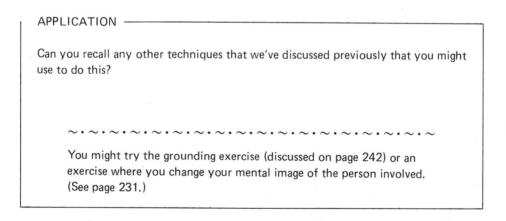

APPLICATION

Can you recall any other techniques that we've discussed previously that you might use to do this?

~ . ~ . ~ . ~ . ~ . ~ . ~ . ~ . ~ . ~ . ~ . ~ . ~ . ~ . ~ . ~ . ~ . ~

You might try the grounding exercise (discussed on page 242) or an exercise where you change your mental image of the person involved. (See page 231.)

The Right Time and Place

Before starting a transaction, an important question to ask yourself is, "Is this the appropriate time and place to transact with this person?" If others are around and your topic is confidential or possibly embarrassing, you might better wait until a later time or perhaps make an appointment to speak to the person involved. This may seem obvious, but have you ever asked yourself, "How did I get into this conversation in front of these people?"

On the other hand, someone else may start a transaction with you at an inappropriate time. Our next application illustrates this.

APPLICATION ───────────────────────────────

Vivian, a toy designer in a toy-manufacturing plant, is discussing the proper procedure for purchasing some new office equipment with Rolf in his office. Mazie enters the office, catches Vivian's attention, and asks, "May I ask a quick question?"

"Sure," replies Vivian.

"Is it all right if I go ahead and order a two-year supply of the parts needed for the computer trucks?"

"How soon do you want to order them?" Vivian asks.

"Today or tomorrow."

"Today or tomorrow? Hmm."

"Are you complaining? After all, with all the other designers I just let them know I'm ordering new parts and they routinely approve it," explains Mazie, her eyes widening. She crosses her arms and says loudly, "I don't know why you need two-months notice before approving a reorder of parts. It seems unreasonable!"

Vivian has a number of reasons why she needs two-months notice, but she doesn't have them clearly organized in her mind at the moment, nor does she wish to discuss them now. Rolf is waiting patiently and observing the conversation between Vivian and Mazie. What might Vivian say now?

~ • ~ • ~ • ~ • ~ • ~ • ~ • ~ • ~ • ~ • ~ • ~ • ~ • ~ • ~

Vivian might best say something like, "I'd like to talk to you about this, Mazie. Can we do it later? I'm discussing something else with Rolf right now."

When you are not prepared to answer a question or you don't want an audience for what should be a private transaction, postpone the conversation. By doing this you may be able to avoid being trapped into a game such as *NIGYSOB*. But be sure that you *do* get back to the other person, otherwise your request becomes a putoff.

Consider the Abilities of the Person

After checking to be sure the time and place are right for a transaction, give some thought to the knowledge and skills of the person you are about to transact with. For example, if Melvin needs to explain to Russell how to carry out a procedure, he might ask himself, "What key terms do I need to use in my explanation? Which of these terms is Russell probably unfamiliar with? What skills or knowledge must Russell have *before* he can do what I want him to do? Can he already do these things or do I need to teach him? What are my expectations and how realistic are they?" After thinking through these questions, Melvin can modify his approach accordingly.

APPLICATION

Suppose Melvin has identified some key terms that he needs to use in a discussion with Russell. He thinks Russell is probably not familiar with them. What do you think Melvin should do?

___ (a) Explain the terms thoroughly just in case Russell is not familiar with them.

___ (b) Simply use the terms and leave it to Russell to ask about them if he needs to.

___ (c) Say, "I'd like to talk to you about X. Here are some key terms I'll need to use. Are any of these words unfamiliar to you?"

~ • ~ • ~ • ~ • ~ • ~ • ~ • ~ • ~ • ~ • ~ • ~ • ~ • ~ • ~

We like (c). Choice (a) is likely to be a putdown and a waste of time if Russell is familiar with the terms. (Have you ever felt like saying, "Why don't you tell me something I don't already know?") Choice (b) is not good because many people are afraid to ask about words they are not familiar with. Even if people aren't afraid to ask, they are likely to feel confused or muddled until the key terms are clarified. Notice that if you asked "Are you familiar with them?" Russell may still be embarrassed. Choice (c) focuses on which words might need explanation and takes Russell off the hook.

Check Out Expectations

If you are fearful that people will respond in an undesirable way when you transact with them, one approach might be to ask them ahead of time how they would be likely to respond.

Example

Mary was concerned about the fact that Sue was often late to work. She was fearful about talking to Sue, thinking Sue would be resentful and think of her as a big bear. Mary solved this problem by going to Sue and checking out this expectation and fear. She said, "Sue, I'd like to talk to you about your lateness, but I'm afraid that you'll think of me as a big bear who's watching your every move. I don't want you to think of me that way. Would you?"

"No, I wouldn't do that," Sue answered, "after all, that's your job."

APPLICATION ―――――――――――――――――――――――――

Suppose you'd like to ask your boss for a raise but you are fearful that he or she
will think that you are dissatisfied and don't like your job. How might you approach
your boss using the technique we've just mentioned?

~ . ~ . ~ . ~ . ~ . ~ . ~ . ~ . ~ . ~ . ~ . ~ . ~ . ~ . ~ . ~ . ~ . ~

You might say to your boss, "I'd like to ask you for a raise, but I'm
afraid that you'll think I'm unhappy here and I don't want you to
think that. Am I right?"

Usually when you're using this technique, the person you're transacting
with will reassure you that your fears are unwarranted. However, if you do
get a response that confirms your fears, you have an out. You don't have
to go through with the action. For example, you might say, "Well, I want
you to know that I really am not dissatisfied. Still I would like to have you
listen to my case for a raise."

Somehow when we express our fearful expectations, we give ourselves
added strength. Also, when we assert ourselves rather than hold back unnecessarily, we help ourselves avoid playing games like *Why Does This Always
Happen to Me?* and *Ain't It Awful about Me?*

After you get a transaction started, you're on your way. Keeping it open
until you reach your objective is another matter though. That's what we'll
discuss now.

KEEPING TRANSACTIONS OPEN

In earlier chapters, we've seen how transactions can easily become blocked.
Such transactions are almost always unproductive since the goal of the transaction isn't met. For example:

Nat: "Betsy, please get me the Carter contract."

Betsy (looking up from her desk with a frustrated expression and whining): "I can't keep track of all these things. All kinds of people
can get into these files and everyone expects me to know where
everything is."

Nat (scolding Betsy, as he rummages through the file looking for the
Carter contract): "Well, if you'd do your job and take care of
the filing like you're supposed to, you wouldn't have that problem, would you?"

Betsy: "If you were smart like Mr. Brown, you'd keep your own copies
and take care of filing them yourself."

When communication lines cross like this, people are likely to turn away from
each other, feeling frustrated, angry, or bewildered. Without ego-state awareness, Nat might turn away, muttering under his breath something like, "All I

did was ask for one lousy contract. Who does she think she is?" To keep the transaction open, we must be sensitive to ego states in others *and* in ourselves.

When faced with a response like Betsy's, it's helpful to mentally sketch an ego-state diagram of the transaction. In other words, Nat might ask himself:

"What ego state was I coming from?"
"What ego state was I sending my message to in Betsy?"
"What ego state in Betsy was activated?"
"What ego state was she aiming her message toward?"

APPLICATION ———————————————————————————————

Complete this diagram:

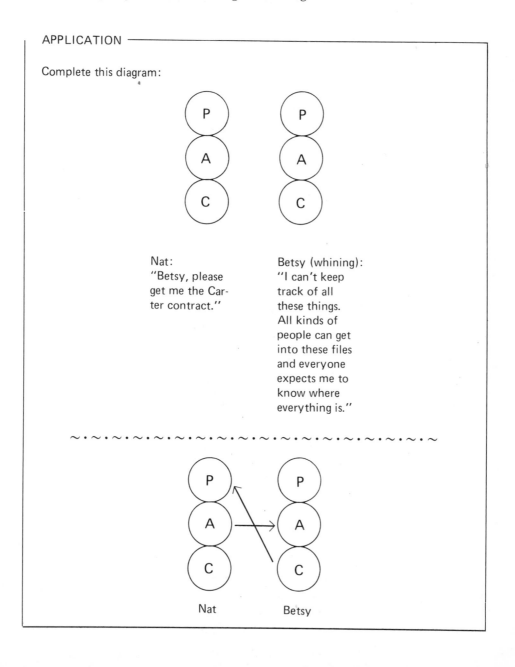

Nat:
"Betsy, please get me the Car-ter contract."

Betsy (whining):
"I can't keep track of all these things. All kinds of people can get into these files and everyone expects me to know where everything is."

~ . ~ . ~ . ~ . ~ . ~ . ~ . ~ . ~ . ~ . ~ . ~ . ~ . ~ . ~ . ~ . ~

Nat   Betsy

By mentally drawing an imaginary ego-state diagram, you become sensitive to which ego state you're coming from and which ego state is activated in the other person. When you send a message to one ego state but hook another, it's usually best to respond to the activated ego state rather than to barrel ahead insensitively.

APPLICATION ────────

1. Since Betsy's Child is activated, what kind of response do you think would be most appropriate in this case?

____ (a) A firm, controlling response.

____ (b) A questioning response.

____ (c) A warm, sympathetic response.

____ (d) An unemotional, factual response.

~ • ~ • ~ • ~ • ~ • ~ • ~ • ~ • ~ • ~ • ~ • ~ • ~ • ~ • ~

A warm, sympathetic (Nurturing Parent) response (c) would be most appropriate here since it would stroke Betsy's Child.

~ • ~ • ~ • ~ • ~ • ~ • ~ • ~ • ~ • ~ • ~ • ~ • ~ • ~ • ~

2. What might Nat say that would enable him to keep the transaction open and get the Carter contract?

~ • ~ • ~ • ~ • ~ • ~ • ~ • ~ • ~ • ~ • ~ • ~ • ~ • ~ • ~

Here are three possible responses Nat might make. Which is closest to the one you gave in the last question?

____ (a) "That really must be tough. You know, you have to be responsible for *all* these files. But I really need the Carter contract. If you could get it to me, I'd certainly appreciate it."

____ (b) "Betsy, you are responsible for all these files and I expect you to keep track of them. After all, that's your job."

____ (c) "Yes, there *is* more work here than one person can handle, Betsy. Do you mean you don't know where the Carter contract is?"

Read the comments opposite your choice.

Choice (a): Congratulations, you've correctly applied the transactional approach we've been discussing.

Choice (b): Recall that if a person's Child ego state is hooked, it's usually helpful to stroke that Child ego state before continuing the conversation with an Adult response.

Choice (c): This choice is better than (b) but *not* as effective as (a). We like choice (a) better because Nat comes back with his original Adult request after first stroking Betsy's Child.

Notice that after stroking the other person's Child, the next step is to return to an Adult-Adult transaction. In general, once the activated ego state has been addressed rather than ignored, the Adult will likely be more open to contact.

The same approach applies when other ego states besides the Child have been activated. For example, if you have asked a question or have given some directions and a subordinate responds in a critical or scolding way (sending a message from the Controlling Parent to your Child), the best thing to do *may* be to respond from your Child briefly in a way that will stroke the other person's Parent. Often this involves agreeing with the other person or restating the problem as you believe the other person sees it, or occasionally apologizing for some goof that you've made. (However, don't make apologies a habit!) This approach increases your chances for opening up the transaction.

APPLICATION

1 Finish the diagram of this transaction between Sid and Nancy by drawing in the proper arrows.

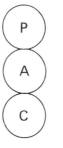 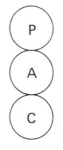

Sid:
"Would you copy this report for me right away? I need it for the meeting I'm having with Mr. Brown after lunch."

Nancy:
"I can't just drop everything and run to the Xerox machine every time someone needs a copy of something. If you want something copied, put it on my desk before 9 a.m.!"

~ . ~ . ~ . ~ . ~ . ~ . ~ . ~ . ~ . ~ . ~ . ~ . ~ . ~ . ~

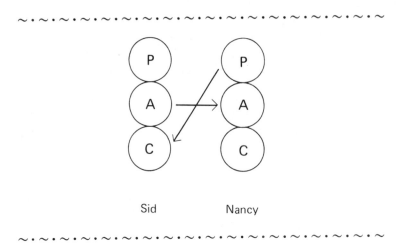

Sid   Nancy

~ . ~ . ~ . ~ . ~ . ~ . ~ . ~ . ~ . ~ . ~ . ~ . ~ . ~ . ~

2 In view of the transactional tactic we've been discussing, which of these responses by Sid would be best?

___ (a) "Listen, Nancy, you're supposed to be my assistant. If I need something copied in an emergency like this, you should be willing to make an exception to the usual procedure and put a rush on this for me."

___ (b) "I'm sorry, Nancy. You're right. I should have gotten this to you sooner, but I really need to have it copied before lunch. I'd appreciate it if you could manage it for me."

___ (c) "I can see that you're upset because you have a lot to do and that you don't like to go to the copy machine except at scheduled times."

___ (d) "I can't always adjust my problems to fit your schedule! You should be able to make an exception if it's necessary."

~ . ~ . ~ . ~ . ~ . ~ . ~ . ~ . ~ . ~ . ~ . ~ . ~ . ~ . ~

Response (b) would probably be the most likely to get Sid his report. Note his approach: he is consciously using his Child to acknowledge Nancy's Controlling Parent. By admitting his error, Sid is defusing Nancy's Parent. He is then able to continue by repeating his original request in an Adult way.

By stroking the activated ego state in another person and then reaching for the Adult, you can avoid making the kind of response that often leads to a game. Instead, you can choose a response that will lead to a successful transaction in which you and the other person reach a mutually satisfying agreement. In the next several pages we will be discussing two specific techniques for stroking the activated ego state:

— active listening, and
— fogging.

Active Listening

A good way to stroke another person's activated ego state is to use a skill called *active listening*. Active listening is especially appropriate when dealing with people in high feeling states—like an irate customer. When people are mad, sad, upset, or frustrated, they are often relieved to discover that someone else is tuned in to their feelings. With active listening, you listen carefully to the *total* message that the other person is sending and then feed back to the other person what you think you heard. We say "total message" to stress that people often send nonverbal messages along with the usual verbal content. Be sure to feed back the total message including any feelings that were expressed or implied.

APPLICATION ————————————————————————

Randy, a car salesperson, is chatting with Terry, a customer. As we look in on the scene, Terry is complaining about a new car he has just bought from Randy. "And after I finally got the automatic choke fixed, I decided to go to one of those fancy carwashes. I got drenched when the water leaked through a crack near the windshield. Now the automatic choke isn't working again." Which of these do you think would be the best active-listening response?

____ (a) "Well, you know it's been six months since that automatic choke was fixed. The service department can't guarantee its work forever."

____ (b) "How is it running now?"

____ (c) "It sounds like you're really upset because you think your car is a lemon."

~ • ~ • ~ • ~ • ~ • ~ • ~ • ~ • ~ • ~ • ~ • ~ • ~ • ~ • ~ • ~

We prefer choice (c). Notice that it reflects the content of Randy's message: both the central idea and Randy's feelings about that idea.

To make an active-listening response, first tune in carefully to what the other person is saying. Look beyond the other person's words. Observe:

— tone of voice,
— body position,
— facial expressions, gestures, actions, eyes.

Be aware of ego states. Ask yourself, "What is this person really saying and feeling?" Some good beginnings for active-listening responses are:

"You seem to be telling me that . . . ."
"I hear you saying that . . . ."
"It's like . . . ."
"I could be wrong but you seem . . . ."
"It sounds like . . . ."

APPLICATION ──────────

Laura, a co-worker, has just come from a meeting with Jack, Bill's boss. Bill has started to discuss Laura's proposal for advertising a new product. He has just asked her how much the proposed campaign would cost. He notices a certain stiffness in her body posture and a hurt look in her eye. She is silent for several seconds. What might Bill say?

~ • ~ • ~ • ~ • ~ • ~ • ~ • ~ • ~ • ~ • ~ • ~ • ~ • ~ • ~ • ~

Bill might say, "Laura, I could be wrong, but you seem upset about something."

We might diagram the transactions between Bill and Laura like this:

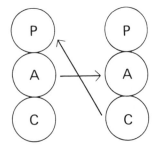

Bill:
"How much will
this advertising
campaign cost
us?"

Laura:
(Silence and
hurt look.)

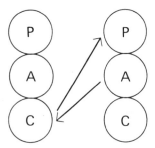

Laura:
(Silence and
hurt look.)

Bill:
"Laura, I could
be wrong, but
you seem upset
about something."

By stroking Laura's activated Child, Bill was able to keep the transaction open. It continued like this:

> Laura: "Jack just chewed me out for leaving early yesterday."
> Bill: "Oh, yeah?"
> Laura: "He really raked me over the coals, and I only left ten minutes early. I had to get to a doctor's appointment and I didn't want to be late."

Notice that by interpreting and responding to Laura's nonverbal message, Bill was able to keep the transaction open. He used his Little Professor to intuit Laura's feelings. Had he continued to try to talk about Laura's proposed advertising campaign, the diagram would have looked like this:

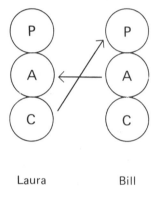

Laura   Bill

The transaction would be blocked and the likelihood that a productive conversation would continue almost nil.

With active listening, you are usually listening to a particular ego state in the other person as you clarify information, opinions, or feelings.

APPLICATION ————————————————————————

1 When you actively listen to a person using his or her Parent, what are you most likely to be clarifying?

____ (a) Information

____ (b) Opinions

____ (c) Feelings

2 When you actively listen to an Adult ego state, what are you most likely to be clarifying?

____ (a) Information

____ (b) Opinions

____ (c) Feelings

3 When you actively listen to a Child ego state, what are you most likely to be clarifying?

___(a) Information

___(b) Opinions

___(c) Feelings

4 What ego state do *you* use during active listening?

~ . ~ . ~ . ~ . ~ . ~ . ~ . ~ . ~ . ~ . ~ . ~ . ~ . ~ . ~ . ~ . ~ . ~ . ~

1 When you actively listen to a person using his or her Parent, you are most likely to be clarifying *opinion:*

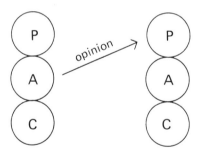

You   The Other Person

2 When you actively listen to a person using his or her Adult, you are most likely to be clarifying *information:*

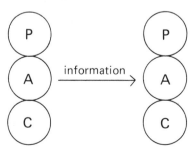

You   The Other Person

3 When you actively listen to a Child ego state, you are most likely to be clarifying *feelings:*

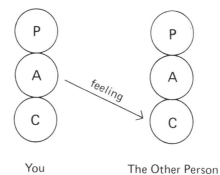

You   The Other Person

4 The Adult is the ego state *you* use when you listen actively. Notice how all of the arrows are coming from the Adult in the diagrams.

Active listening is not an easy skill for everyone to learn. Sometimes it helps to keep in mind a number of taboos—things you don't do while you're in an active-listening transaction.

APPLICATION

Which of the following would make sense as taboos to observe when practicing active listening?

____ (a) Don't use your Adult.

____ (b) Don't give advice.

____ (c) Don't summarize.

____ (d) Don't talk about feelings.

____ (e) Don't teach.

____ (f) Don't preach.

____ (g) Don't observe body language.

____ (h) Don't sidetrack.

____ (i) Don't disagree.

____ (j) Don't introduce new ideas.

~ • ~ • ~ • ~ • ~ • ~ • ~ • ~ • ~ • ~ • ~ • ~ • ~ • ~

These items make sense as taboos: (b), (e), (f), (h), (i), (j). Item (a) is not a taboo because you need to use your Adult to listen actively.

> Item (c) is not a taboo because active listening often involves summar-
> izing what a person has said in just a few words. Item (d) is not a taboo
> because an important part of active listening involves guessing what the
> other person is feeling. Item (g) is not a taboo because it's important to
> observe body language while listening actively. Often people show their
> feelings with their body language.
>
> The other items make sense as taboos because when you give
> advice, teach, preach, sidetrack, disagree, or introduce new ideas, you
> do not achieve the active-listening goal of clarifying what the other
> person seems to be communicating.

As you've seen, active listening is an effective means of stroking an ego
state that has been activated in another person. It's especially effective for
recognizing a person's Child. We'll discuss more about active listening shortly.
But for now, let's turn to another technique for stroking an activated ego
state: *fogging.*

Fogging

Manuel J. Smith's description of fogging makes it an effective transactional
technique for stroking a person's Parent ego state. Using the fogging technique, you agree in some meaningful way with what the other person is
saying. You do this by agreeing:

— with truth,
— with the odds, or
— in principle.

The Parent ego state tends to be inflexible and looks for compliance.
When you agree with people coming from their Parent ego states, you give
them what they are looking for. You also help yourself to stay in your Adult
and avoid making a rebellious Child response. The technique is called fogging
because in a way it resembles a fog bank. Here's how Smith explains it:

> A fog bank is remarkable in some aspects. It is very persistent. We cannot clearly see
> through it. It offers no resistance to our penetration. It does not fight back. It has no
> hard striking surfaces from which a rock we throw at it can ricochet back at us,
> enabling us to pick it up and throw it at the fog once more. We can throw an object
> right through it, and it is unaffected. Inevitably, we give up trying to alter the persis-
> tent, independent, nonmanipulative fog and leave it alone. Similarly, when criticized,
> you can assertively cope by offering no resistance or hard psychological striking sur-
> faces to critical statements thrown at you.[1]

Now, let's discuss each aspect of the fogging technique separately. We'll
begin with "agreeing with the truth."

Agreeing with the Truth

In agreeing with the truth, you simply say something like, "What you say is
true; I did . . . ." For example:

Boss: "Your production was way down last week. You only processed 25 loan applications!"

Alvin (*fogging response*): "You're right, boss. I did slow down last week."

Agreeing with the Odds

Another way to make a fogging response is to agree that your critic might be or probably is right. (In this next example, note that fogging can be used by a boss as well as a subordinate.)

Anne (subordinate—angrily): "I can't understand your directions. They are really confusing and it is hard to read your writing."

Boss (*fogging response*): "You're probably right. My directions may not be clear enough and my handwriting may be hard to read, too."

Agreeing in Principle

When agreeing in principle, you agree that what the other person is saying is basically logical or generally true. When agreeing in this way, you might start with statements like:

"What you are saying makes sense. . . ."
"That's logical. . . ."

For example:

Chuck: "Bernie, if your desk wasn't such a mess, you wouldn't have to waste so much time looking for things."

Bernie (*fogging response*): "You know, Chuck, that makes a lot of sense. I wouldn't have to look under these papers to find my progress report if my desk were neater."

APPLICATION ─────────────────────

Here's some practice in making different kinds of fogging responses. For each of the following Controlling Parent statements, make up the type of fogging response indicated.

(a) "You've got the wrong attitude. You should be willing to make some calls on the Bixby people. Sooner or later they'll come around."   (Agree with the odds)

(b) "You didn't use the drafting board and T-square as I asked you to in doing the lettering for that cover."   (Agree with the truth)

(c) "If you'd take the time to put   (Agree in principle)
    your tools back where they
    belong when you finish using
    them, you'd save yourself a lot
    of time in the long run."

~ • ~ • ~ • ~ • ~ • ~ • ~ • ~ • ~ • ~ • ~ • ~ • ~ • ~ • ~ • ~

Here are some possible fogging responses:

(a) "Maybe I do have the wrong attitude. It might do some good to
    make some calls on the Bixby people."
(b) "That's right. I didn't use the drafting board and T-square."
(c) "Yes, it's generally true that you can save time by having a place
    for everything and keeping everything in its place."

You've seen two techniques for stroking activated ego states: active listening and fogging. After stroking a person's activated ego state, it's important to follow through with an Adult-Adult transaction. Usually emotions will have subsided because they've received some attention. Then the Adult becomes more receptive to action.

Adult Questions

An effective way to activate another person's Adult ego state is to ask an Adult question. That's because to answer an Adult question, a person usually must process information, assign probabilities, consider alternatives, anticipate consequences, and so on. As a result, the person moves into the Adult ego state. In framing Adult questions, it's useful to keep in mind these familiar question words:

— What?
— Where?
— When?
— Why?
— How?

For example, you might ask questions such as:

"How do you see the situation?"
"How would you like it to be?"
"What is your plan of action?"
"Why do you think your plan will work?"
"When do you think you need to start?"
"Are there any people that you need to help you?"
"What supplies and equipment do you need?"

Adult questions are often useful in avoiding Ain't It Awful sessions. For example, without the use of Adult questions, time may be spent like this:

Jerry: "How's it going, Tom?"
Tom (hangs his head): "Oh, terrible."

Jerry: "That's par for the course around here. What's the problem this time?"

Tom: "These people just don't believe in following proper procedure."

Jerry: "Yeah, I know what you mean."

Tom: "You know what happened? Someone nominated Bert for president of the board. I got the floor and started to explain that Bert wasn't eligible, but nobody would listen. Nobody listens these days."

Jerry: "Right. I talk to my boss until I'm blue in the face. It never does any good."

Tom: ". . . And just as I was trying to make my point, Pete jumps up and starts screaming, 'I object! I object!' And then his friend chimes in with, 'Tom is just electioneering.' "

Jerry: "Isn't it awful the way nobody listens! I've tried every way I know how to get through to my boss. Nothing works, nothing."

Tom: "What's the use? There's no future in it. Pete now is watching every move I make. He thinks I'm out to get him next. He thinks I'm a spy for that 'Leadership Inquiry' group. You know, the one that goes around defaming everyone."

Jerry: "Yeah, it's a hopeless case around here. Like the time when I . . . ."

As you can see, Ain't It Awful goes nowhere. It only serves to pastime and reaffirm bad feelings.

APPLICATION ———————————————————————————

Take a moment to visualize what might happen if Jerry were to respond with Adult questions. Make some notes about the scene as you imagine it. What is Jerry asking? What is Tom replying? (Make your notes on a separate sheet of paper.)

Everyone will imagine the scene differently. Here is one possibility:

Jerry: "How's it going, Tom?"

Tom (hangs his head): "Oh, terrible."

Jerry: "Terrible, huh?"

Tom (slowly and softly): "Yeah."

Jerry: "What happened?"

Tom: "Didn't you hear? At the board meeting they tried to nominate Bert, and Pete jumped on me just because I brought up Bert's record."

Jerry: "What do you mean?"

Tom: "I had the floor and I said, 'I hate to bring this up, but according to the handbook, Bert should not be nominated because he's had some difficulties with his staff that haven't been resolved yet.' Before I could finish, Pete jumped up and screamed, 'I object! I object!' Then his friend chimed in with, 'Tom is just electioneering.' "

Jerry: "What happened next?"

Tom: "Well, Bert's name was removed from the list of nominees, but now a lot of people have got the wrong impression about me. They think I'm a spy for that 'Leadership Inquiry' group—you know—the one that seems to be going around defaming everyone."

Jerry: "How would you have wanted things to go at that meeting?"

Tom: "I'd like to be able to present some data about a potential nominee without the person who nominated him jumping to conclusions and making a scene."

Jerry: "Is there anything you might do to make that happen?"

Tom: "Naah. It's hopeless."

Jerry: "You seem pretty sure about that."

Tom: "I sure am. The same thing happened to me last month. I just don't think that Pete understands where I'm coming from."

Jerry: "What would happen if you had a heart-to-heart talk with Pete before the next meeting?"

Tom: "I don't know. I tried to do that last time but Pete was on vacation and I couldn't get hold of him. I did try."

Jerry: "If you did have a talk, what's the worst possible thing that might happen?"

Tom: "He might tell me to get lost."

Jerry: "Would that be any worse than what he's saying to you now at the board meetings?"

Tom: "No, I guess not."

Jerry: "What's the best possible thing that might happen?"

Tom: "I'd be able to level with him. We'd be able to straighten things out and start working together."

Jerry: "How about the board meetings?"

Tom: "I'd be able to relax and really contribute something instead of feeling all locked up inside."

Jerry: "Is that something you really want?"

Tom: "You bet it is. You know, maybe it's worth a try. I've really got nothing to lose. Thanks, Jerry."

In this last example, Adult questions worked well (as we described the scene). But sometimes Adult questions may be perceived as being too cold and calculating. A person who is angry, for example, is probably not in the mood to respond right away to an Adult question.

APPLICATION ———

What might you do first—before asking an Adult question—when a person is coming from a feeling Child or prejudiced Parent ego state?

~ . ~ . ~ . ~ . ~ . ~ . ~ . ~ . ~ . ~ . ~ . ~ . ~ . ~ . ~

Stroke the ego state that is activated in the other person. You might consider using active listening to stroke the Child ego state and fogging to stroke the Parent, or vice versa.

Negative Inquiry

People who play the Persecutor role in games like *Blemish* or *NIGYSOB* often criticize in very vague ways to keep their Victims powerless. Their Victims find it hard to change, because they don't know *what* to change. In such cases, Adult questions can work well for clarifying the negative comments the other person is making. We call this *negative inquiry.* For example, you might say, "I don't understand. What is it about _____ that is unsatisfactory?"

If you use negative inquiry to break up a game, be prepared for some resistance when you first use it. In fact, the other person is likely to answer you with another abstraction rather than something specific. If that happens, rephrase your Adult question but keep focusing on the same target: what you are doing that is unacceptable.

Negative inquiry is useful in breaking up such games because it encourages the Persecutor to talk about specific unacceptable behaviors. Once you identify what you are doing that is unacceptable, you can deal with the situation in a more rational way. You can either change your behaviors or, perhaps, explain why they're appropriate.

APPLICATION

As we look in on this scene, Vince, the manager of a bar, is criticizing Joe, a bartender.

Vince: "You just don't have the right attitude, Joe. I'm afraid we're going to have to let you go if you don't shape up."
Joe (*fogging*): "Maybe my attitude isn't right."
Vince: "Well, maybe you just need more time. You don't learn to be a good bartender overnight."
Joe: "I don't understand. What is it about the way that I serve drinks that you find unacceptable?"
Vince: "You just don't have the right spirit."

What would Joe say now, following the guidelines we just mentioned:

___ (a) "How many days do you think I have before you'll have to make a decision about whether to keep me?"

___ (b) "OK, I'll try to do my best to improve."

___ (c) "I really don't understand. What would you like me to do to show that I have the right spirit?"

~ . ~ . ~ . ~ . ~ . ~ . ~ . ~ . ~ . ~ . ~ . ~ . ~ . ~ . ~ . ~ . ~

We like choice (c). By persisting with negative inquiry, Joe was able to discover that Vince was dissatisfied because he wasn't smiling enough. The fact that Joe wasn't smiling *sounded* trivial so Vince was reluctant to mention it. Once Joe found out what Vince wanted, he started smiling more. The customers began to respond better and Joe started smiling even more. Not only was he happier, but he kept his job.

When using negative inquiry, you may be tempted to use a sarcastic tone of voice. Don't. Remember, sarcasm is characteristic of the negative part of the Adapted Child (or the Controlling Parent). The goal in using negative inquiry is to transact from your Adult and to activate the other person's Adult. With sarcasm you're likely to get into a Child-Child or Child-Parent dialogue.

Criticizing Others

So far we've talked mainly about using Adult questions to activate the Adult ego state in others and about how to respond to criticism from others. Equally important is the approach we take when *we* criticize others. Because criticism can be a negative payoff that people seek unwittingly, it is often more effective to stroke what you want in a positive way, rather than to criticize. But sometimes we need to pass on constructive criticism. The most effective criticism is growth-oriented and helps to educate or to protect the other person. When faced with a touchy problem, ask yourself:

"Is what I need to tell this person going to facilitate his or her growth, potential, and success?"
"Will it strengthen this person and add to her or his resources?"
"Is my criticism cushioned by caring?"

Criticism affects people most productively if the relationship is basically a sound, positive one. In fact, before passing on constructive criticism to another person, it's important to establish an agreement—a contract—that passing critical information back and forth is OK. This helps to decrease the possibility of collecting resentment.

When phrasing critical comments, it is often helpful to begin with a statement of how you feel when the other person does whatever it is that you don't like. A useful four-step pattern:

"I feel . . . ." Express your feeling.
". . . when you . . . ." Describe what you don't like.
"I would like you to . . . ." Describe what you would like.
". . . because . . . ." Explain why.

When criticizing, it's important to express your feelings through your Adult ego state. With your Adult as interpreter, you are more likely to hook the other person's Adult and to remove some of the sting. Remember, if you suppress your feelings of frustration, anger, or uneasiness when passing on criticism, those feelings are likely to be expressed nonverbally anyway and can hook an undesirable ego state in the other person. Of course, sometimes your feelings will be positive. For example, you may feel good about what someone has done and still want to make some constructive comments. You may want to say something like, "Under the circumstances I feel good about the way you handled the situation. Next time, please set a deadline whenever you give Tabatha any work to do." With this approach the person you are criticizing may be less likely to become defensive.

It is equally important for you to describe the other person's undesirable behavior. Avoid abstractions such as "You've got the wrong attitude." In addition, avoid *negative* implications about the other person's being or inner self. Don't imply that the other person has certain unchangeable personality characteristics. People aren't problems. They *have* problems.

APPLICATION ──────────────────────────

1 David is upset because Del has been making company purchases without going through the proper authorization procedures. In following our guidelines for criticism, what would David say?

___(a) "I get nervous when you continue to purchase items over $10 on your own without proper authorization. I'd like you to get John's signature on a purchase order for any such items because it is required by the accounting office and I'm the one they come to when things are wrong."

___(b) "Del, you shouldn't be ordering things over $10 without John's signature. I expect you to get his signature from now on because if any deviation from standard purchasing procedure occurs, the accounting department comes down on me."

___(c) "Del, you make me mad when you don't follow the company's purchasing procedures. Last month you spent $300 extra on textured toilet paper. Do you have any justifications for this? Is it supposed to boost morale?"

~ • ~ • ~ • ~ • ~ • ~ • ~ • ~ • ~ • ~ • ~ • ~ • ~ • ~ • ~ • ~ • ~

Choice (a) is the one we prefer. Notice in choice (a) that David is:

— expressing his feeling;
— describing Del's undesirable behavior;
— telling Del specifically what he would like him to do;
— giving the reason why.

In choice (b) the speaker is using words ("should," "expect") that are likely to activate an undesirable Adapted Child ego state. Also notice that choice (b) does not contain an expression of feeling. Choice (c) contains an expression of feeling, but notice that the speaker is blaming Del for the feeling rather than taking responsibility for it. Also, the speaker is interrogating Del rather than explaining desired performance.

~ • ~ • ~ • ~ • ~ • ~ • ~ • ~ • ~ • ~ • ~ • ~ • ~ • ~ • ~ • ~ • ~

2 Think of someone you criticized recently. Did you include the four steps we recommend? Would it have been appropriate to do so? How might you have phrased your criticism to include the four steps?

Closely related to the skill of criticizing constructively is the skill of disagreeing assertively. Both skills—if *not* used with care—may activate a person's not-OK Child or Controlling Parent ego state.

Disagreeing Assertively

What do you do when someone says something you disagree with? Do you nod your head politely and then kick yourself later for not speaking up? Do you ever abruptly contradict the other person and later feel sorry that you did? Do you sometimes find yourself trapped into an argument that is not worth your energy or may be steering you away from your goals? If you answered *yes* to any of these questions, you may find the following approach helpful. As we discuss each step in the text, we will also add it to a flowchart.

DISAGREEING ASSERTIVELY

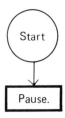

The first step in disagreeing assertively is to pause. Often a quick, automatic response comes from our Parent ego state. If you pause for about four seconds before responding, you'll help to ensure that your Adult is in gear. As you pause, activate your Adult by mentally working out an active-listening response.

DISAGREEING ASSERTIVELY

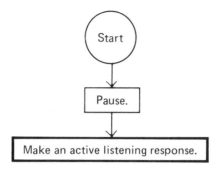

As a rule of thumb, it is usually best to make an active-listening response after pausing. Here's why:

— An active-listening response reassures people because they can see they are getting through to you.
— By making an active-listening response you activate *your* Adult. With your Adult in gear, you'll be better able to avoid locking horns with the other person.
— Active listening helps to *clarify* the other person's message. After such clarification you may find out that you don't disagree after all! Have you ever argued with a person for some time only to discover later that you agreed all along? Active listening can help you avoid that.

APPLICATION ──

You have just boarded a plane on a cross-country flight and are sitting next to a character who reminds you of Archie Bunker. As you look down the aisle, you notice that most people are smartly dressed in business suits with the exception of a few teen-agers in jeans and T-shirts, carrying knapsacks. Archie nudges you and says in an irritated voice, "Just look at them. Isn't it terrible the way they're dressed?" How would you respond to Archie if you didn't choose to pastime or argue?

~·~

Many answers might work. We would suggest listening to Archie's Parent and feeding back his opinion by saying something like, "You seem upset about the way these kids are dressed."

DISAGREEING ASSERTIVELY

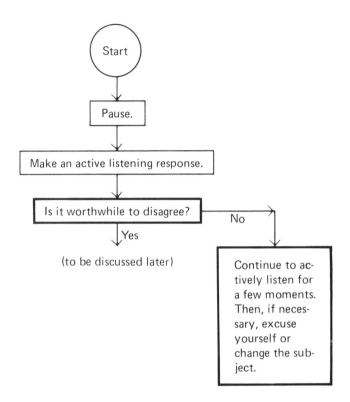

After making an active-listening response, consider whether it would be worthwhile to pursue the matter with this person. Will doing so help you reach your goal? Is it worth your time and energy? In a moment, we'll discuss how to proceed if your answer is *yes*.

If you decide against expressing your disagreement, we recommend that you continue active listening briefly and then change the subject or excuse yourself. In this case Archie seems to be trying to *hook* you into a pastime of Ain't It Awful. Your first active-listening response may be enough to get you off the hook. But sometimes it's necessary to give one or two more such responses. After that the other person will be more relaxed and unlikely to hook you into either an argument or an Ain't It Awful session.

APPLICATION ─────────────────────────

Let's go back to Archie. Suppose you have a lot of work to do on your flight and you don't want to get hooked into Ain't It Awful. After your first active-listening response, Archie continues, "Right! Probably their old man is paying for the ticket." Following our suggestion, what might you say next?

~·~·~·~·~·~·~·~·~·~·~·~·~·~·~·~·~·~·~

You might give another active-listening response and say, "It's not only bad the way they're dressed but their dad probably paid for the ticket." At this point you just might be off the hook. In an actual situation much like this one, Archie simply said, "Yeah!" and that was the end of it. So when you want to *avoid* getting into Ain't It Awful or an argument, put your active-listening skills to work. Then, if necessary, excuse yourself or change the subject.

DISAGREEING ASSERTIVELY

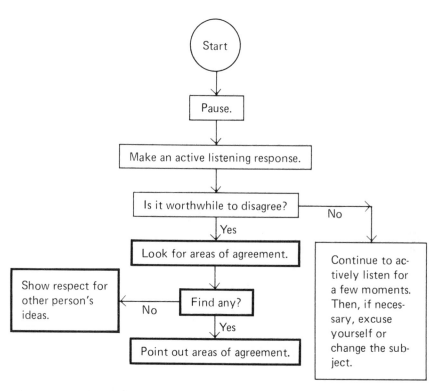

If you *want* to disagree, we suggest that you look for areas of agreement. Before expressing any disagreement, ask yourself, "Is there anything about what this person is saying that I agree with?" If the answer is *yes*, point them out. By doing this, you may help the other person to relax and avoid becoming defensive. For example, you might say, "It seems we're both in agreement that . . . ." Even if you can't find any areas of agreement, you can usually use the fogging techniques we discussed earlier. For example, you might agree with the odds. You might say, "You know, you *may be* right." (Notice that in agreeing that there is a chance that a statement is correct, you are not agreeing that it *is* correct.)

If you don't want to admit to the *possibility* that the other person is right, it is often useful to show in some way that you respect the other person's opinion or right to his or her opinion. For example, you might say:

"That's an interesting point . . . ."
"I respect your opinion on this . . . ."

Your tone of voice, facial expressions, gestures, and body position can also help to convey the idea that you respect the other person's ideas.

DISAGREEING ASSERTIVELY

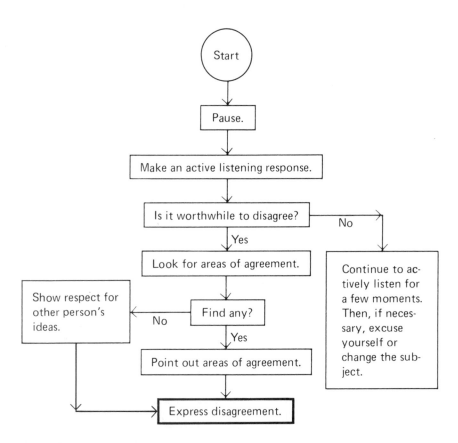

Then the way is prepared for you to express disagreement. When expressing your disagreement, do it firmly but courteously. Avoid making dogmatic, Parent-sounding statements that lock you into an unyielding position such as:

Accusative Statements
Beginning with "You"   *Prejudicial Statements*

"You always . . . ."   "The *fact is* that . . . ." (pompously)
"You never . . . ."   "I happen to know that . . . ."

When expressing your disagreement, it's often useful to give reasons or examples that support your position. Otherwise your statement of disagreement may seem unnecessarily curt.

DISAGREEING ASSERTIVELY

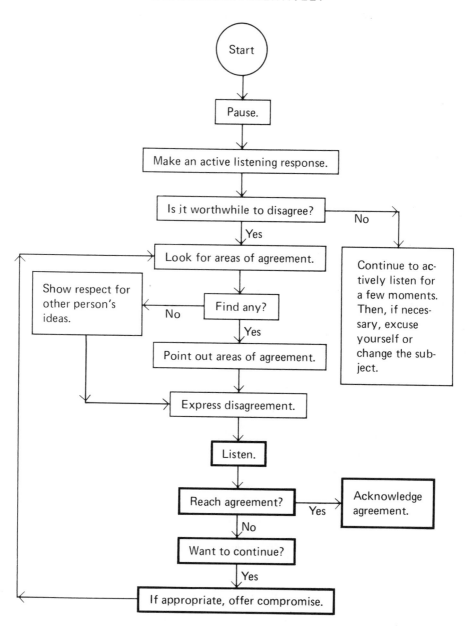

As important as what came before is what you do *after* expressing your disagreement. Listen to what the other person says in response. *Don't rehearse your next comeback in your head.* Instead focus on the other person. Surrender your attention. If you reach an agreement, acknowledge it quickly so that you don't waste time going through the motions of disagreeing when no disagreement exists.

If you still disagree after listening to the other person's response, consider whether it's worthwhile for you to continue the discussion. If you think it is and you want to continue, you might want to consider making a compromise. If you wish to continue the conversation, you repeat the cycle.

DISAGREEING ASSERTIVELY

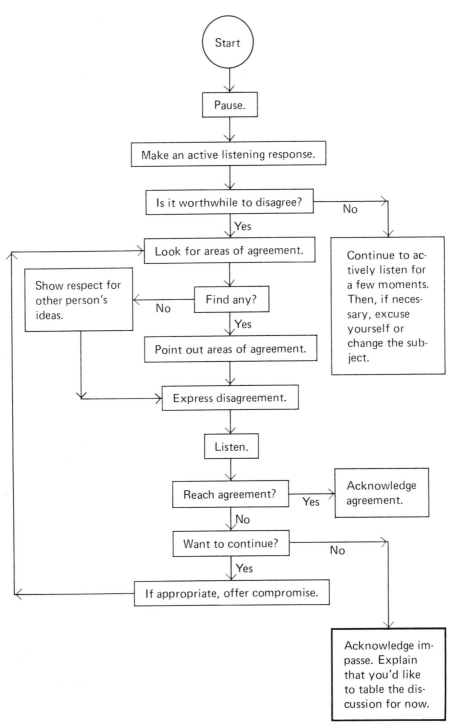

In spite of your efforts to compromise and reach an agreement, you may reach an impasse. If so, it's often useful to acknowledge that rather than to continue to escalate your discussion into an argument. You can save a lot of time and hurt feelings that way. Here's one way you might phrase it:

"Mike, I can see that we've both got some very definite ideas on this matter. We seem to have reached an impasse. I'd like to end this discussion for now. OK? Is there something else you want to discuss?"

APPLICATION ————————————————————————

This conversation is designed to help you practice applying some of the ideas we've just presented about how to disagree assertively. You'll be looking in on Rosalie and Jeanette, who are discussing the advisability of putting up barriers in the middle of city streets to divert traffic.

Read through the conversation and note Rosalie and Jeanette's approaches in disagreeing with each other. Identify any good features, as well as bad ones, about their approach.

Rosalie: ". . . and I think we should put in those street barriers to divert traffic. It makes the street a lot safer for our children, and . . . ."

Jeanette: "Yeah, but the fact is that just because of those barriers, it takes me a half an hour longer every day to get to work."

Rosalie: "Well, it's worth an extra half-hour."

Jeanette: "Actually, it's an hour. A half-hour *to* work and a half-hour coming back home."

Rosalie: "Well, maybe if you were inconvenienced enough, you'd stop polluting our environment with your smog-producing car."

Jeanette: "That's a stupid thing to say. Apparently you're not aware of all the extra fumes that are being thrown into the atmosphere as a result of those barriers."

Rosalie: "It seems to me that you're concerned about all the pollution that cars are producing, too, and you seem to be really angry. Am I right?"

Jeanette: "Sure! We're destroying the air. I bet if we put as much money into research on smog-control devices as we do into interior design of cars, we'd move a long way toward getting some clean air."

Rosalie: "Well, I think we both agree that smog emissions from cars are dangerous and a serious problem. I *do* feel that barriers are a good thing even though they do inconvenience commuters, because people who live in a city — well — their rights come first, I think."

Jeanette: "That's an interesting point, but I think that city officials should consider the rights of commuters, too, because commuters bring city people a lot of business."

Rosalie: "Yes, you *do* have a point there. Say, I can see we do agree on some points, but we seem to be at a standoff about others."

Jeanette: "Talking to you has clarified my thinking somewhat. You pose some good arguments and I find myself starting to reconsider some of my first ideas. At any rate, I think we've exhausted the subject for now."

Rosalie: "OK. I'm sorry, I kind of got a little overreactive."
Jeanette: "Yeah. I guess I overreacted, too."

1 Which of the steps that we suggested for assertive disagreement did Rosalie follow?

2 Jeanette?

3 Which ones did Rosalie *not* follow?

4 Jeanette?

~ • ~ • ~ • ~ • ~ • ~ • ~ • ~ • ~ • ~ • ~ • ~ • ~ • ~ • ~ • ~ • ~

1 Steps followed by Rosalie: active listening ("It seems to me that you're concerned about all the pollution that cars are producing, too. And you seem to be really angry. Am I right?"), identifying areas of agreement ("Well, I think we both agree . . . .").
2 Steps followed by Jeanette: acknowledging that the other person's idea has some value ("That's an interesting point but . . . .").
3 Steps *not* followed by Rosalie: avoiding Parent-sounding statements ("Well, maybe if people like you were inconvenienced enough . . . .").
4 Steps *not* followed by Jeanette: avoiding Parent-sounding statements, active listening to check on communication, identifying areas of agreement, acknowledging value of the person's point of view (*exception:* Jeanette *did* say, "That's an interesting point," but only after Rosalie used active listening and pointed out areas of agreement).

ENDING TRANSACTIONS

Have you ever found yourself locked into a conversation when you have more important things to do? If so, you realize how important it is to be skillful in ending transactions.

You can do a number of things to signal that you want to end a transaction. For example, you can:

— send nonverbal messages;
— summarize;
— explain your need to leave;

— express enjoyment, appreciation, or thanks;
— indicate a desire to meet again;
— ask if there is anything else to discuss.

APPLICATION

In the left column we've listed the ways to end a transaction. In the right column are some examples of these ways. Match each example with the way that it illustrates.

Ways to End a Transaction		*Examples*
___ (a) Send nonverbal message.	(i)	"It's felt really good to talk to you about this!"
___ (b) Summarize.	(ii)	"So you'll contact Mrs. Baker and then give me a written report of what you find out."
___ (c) Explain your need to leave.	(iii)	"Is there anything else we should cover?"
___ (d) Express enjoyment, appreciation, or thanks.		
___ (e) Indicate a desire to meet again.	(iv)	"Please excuse me. I need to get started on a project I'm working on."
___ (f) Ask if there is anything else to discuss.	(v)	Break eye contact for a moment and stand up (if seated).
	(vi)	"Let's get together the early part of next week to discuss this."

~ • ~ • ~ • ~ • ~ • ~ • ~ • ~ • ~ • ~ • ~ • ~ • ~ • ~ • ~

(a) v; (b) ii; (c) iv; (d) i; (e) vi; (f) iii.

You may find it useful to combine one or more of these methods. For example:

"So I will have that report to you by next Thursday. I've got a number of other things I have to do, too. Is there anything else? . . . OK, I'll talk to you later. Thanks for taking the time to talk to me about this."

The technique of closing a transaction by asking if there is anything else to discuss needs some special comment. This technique can help a person who is rambling to focus on the purpose of the transaction and decide whether or not it is necessary to continue. However, use this method only if you are prepared to continue the transaction if the other person indeed has something further to discuss. If you need to cut off a transaction quickly and you can't afford to discuss other matters, then use a more direct approach, such as excusing yourself and expressing your need to get on with something else.

Also, be sensitive to how others are signaling you that they would like to bring a transaction to a close. Besides using the preceding methods, people may signal the end of a transaction by saying things such as:

"OK?" (said with a rising inflection)
"Right?"
"Is that all?"

Some people indicate a desire to end a transaction by:

— looking at their watches;
— fidgeting;
— wringing their hands;
— pointing their bodies toward an exit;
— sitting on the edge of their chair.

Be sensitive to these nonverbal signs, so that you don't extend any transaction unnecessarily.

Whatever method you use when ending a transaction, be sure that you are courteous to the other person. Avoid discounting him or her as a person; try seeing things from his or her perspective. If you do that and show your empathy with a warm, friendly facial expression, you won't have to worry about putting that person down when you excuse yourself.

EGO STATES IN WRITING

Written messages—whether they be notes, letters, memos, proposals, or reports—are also transactions. Our ego states show up both in our writing and in our reactions to other people's writing.

APPLICATION

Ralph Zimmerman happened to see a letter from Ron Smith to a Mr. Green, a letter that contained some errors. Read Ralph's memo.

Memo to all clerical staff:

By chance a number of staff-written letters recently crossed my desk. I was appalled at the poor grammar, spelling, and general appearance of those letters. They certainly do not reflect well upon our firm.

Let this be a reminder to all of you to pay close attention to your letters. They should be neat with no grammar or spelling errors. They should uphold our good image.

Plainly a course in basic English is needed. If enough of you are interested, I will arrange for Tom Gadsworth to teach a course on basic letter-writing skills.

The course could be held either on Tuesday or Thursday afternoons from 3 to 4 P.M. If you're interested, please send me a note indicating your time preference. Attendance will be voluntary, of course.

Ralph A. Zimmerman

Ralph A. Zimmerman

1   What ego state was the writer probably coming from?

2   What ego state is it likely to hook in the reader?

3   Is the memo likely to be effective?

~·~·~·~·~·~·~·~·~·~·~·~·~·~·~·~·~·~·~

Ralph sounds as if he were in his Controlling Parent when he wrote the memo, and it's bound to hook the readers' rebellious or sabotaging Child ego states (in some cases maybe the compliant Child). Notice particularly his use of the following words: "appalled," "carelessness," "tolerated," "pay close attention," and "should." Because of this, the memo comes across as a big putdown. So if Ralph's goal is to get better letter writing, he's not likely to achieve it. It's not necessarily wrong to use the Controlling Parent in a memo, but note that Ralph's use of it here leaves a lot to be desired.

~·~·~·~·~·~·~·~·~·~·~·~·~·~·~·~·~·~·~

4   Take a few moments and think about what ego state(s) might be useful in writing the previous memo. Also consider who should get the memo and what ego states in the reader Ralph wishes to activate. Then, with these in mind, rewrite the memo to improve it. (Use a separate sheet of paper.)

~·~·~·~·~·~·~·~·~·~·~·~·~·~·~·~·~·~·~

There's no one right answer for this question, of course. Here's one possibility:

Memo to Ron Smith:

Recently a letter you wrote to Mr. Green concerning his account was forwarded to me for approval. As I'm sure you know, it is important that all official company letters make a good impression on our customers. In reading over your letter, I noticed certain errors in spelling and grammar. I've attached a copy of your letter with the errors circled and some suggested corrections written in. Please use your own judgment in rewriting the letter, giving consideration to my suggested corrections.

The tone and content of your letter are excellent. I suspect you will get a good response from Mr. Green. I'm looking forward to seeing the revised version.

Ralph A. Zimmerman

Ralph A. Zimmerman

Notice that Ralph is now making more use of his Adult ego state. He is writing to a specific person rather than directing his memo to all staff members. Notice the absence of words like "should," "careless-ness," and "expect." Note also that Ralph returns the letter to Ron and trusts him to use his own judgment in rewriting it. This version is much more likely to hook Ron's Adult and result in a rational response.

Besides Adult information, other elements are important for effective writing. A sense of humor or excitement (Child) and concern or caring (Parent) also add zip to your writing.

APPLICATION

Imagine that this letter arrives in a business office:

Please forward this letter to my husband, Mr. Grumbach. I don't know where he has gone! He left me last month and I do want so much to find him. Can you help me, please!

Now examine the reply to Mrs. Grumbach's letter:

Regarding your request to forward a letter to your husband, Mr. Grumbach, we would like to inform you that our office cannot take the time to provide such services.

You should know that we cannot be expected to have such information regarding your husband's whereabouts. We expect that in the future you will look elsewhere for such information. Thank you. Returned herewith is the letter you wanted sent on to Mr. Grumbach.

1 What ego state was the writer probably using? _____

2 What ego state is likely to be actived in Mrs. Grumbach? _____

~ • ~ • ~ • ~ • ~ • ~ • ~ • ~ • ~ • ~ • ~ • ~ • ~ • ~ • ~

The letter seems to come from the Controlling Parent and will probably hook Mrs. Grumbach's Adapted Child or Parent.

~ • ~ • ~ • ~ • ~ • ~ • ~ • ~ • ~ • ~ • ~ • ~ • ~ • ~ • ~

3 Now try your hand at rewriting the letter to Mrs. Grumbach. (Consider using some active listening.)

~ . ~ . ~ . ~ . ~ . ~ . ~ . ~ . ~ . ~ . ~ . ~ . ~ . ~ . ~ . ~ . ~ . ~

You could rewrite this letter in many ways. You may wish to compare your answer with the actual letter written by the Social Security Administration (an excellent one!):

> We are sorry that we cannot help you by forwarding the enclosed letter to your husband, Mr. Grumbach.
>
> We can understand your desire to get in touch with your husband and realize that you are anxious to obtain information about him. Unfortunately, we can be of no help to you in forwarding the enclosed letter as we have no record of any address at which your husband could possibly be contacted.[2]

You've seen that it can be useful to consider your ego states as a writer and also the ego states that are likely to be activated in your readers. This is particularly important in writing memos that are designed to implement new management decisions. Such memos, if they are written from a critical Parent position, will often activate an undesirable Child ego state in the reader.

The overuse of the Controlling Parent is classical in organizational writing. But there can be other ego-states problems. For example, a memo can have too much Adult and consequently be boring and lifeless. Or the over-Adapted Child may smother the pages with big words in an attempt to impress rather than express.

SUMMARY

In this chapter you've learned to:

— do something to activate your Little Professor, Natural Child, or Adult when you feel fearful of starting a transaction;
— recognize situations in which it would be better not to transact, and then find a way to excuse yourself;
— when appropriate, keep transactions open until you achieve your goals by:

> stroking people's activated ego states with such techniques as active listening and fogging;
> asking adult questions;
> making your criticism constructive;
> disagreeing assertively;

— choose from a variety of techniques to end transactions when necessary—for example:

> explain your need to leave;
> show a desire to meet again;
> summarize;
> give a nonverbal signal;

— consider ego states in written messages.

We've designed these tips to increase the productivity of your transactions. In the next chapter you'll learn how to give and get more autonomy.

SOURCE NOTES

[1] Manuel J. Smith, *When I Say No, I Feel Guilty* (New York: Dial Press, 1975), p. 104.
[2] Rudolf Flesch, *How to Say What You Mean in Plain English* (New York: Harper & Row, 1974), p. 99.

16

Encouraging Autonomy

As you are aware, autonomy is one of the main goals of transactional analysis. Unfortunately, many jobs do not promote the awareness, spontaneity, and authenticity that autonomy releases. All too often people think of themselves as cogs in a wheel and their uniqueness gets swallowed up by their jobs. In this chapter we'll give you some ideas on how to attack this problem, how to strengthen autonomous behavior. Every time workers increase their self-reliance level, the boss's freedom level rises, too. Everybody wins.

OBJECTIVES

When you finish this chapter, you'll be able to:

- identify and draw ego-state diagrams of symbiotic relationships;
- suggest ways of redesigning jobs to promote greater worker autonomy;
- predict what will likely happen to productivity, job turnover, absenteeism, and learning time when jobs are redesigned to permit more worker autonomy;
- identify ways of conveying positive expectations to subordinates;
- identify appropriate ways to ask for greater autonomy in your job.

Let's start with the idea of symbiosis.

SYMBIOSIS

If supervisors come on consistently from their Parent and Adult ego states, the Parent and Adult are then discouraged in subordinates. The Child is encouraged. The result is a symbiotic relationship, which we can diagram as shown on the next page.

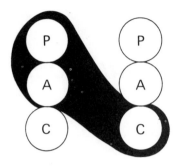

Superior   Subordinate

The word *symbiosis* literally means the living together of two dissimilar organisms (*sym* meaning "together" and *biosis* meaning "live"). Notice that together the supervisor and the subordinate make up what we normally think of as total personality: Parent, Adult, and Child. But notice that neither person is whole. The supervisor doesn't function from the Child and the subordinate makes little use of the Parent and Adult ego states.

APPLICATION ─────────────

Would you say that a symbiotic relationship between a supervisor and a subordinate is a desirable one? Why or why not?

~ . ~ . ~ . ~ . ~ . ~ . ~ . ~ . ~ . ~ . ~ . ~ . ~ . ~ . ~ . ~ . ~ . ~

We believe that in most cases a symbiotic relationship is undesirable because only part of each person's resources are being used. Consequently, the organization suffers because of the wasted human resources —energy as well as talent.

Here's a classic example of a nonproductive symbiotic relationship.

Example

At a well-known stock-brokerage firm the processing of stock certificates was broken into many small, simple tasks. Clerks carried out only a few of these tasks and had little, if any, knowledge of the end result. So the clerks could make no Adult decisions regarding the processing of the certificates. Similarly they could not use their Parent ego states. For example, they couldn't reject improperly prepared certificates. In effect, their *supervisors* were supplying their Parent and Adult ego states. This was tiring for the supervisors! Sometimes they spent four hours on the phone just answering questions from brokers.

APPLICATION ———————————————————————————

1 Picture a situation like the stock-brokerage firm in which one supervisor has a symbiotic relationship with, say, five subordinates. In the ego-state diagram below, draw the lines needed to show the symbiotic relationship.

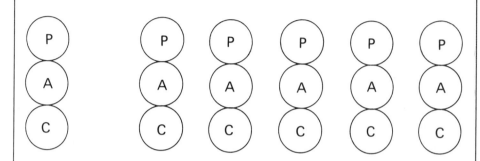

Superior   Subordinates

~ · ~ · ~ · ~ · ~ · ~ · ~ · ~ · ~ · ~ · ~ · ~ · ~ · ~ · ~ · ~ · ~ · ~

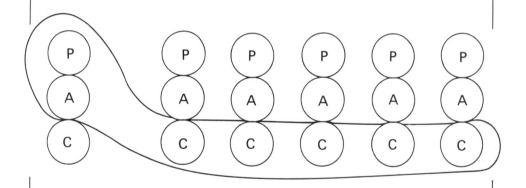

~ · ~ · ~ · ~ · ~ · ~ · ~ · ~ · ~ · ~ · ~ · ~ · ~ · ~ · ~ · ~ · ~ · ~

2 In the situations where one superior is supervising five subordinates, how many ego states are available to work for the organization? _____

3 How many ego states seem to be doing most of the work in the above symbiotic relationship? _____

~ · ~ · ~ · ~ · ~ · ~ · ~ · ~ · ~ · ~ · ~ · ~ · ~ · ~ · ~ · ~ · ~ · ~

   2 There are potentially eighteen ego states.
   3 It seems that only seven ego states are doing most of the work: the five subordinates' Child ego states and the supervisor's Parent and Adult.

~ · ~ · ~ · ~ · ~ · ~ · ~ · ~ · ~ · ~ · ~ · ~ · ~ · ~ · ~ · ~ · ~ · ~

4 Now let's take a look at another example:

> Karen was given the task of sorting bills into three piles. She made one pile
> for bills under $10, another for bills between $10 and $25, and a third for
> bills over $25. After doing this, she was to pass the pile of bills to another
> worker.

On the basis of what you've learned, would you say that this person's job was
well designed? Why or why not?

~ . ~ . ~ . ~ . ~ . ~ . ~ . ~ . ~ . ~ . ~ . ~ . ~ . ~ . ~

4 We would say that the job design leaves a lot to be desired. After
months of work, Karen was bored stiff and ready to quit.[1] She had
no challenge for her Parent or Adult ego states, a classic case of a
symbiotic relationship.

REDESIGNING JOBS FOR GREATER AUTONOMY

Fortunately, we can redesign jobs and give employees at all levels more autonomy. For example, the department redesigned Karen's job and put her in
charge of handling an entire account, from credit payments to returning un-
signed checks to customers. "This is really great," Karen was overheard saying,
"I feel like I'm really accomplishing something now. I feel that what I do
directly affects what the customer gets."[2]

Notice the difference. When Karen had little autonomy, she was ready to
quit. With the new job structure, she was happy with her work. A number of
studies have shown that when workers are given more autonomy, they are
not only happier but also more productive. Problems associated with lateness
and absenteeism also tend to disappear.[3-6]

If desired, it's possible to give workers at many levels more autonomy in
a number of ways. One is to arrange things so that when employees finish a
meaningful increment of work, they can look back and say, "That's what I
did." In this way they can take pride in what they've done and feel a sense
of accomplishment.

Mike, a laborer in a steel mill, is quoted by Studs Terkel in his book
Working:

> . . . I would like to see a building, say, the Empire State, I would like to see on
> one side of it a foot-wide strip from top to bottom with the name of every bricklayer,
> the name of every electrician, with all the names. So when a guy walked by, he could
> take his son and say, "See, that's me over there on the forty-fifth floor. I put the
> steel beam in." Picasso can point to a painting. What can I point to? A writer can
> point to a book. Everybody should have something to point to.[7]

In a study at AT&T by Ford,[8] it was found that employees were more
productive when they were encouraged to be more autonomous. In one
situation a group of women were in charge of correspondence. Typically,

every letter they prepared had to be checked by a supervisor before it could be mailed. When the job was redesigned, the women took responsibility for their own letters and signed them themselves. Also, the writers were encouraged to be original and to avoid a strict form-letter approach. From a TA viewpoint, the original job's design established an unproductive, symbiotic relationship between the letter writers and their supervisors. In the new arrangement the supervisors stroked the correspondents' Adult ego states and avoided forcing them to get Parental approval.

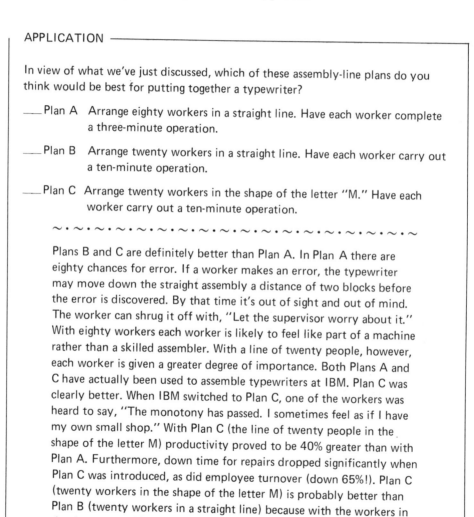

APPLICATION

In view of what we've just discussed, which of these assembly-line plans do you think would be best for putting together a typewriter?

____ Plan A   Arrange eighty workers in a straight line. Have each worker complete a three-minute operation.

____ Plan B   Arrange twenty workers in a straight line. Have each worker carry out a ten-minute operation.

____ Plan C   Arrange twenty workers in the shape of the letter "M." Have each worker carry out a ten-minute operation.

Plans B and C are definitely better than Plan A. In Plan A there are eighty chances for error. If a worker makes an error, the typewriter may move down the straight assembly a distance of two blocks before the error is discovered. By that time it's out of sight and out of mind. The worker can shrug it off with, "Let the supervisor worry about it." With eighty workers each worker is likely to feel like part of a machine rather than a skilled assembler. With a line of twenty people, however, each worker is given a greater degree of importance. Both Plans A and C have actually been used to assemble typewriters at IBM. Plan C was clearly better. When IBM switched to Plan C, one of the workers was heard to say, "The monotony has passed. I sometimes feel as if I have my own small shop." With Plan C (the line of twenty people in the shape of the letter M) productivity proved to be 40% greater than with Plan A. Furthermore, down time for repairs dropped significantly when Plan C was introduced, as did employee turnover (down 65%!). Plan C (twenty workers in the shape of the letter M) is probably better than Plan B (twenty workers in a straight line) because with the workers in the shape of an M each worker can see the typewriter as it is passed from person to person. If a problem develops at one point, an assembler can easily walk over and talk to a fellow worker.

In another study, at a one-year-old plant of the Butler Manufacturing Company, similar results were obtained through job redesign. In the traditional job structure, employees worked in assembly-line fashion. Each worker knew how to do one quick assembly procedure but knew little, if anything, about the total assembly process. The *World of Work Report* explains that under a new system, employees were given more responsibility:

> The employees, who work together as team members, handle most production scheduling and support functions by themselves. Most workers are knowledgeable about all of the production steps necessary to assemble Butler's $25,000 two-story-high grain dryers, involving the assembly of as many as 3,000 parts, in Story City, Iowa (population 2,000).[9]

As part of their work, these employees also help to design new products, tools, and ways of handling equipment. In some cases, they are able to buy tools and materials themselves with authorization from the supervisor needed only for purchases amounting to more than $200.

Benefits to the Butler plant include reduced absenteeism (down to 1.2% from a typical 4–5%) and turnover cut to 12% (compared to an average of about 35%). The plant manager, Mr. Hayes, has high praise for the new system: "We are probably 10% higher in profitability than comparable operations elsewhere which have been in business for 10 years or more."[10]

So in giving workers a greater degree of autonomy, we suggest giving them a special domain. For example, give them a certain group of customers, a certain section of a building, a certain part of the machine—a certain something—that they and they alone are responsible for. Then give them the authority to do what they need to do to choose success in their particular domain. Now, let's return to the stock-brokerage firm and see how this might work.

APPLICATION

As you will recall, in the stock-brokerage firm the processing of stock certificates was broken down into many small, simple tasks. Each clerk carried out a few tasks and had little, if any, knowledge of the end result. Only the supervisors could answer questions from brokers and they often spent half their day doing just that. How might this job situation be redesigned to improve productivity?

~ . ~ . ~ . ~ . ~ . ~ . ~ . ~ . ~ . ~ . ~ . ~ . ~ . ~ . ~ . ~ . ~ . ~

At Merrill Lynch, where a dependent relationship between clerical workers and supervisors seemed to exist, the clerical job was redesigned so that each clerk could handle all of the office work on a single certificate and take responsibility for it. When a clerk disallowed a certificate that was unacceptable, the clerk signed his or her name and telephone extension and handled any calls from brokers. In a *Wall Street Journal* article, one of the supervisors praised the new system like this:

"This has cut 70% of my phone calls . . . . Now for the first time, I really have time for planning," he says. Among other things, he now is planning how the office can add an additional function without increasing the number of workers.[11]

A big advantage in giving workers more autonomy is that it is possible to give them more meaningful feedback about the quantity or quality of their work. For example, at Merrill Lynch when clerks were allowed to handle all of the office work on a certificate, it was easy to give them feedback on the quality of their work on that certificate. As a result, productivity climbed and error rate dropped.[12]

APPLICATION

Suppose the janitorial service in a large firm is poor. Crews of maintenance people work on cleaning the entire office building. On a rotating basis, one person is assigned to sweeping the floors, another person cleans the restrooms, another person empties waste cans, and so on. If a worker does an especially good job of cleaning the floors but the one in charge of cleaning the windows doesn't do his or her job, no one notices the clean floors but many people complain about the dirty windows. What changes might be made to improve this situation considering the guidelines for job design that we have been discussing?

~ . ~ . ~ . ~ . ~ . ~ . ~ . ~ . ~ . ~ . ~ . ~ . ~ . ~ . ~ . ~ . ~

One solution might be to divide the plant into sections and make each worker the boss of his or her own section. Each person would be responsible for keeping his or her section clean — everything from sweeping the floor to cleaning the toilets. That way each person could feel a sense of accomplishment for taking care of an area designated as his or her own.

Interestingly, the above solution was proposed by a janitor who surprised his boss by complaining, "I never get to clean the toilets." But the janitor's complaint made a lot of sense:

All I do is sweep the floor. Nobody ever notices if the floor is really clean when the rest of the place is dirty. Would you let me have one section of the plant, 1/40 of it, and let me sweep the floor, clean the desks, dump the wastepaper baskets, clean the toilets, do everything there is to do? Just let it be my section. Then all I'll ask is that you'll look at my section every morning and compare it to someone else's section. I think I can do the best job on the crew and I want to prove it.[13]

The boss was Clair Vough. He has since become an expert on designing jobs for maximum worker productivity.

So far we've stressed the importance of allowing workers to:

— be responsible for meaningful outcomes;
— see the outcome of their work in some real way;
— get meaningful feedback;
— feel they are their own bosses.

Another good way to encourage people toward autonomy is to give them some responsibilities normally reserved for management. For example, workers can be taught to test and inspect their own work, set their own goals, participate in problem-solving discussions, and develop improved work procedures.

In his book, *Creating More Meaningful Work*, Fred Foulkes describes how this management philosophy increased productivity at a division of Texas Instruments (TI).[14] A group of women at TI were paid hourly wages to assemble a complex instrument for a government contract. The assembly procedures had been set up by an engineering department. The group was assembling one unit in about 138 hours. At this rate the company was losing money fast. The supervisors decided to try giving the women more autonomy in deciding how to do their jobs. They held a meeting and asked the women to decide on new work procedures that might improve production. They also asked the workers to set a production standard—that is, to decide on about how many hours they needed to produce one unit. The group arrived at a standard of 86 hours (the industrial engineers had set a standard of 100 hours—the actual time, remember, had been 138 hours).

In granting the workers more autonomy, the supervisors gave them much more information than such workers would normally have access to, even information about costs and the details of the government contract normally seen only by managers. Furthermore, workers were allowed to interview engineers and ask for their help in arranging the work flow.

APPLICATION ───

What do you think happened?

____ (a) The workers ended up taking more time than before to assemble one unit.

____ (b) The group made no improvement.

____ (c) The group met their goal of producing one unit in 86 hours.

____ (d) The group exceeded their goal.

~ • ~ • ~ • ~ • ~ • ~ • ~ • ~ • ~ • ~ • ~ • ~ • ~ • ~ • ~ • ~ • ~

In fact, they exceeded their goal (d). They were able to assemble one unit in 75 hours, three-fourths of the engineering standard! Even more exciting: the group of workers held successive meetings to brainstorm new and better procedures and the time needed to assemble one unit dropped to 57 hours and later to 32 hours!

The approach spread to other groups within the division at Texas Instruments. As a result the entire division began performing much better. Foulkes reports that the approach helped TI to get extra government contracts for the particular product involved.[15]

APPLICATION ────────────────────────────────

What effect do you think this approach had on such things as: absenteeism, turnover, learning time, complaints, and so on?

~ • ~ • ~ • ~ • ~ • ~ • ~ • ~ • ~ • ~ • ~ • ~ • ~ • ~ • ~ • ~ • ~

At Texas Instruments, there were fewer complaints, workers took *less* time to do their jobs, and absenteeism and turnover dropped.

The role of a supervisor is quite different when workers can use all three ego states on the job. This is illustrated in our next application.

APPLICATION ────────────────────────────────

Below are some actions typical of supervisors. The actions are grouped in pairs. In each pair check the action that *best* characterizes a supervisor who is helping subordinates develop more autonomy.

1 ___ (a) Determine objectives and work standards; meet with subordinates to inform them of such.

___ (b) Work with subordinates in setting up goals and work standards.

2 ___ (a) Offer workers a variety of learning resources about their jobs.

___ (b) Train workers how to do their jobs.

3 ___ (a) Show workers how they can check their own performance.

___ (b) Check all work done by subordinates to make sure it is correct.

4 ___ (a) Develop and implement new work methods so that subordinates can maximize their productivity.

___ (b) Give workers a chance to learn principles of work simplification and apply them to their own jobs.

5 ___ (a) Reward employees for doing their job according to the company operations manual.

___ (b) Reward employees for inventing time- or cost-saving procedures.

6 ___ (a) Encourage subordinates to work smarter.

___ (b) Encourage subordinates to work harder.

~ . ~ . ~ . ~ . ~ . ~ . ~ . ~ . ~ . ~ . ~ . ~ . ~ . ~ . ~ . ~

1 (b); 2 (a); 3 (a); 4 (b); 5 (b); 6 (a).

Although research shows that encouraging autonomy often produces good results, employees who are not used to self-reliance in work situations can have difficulty if they are suddenly asked to use their own initiative to solve problems. One good way to minimize this problem is to expect that others will be able to handle the assignments you give them. Research suggests that when supervisors expect good performance from subordinates, they are more likely to get it than when they have no special expectations. For example, the following experiment is reported in the McGraw-Hill film, *Productivity and the Self-Fulfilling Prophecy: The Pygmalion Effect.*

> At a vocational training center for the hardcore unemployed, an experimenter, Dr. Alfred King, told a welding instructor that 5 of his trainees had an exceptional aptitude for welding. In reality, of course, the 5 men had been chosen at random. During the 6-month period, however, those high aptitude personnel, or HAPS as they grew to be called, changed their behavior significantly. They were absent fewer times than the control group. They learned the fundamentals of welding at little more than half the time. They scored 10 points higher on a comprehensive welding test.[16]

Robert Rosenthal points out that we can convey positive expectations to subordinates in four basic ways.[17] We can do it by:

— *Creating a positive climate when we interact.* If our tone of voice is cordial, if we make relaxed eye contact, smile appropriately, and turn our body toward the person we're talking with, we will convey a feeling of trust to others.

— *Giving others adequate feedback on their performance.* If we expect that others *can* handle challenges, think creatively, assume responsibility, and so on, then we will give them the feedback they need to be successful. (Conversely, if we doubt that people can be autonomous, we will tend to withhold feedback, thinking that it won't be used anyway. In one particular case, for example, typists performed poorly because they were not given feedback about the accuracy of their work. Instead, pages with typing errors were forwarded to a special "corrections group.")[18]

— *Giving people adequate input.* If we have positive expectations, we will not only provide feedback but will give people whatever information, supplies, or resources they need for success. The people at Texas Instruments did this when they gave the women who were assembling the complex electronic instruments access to engineering consultants and to other information normally reserved for management.

— *Encouraging output.* If we expect that employees can assume more responsibility, we will give them opportunities to expand their potential and, perhaps, even reward them for doing so. For example, at the IBM typewriter-assembly plant, workers are encouraged to take more responsibility. All employees are trained in work-simplification procedures. If a worker thinks of a way that he or she can assume more responsibility and thus become more productive, the worker is allowed to do so and is given a corresponding bonus in pay.

You can also convey your positive expectations to others by asking Adult questions rather than sending solution messages. When another person comes to us with a problem, our first impulse is often to play the Rescuer and say, "Why don't you . . . ?" or "I suggest that you . . . ." or "The best way to do this is . . . ." Although this *may* or may not solve the person's immediate problem, it does little to encourage that person to be autonomous. In fact, it may encourage a sense of being a Victim. A more productive approach is to ask a series of Adult questions such as:

"How do you think things are going now?"
"How do you feel about that?"
"How would you like them to go? To look? To feel?"
"Is there anything you might do?"
"What is your plan?"
"Is there anything I can do to help?"

At a more advanced level, you might ask, "What questions might you ask yourself that would help you solve this problem?"

APPLICATION ──────────────────────────────

1 In the following example, Jack is giving Rick an assignment. In what way is Jack conveying positive expectations regarding Rick's ability to operate as an autonomous person? (Make notes beneath the illustrations.)

~.~

As far as we can tell, Jack is conveying no positive expectation at all.
He is creating a negative climate with his lack of eye contact, flat facial
expression, and turned-away body position. Notice too that Jack did
not give Rick any clear feedback on his proposal but merely made a
sweeping statement that it didn't hang together. When Rick asked for
more responsibility, Jack discouraged him.

~.~

2   Now here's another example. In what way is the supervisor (Steve) conveying his
positive expectations? (Make notes beneath the illustrations.)

Steve is conveying his positive expectation by his body language
(pleasant facial expression, eye contact, gestures, and body position),
by providing specific feedback (need for better transitions), by providing input (the suggestion to see Irene, the editor), and by encouraging
output (lining up additional challenging projects).

WHEN YOU WANT MORE AUTONOMY

So far we've been talking about autonomy from the viewpoint of a superior
who may want to redesign jobs for subordinates. But chances are that you
yourself may be restless or frustrated because you have not been given the
responsibility you believe you can handle. If that's the case, you might consider having a leveling session with your superiors in which you let them

know what you would like. (See "Leveling" on page 344.) Or you might consider writing a memo in which you outline in detail what you believe you can do.

You might also try assuming responsibilities on your own. For example, one clerk was given the job of keeping track of the sale of certain items in her department. (The department was primarily research-oriented and the sale of certain research publications was a sideline.) The clerk studied accounting on her own and developed a well-organized bookkeeping system. Consequently, as sales expanded, the clerk was given increased responsibility with an increase in salary.

Caution! In taking new responsibilities, don't go against the existing company policy or procedure. And be careful not to invade someone else's territory on your own. Also, when asking for more responsibilities, use good transactional techniques:

— Keep your Adult in gear.
— Stroke your supervisor's activated ego states.
— Ask Adult questions.

Show your strengths in acceptable ways.

APPLICATION ————————————————————

Lawrence was a clerk in a credit department of a large department store. Frequently irate customers called him to complain about losing a credit balance of 47¢ or so. When this happened he was required by his supervisor to tell the customer that it was the store's policy to drop a credit balance of less than $1.00 if the credit balance had not been used within six months. He was also to tell the customer that this policy was explained on the back of each monthly statement. If a customer continued to complain, Lawrence was required to refer the customer to his supervisor, who always OK'd a small credit balance. Lawrence not only felt angry, but he also felt that he would be able to save his supervisor a lot of time if he were given authority to reinstate credit balances as long as they didn't exceed a specified amount.

Suppose Lawrence decides to ask his supervisor for more responsibility. Which of these ways would probably get the best results?

____ (a) "I have an idea that I think can save you some time. You know those angry customers that call you from time to time complaining about the fact that we've canceled their credit balance? Since you always OK it, how about giving me the authority to OK it for you as long as the credit doesn't exceed a certain amount. That way you won't have to use your time handling those customers. Also the customers will be happier because I'll be able to give them an immediate answer."

____ (b) "You know those customers who have been upset because they feel they've been cheated out of 50¢ or so? It makes me really mad that you haven't given me authority in the first place to handle these customers' requests.

> You should delegate the authority to me to make 50¢ decisions. After all, you always OK their requests anyway. It's just a waste of your time to have to deal with these customers. How about letting me OK the credit as long as it isn't above a certain amount?"

___ (c) Lawrence starts OKing credit himself. Then he goes to his supervisor and says: "I just wanted to tell you that I've been OKing credit when customers call in complaining about losing a credit balance. I think you should delegate to me the authority to make 47¢ decisions. If you had done this earlier, you'd have saved yourself a lot of time. I'm perfectly willing to take the responsibility for it. It's really upsetting for me to have to argue with customers about such matters. It's really unfair to them since they feel that they are truly being cheated."

~ • ~ • ~ • ~ • ~ • ~ • ~ • ~ • ~ • ~ • ~ • ~ • ~ • ~

We prefer choice (a). Notice that in choice (a) the speaker is phrasing the request in terms of the benefits to the supervisor. Notice, too, that in choices (b) and (c) several words and phrases sound rather Critical Parent. Such an approach is likely to hook the supervisor's not-OK Child. If this happens, the supervisor is likely to get angry and come back with a scolding response, trying to out-Parent the subordinate.

SUMMARY

In many work situations a symbiotic relationship exists between superiors and subordinates, which tends to be wasteful because not all ego states are given a chance to function. When workers are given greater autonomy, they can use all their ego states. As a result, both productivity and job satisfaction tend to increase. When redesigning jobs for greater worker autonomy, it's useful to:

— allow workers to see in some meaningful way how their work contributes to the final product;
— give workers feedback on how what they are doing is affecting the final product;
— allow workers to plan, set goals, deadlines, and work procedures;
— let employees learn and apply work-simplification theory;
— arrange a way for them to be rewarded for working smarter rather than harder.

You can encourage self-reliance in others by sending positive messages, offering meaningful feedback, giving adequate input, and providing opportunities for growth. In addition, you can encourage autonomy by asking Adult questions to help people solve their own problems rather than always giving solutions.

On the other hand, if you'd like more autonomy in *your* job, you may need to ask for it or to begin to assume it on your own. If so, use all the transactional techniques you have learned and keep your Adult in gear!

SOURCE NOTES

[1] Roger Rickleff, "Boredom Fighters Put Variety in Many Jobs, Find Productivity Rises," *The Wall Street Journal*, August 21, 1972.

[2] *Ibid.*

[3] W. W. Dettleback and P. Kraft, "Organization Change Through Job Enrichment," *Training and Development Journal*, 1971, 25:2-6.

[4] F. P. Doyle, "Job Enrichment Plus OD—A Two-Pronged Approach at Western Union," in J. R. Maher (ed.), *New Perspectives in Job Enrichment* (New York: Van Nostrand Reinhold, 1971), pp. 193-205.

[5] E. M. Glaser, *Improving the Quality of Worklife . . . And in the Process, Improving Productivity* (Los Angeles: Human Interaction Research Institute, 1974), pp. 53-56, 106-112.

[6] Raymond A. Katzell, Penney Bienstock, and Paul H. Faerstein, *A Guide to Worker Productivity Experiments in the United States, 1971-1975*, prepared for Work in America Institute, Scarsdale, N.Y. (New York: New York University Press, 1977).

[7] Studs Terkel, *Working*. (New York: Random House—Pantheon, 1974), p. xxxii.

[8] Robert Ford, *Motivation Through the Work Itself* (New York: American Management Association, 1969), p. 26. See also Dorothy Jongeward, *Everybody Wins: Transactional Analysis Applied to Organizations* (Reading, Mass.: Addison-Wesley, 1976), p. 74.

[9] "Self-Managed Teams at Butler Plant Cut Costs, Raise Profitability," *World of Work Report*, November 1977, 2(II):124.

[10] *Ibid.*, p. 125.

[11] Rickleff, *op. cit.*

[12] *Ibid.*

[13] Clair Vough with Bernard Asbell, *Tapping the Human Resource* (New York: AMACOM —a division of American Management Associations, 1975), pp. 83-84.

[14] Fred Foulkes, *Creating More Meaningful Work* (New York: American Management Association, 1969), p. 62.

[15] *Ibid.*

[16] *Productivity and the Self-Fulfilling Prophecy: The Pygmalion Effect*, Joan Owens, producer/director (Del Mar, Calif.: CRM/McGraw-Hill Films, 1975).

[17] *Ibid.*

[18] Dettleback and Kraft, *op. cit.*, p. 2.

17

Transacting Authentically

Autonomy paves the way for the possibility of transacting authentically. When you transact authentically, you are being yourself as a whole person. You are using the resources from all your ego states, rather than being an actor playing phony roles. Authentic transactions are open, honest, and straightforward. They can stir in us feelings of tenderness, empathy, and affection—intimacy. When you transact authentically, you genuinely care about the other person. You're not just passing time, engaging in ritual strokes, playing games, or exploiting people. Rather, you are relating at a much deeper level—a level that tends to hold meaning for both parties and reaffirms the significance of people.

OBJECTIVES

When you finish this chapter, you'll be able to apply some skills that encourage authentic transactions. It's important to realize that authentic transactions *can* occur at work. As expressed in *Born to Win*, "Any activities such as going to a concert, digging in a garden, burying a dog, or working on a proposal serve as a context in which intimacy can occur."[1] For example:

> A father looks into the tear-soiled face of his son who has just buried his dog. He puts his arm around the boy and says, "It's tough to bury a good friend." The boy melts into his father's arms, releasing his grief. For that moment they are close.
> Two men work together for several weeks preparing an important proposal for the company. One presents it to management and the proposal is rejected. When he returns, his colleague looks into his face, and without words a feeling of understanding for their mutual disappointment passes between them.[2]

True, many times authentic transactions seem scary. Whenever we start a transaction that may involve closeness, we're taking a chance—a chance that we may be rejected or otherwise hurt. But for many people it's worth the chance. In fact, many people say that they would never go back to their old ways of being a slave to Parent tapes that say, "Keep your distance."

Caution: We're not suggesting that you go charging off and immediately hug all the people you work with. But we are suggesting that you recognize the significance of people as frequently as possible. And, who knows, maybe there's someone that it would be perfectly OK for you to hug!

In reaching for more authentic transactions, you need not set yourself up to be hurt. The transactional skills you'll learn in this chapter will help to increase your chances of being successful at transacting authentically.

LEVELING

One way to risk authenticity is to express genuine thoughts and feelings in straightforward leveling transactions. Here are some guidelines to help you level more effectively.

Make an Appointment But Deal with the Problem as Soon as Possible

To "make the appointment," say something to let the other person know you have something important on your mind that you want to talk over. This gives that person a mental set. Once you say something like, "There's something I need to talk with you about," arrange to have the discussion right away so that no unnecessary time is spent on worrying about "what's in store."

Arrange Your Physical Positions for Maximum Openness

Let's say you're leveling with George, one of your co-workers. If George is sitting and you're standing, this arrangement may promote a Parent-Child atmosphere, hardly conducive to an Adult-Adult transaction. To avoid this, make sure your eye level is approximately the same as George's. (It might be helpful to use the word "level" to remind yourself that if you transact face to face at eye level, you'll have a much better chance of transacting authentically.)

If George is sitting, pull up a chair and join him. Move comfortably close. Sitting close helps you to focus on the other person, to be aware of facial expressions, eye movements, and other nonverbal messages. If you keep too much distance physically, you're not likely to get close psychologically. In addition, avoid things coming between you, such as a large desk.

Get Right to the Problem

A warm hello is important to help the other person feel at ease and a brief pastime may help break the ice, but too much meaningless chatter only tends to increase tension. State the problem as directly as you can from your point of view. Avoid sending ulterior messages. Some of us "talk crooked," especially if we were brought up in families where people didn't say what they meant. As a result, rather than talking straight now, we may still state wishes and send out innuendoes that need to be interpreted by others. For example, we might say, "I really like potatoes," rather than, "Please pass the potatoes. They're really good." Or we might look longingly into our empty glass instead of asking, "May I have a refill, please?" So, later on the job we may say things like, "Gee, I wish I had a copy of that last printout," rather than, "Would you send me a copy of that last printout?"

When leveling, put the problem as straight as possible. Avoid asking the other person to read your mind.

Send "I" Messages Rather Than Accusative "You" Messages

"I am disappointed that your report is not ready for the board meeting," is more effective than, "You never get anything done on time." Such a "you" message is threatening and may encourage others to feel defensive and angry. Furthermore, it probably won't improve performance. In contrast, an "I" message presents the problem from your point of view and allows both of you to deal with it in a more Adult way.

Stress the Positive Whenever Possible

Often when we express our thoughts and feelings, we focus on the negative things that other people have done. When we do this, we are stroking others for their undesirable behavior and maybe strengthening it. To avoid this problem, we can stress the positive in a number of ways. For example, we can refer to a person's past good performances or accomplishments. In doing this, our goal is to strengthen the assumption that the person is OK: that he or she is basically confident, competent, and intelligent.

Avoid Discounting

Discounting reflects a lack of positive affirmation. Otto Altorfer points out that "discounts come from a not-OK position" and that "they distort the reality of self, others, or a situation through exaggeration, minimizing, or ignoring."[3] Discounting shows up in many ways around problem solving. Both people and situations can be perceived of as "less" than they really are in at least four ways:

— The problem itself is not taken seriously. You may have experienced this when someone unnecessarily gabbed on the phone while you sat anxiously waiting for their attention. You got the message, "Nobody cares."
— The significance of the problem is denied. You may have heard the complaint, "You're just making something out of nothing—always making mountains out of molehills. Don't take it so seriously."
— The solvability of the problem is denied. "There is nothing that can be done about people who keep turning up late for work. It's just impossible."
— A person denies her or his own capacity, or the capacity of others, to solve a problem. "I can't help it if I didn't get that information for you on time. Everything's not always my fault." Or, on the flip side, someone may have denied *your* capacity to solve a problem: "I don't think you can handle it."[4]

Being discounted not only is painful, but it also blocks problem solving. When problems are denied or not taken seriously, they go unsolved and our leveling session becomes a waste of time.

Listen

When leveling, probably the most important thing to do is to listen. Instead of asking questions like, "Don't you agree that . . ." reflect back what you hear other people saying and guess how they're feeling. This gives you a chance to understand their side of the issue. More importantly, you will let them know you are genuinely concerned about their ideas and opinions and are not discounting them.

Avoid Talking About Past Mistakes

Sometimes it's a temptation to dump everything on a person once we get started. If you find yourself reaching back to irrelevant previous errors, you could detract from the importance of the matter under discussion. Also, by throwing in the kitchen sink, you may encourage others to indulge in unproductive feelings of guilt or resentment. Check your motive: Is it to cash in stamps or solve a problem?

Reach a Mutual Agreement

If you both agree on a solution, the leveling session can be satisfying for both of you. This may mean a compromise of some sort. If you simply dictate a solution, the other person may not feel committed to follow through.

Reconfirm Your Agreement

"So, let me restate what I think we've decided . . . . Is that the way you see it, too?" Doing this will help to ensure that you have both agreed to the same thing. At this point a good handshake will affirm your agreement and conclude your session.

Caution: This leveling process is useful when you want to set up mutual Adult problem solving and to express genuine feelings. But if these are *not* your objectives, a leveling session will probably look, feel, and be phony to you. For example, if your Critical Parent is in control and you have an ulterior objective to punish the other person, or if your Child wants to cash in resentments, a phony leveling session will only hurt future communications.

To ensure that your Adult is in charge when you want to level, ask yourself these questions. "Will I:

- deal with this problem as soon as possible?"
- arrange the setting for maximum openness?"
- get right to the problem?"
- send 'I' messages and avoid accusative 'you' messages?"
- stress the positive?"
- avoid discounting?"
- listen?"
- avoid talking about past mistakes?"
- arrive at a mutual agreement?"
- confirm the final decision?"

APPLICATION ───

In the following incident an office worker, whom we'll call Edwin, "levels" with a subordinate. Read over this incident and decide which of the ten guidelines Edwin is following. Also, decide whether or not Edwin is effective in his attempt at leveling.

Edwin felt embarrassed because Roy, his subordinate, criticized him loudly several times within earshot of the department manager and two other workers. Although Edwin was upset about the situation, he hadn't confronted it because Roy was one of his most productive workers.

Edwin stewed about this for awhile and finally decided to level with Roy. The next day, when Roy stopped by, Edwin took advantage of the opportunity.

Roy (poking his head into Edwin's office): "Just wanted to let you know that I am taking my lunch hour now."

Edwin: "That's fine. There is something I need to talk about with you, though. Can we meet this afternoon?"

Roy: "Sure. What's it about?"

Edwin: "I'd like to save it for later, Roy, when we have the time to talk. I'd prefer meeting in your office. OK?" (Roy's office was located in a more isolated and soundproof area.)

Roy: "OK. Anytime this afternoon is fine. I'll be there."

That afternoon Edwin walked into Roy's office feeling a bit nervous about what he was about to say. Roy was sitting at his desk typing. After exchanging greetings, Edwin got right down to business.

Edwin (standing): "Roy, whenever you talk to me, you always raise your voice. Please stop doing that. It is really upsetting to me."

Roy: "I don't always do that. Besides, if I didn't have so much to complain about, I wouldn't have to raise my voice."

Edwin: "Well, I'm sorry. I guess you don't *always* do it. I do feel embarrassed when you criticize me in such a loud voice in front of others. You know, Wally's and Max's offices are right next to mine."

Roy (nods his head knowingly as if he's been criticized before for speaking loudly): "Sorry, I didn't really intend to criticize you today. I was just, you know, giving you some feedback."

Edwin: "OK. I can accept that. It's just that I'm concerned about what my boss thinks when he hears you. Is there some way you can give me feedback in a normal voice and just for my ears?"

Roy: "I could save my feedback for when we go over our agenda for the day. We could do that here in my office—that is, if you don't mind meeting here."

Edwin: "Yes, perhaps. But another thing. When I give you work to do and you don't understand something, you always assume that *my* directions are unclear. Could it be, perhaps, that you haven't read them correctly?"

Roy: "Your directions often aren't clear!"

Edwin: "Maybe not to you. If you can't understand plain English there is nothing I can do about it. And I don't like the idea of discussing problems in my office unless, perhaps, we close the doors, and—"

Roy: "No, I said we could meet in my office, not yours."

Edwin: "Oh, OK. Let's do that from now on. Is there anything else?"

Roy: (shakes his head "No" and remains silent)

Edwin (still standing): "Well, good. That's settled. I need to get back to my office now. I'll talk to you later."

Roy: "OK."

1 What guidelines did Edwin follow?

____(a) Deal with the problem as soon as possible.

____(b) Arrange the setting for maximum openness.

____(c) Get right to the problem.

____(d) Send "I" messages; avoid accusative "you" statements.

____(e) Stress the positive.

____(f) Avoid discounting.

____(g) Listen.

____(h) Avoid talking about past mistakes.

____(i) Arrive at a mutual agreement.

____(j) Confirm the final decision.

2 Do you think Edwin was effective in his effort to level with Roy?

~ • ~ • ~ • ~ • ~ • ~ • ~ • ~ • ~ • ~ • ~ • ~ • ~ • ~ • ~ • ~ • ~ • ~

1 Edwin followed guidelines (a), (c), and (i). Let's consider the ones he didn't follow:

(b) Arrange the setting for maximum openness: He remained standing during the entire discussion, forcing Roy to look up to him. A better approach would have been for Edwin to pull up a chair and meet Roy on his level.

(d) Send "I" messages rather than accusative "you" messages: Edwin went against this guideline with his opening sentence: "Roy, whenever you talk to me, you always raise your voice." Later, he did use an "I" message when he said, "I do feel embarrassed when you criticize me in such a loud voice in front of others." But by that time the damage done by the accusative "you" message had already put Roy on the defensive. A more effective approach would have been to simply start with the "I" messages and avoid the accusative "you" message altogether.

(e) Stress the positive: Edwin gave little if any positive feedback. He missed a good chance to stroke Roy when Roy said, "I could save my complaints for when we go over our agenda for the day." He could have responded with something like, "Yes, that's a good idea, and I'll do the same if that's all right with you."

(f) Avoid discounting: Edwin seems to be discounting Roy's intelligence and importance throughout the conversation in the way he speaks to him. For example, when Roy says, "Your directions often aren't clear!" Edwin simply brushes the statement aside with, "Maybe not to you. If you can't understand plain English, I guess there's nothing I can do about it." Edwin might have avoided discounting by following guideline (g).

(g) Listen: When Roy suggested meeting in his office, Edwin didn't listen. He just went ahead with a negative comment about Roy's inability to understand directions. When Edwin did come back to Roy's suggestion, he repeated it incorrectly showing that he probably didn't hear it correctly in the first place. Edwin could have listened to Roy's suggestion and then responded positively to it right away.

(h) Avoid talking about past mistakes: Edwin went against this guideline when he brushed aside Roy's suggestion and brought up the matter of the clarity of his directions and Roy's "inability" to understand them. Edwin should have stuck to the subject at hand and brought up this matter at another time.

(j) Confirm the final decision: Instead of saying, "Well, that's settled," Edwin could have said, "OK, let me give you my understanding of what we've decided . . . . Is that the way you understand it?" Something like that followed by a handshake would have helped to confirm the final decision.

2 If Edwin had followed the ten guidelines, he might have left Roy's office with a good feeling and a lasting solution to the problem. But the way Edwin handled the situation, he is probably in for more trouble with Roy.

Here's what the transaction might have sounded like if Edwin had followed all of our guidelines. After he had greeted Roy and passed a little time with him about the impending storm, Edwin took a seat as shown in this diagram:

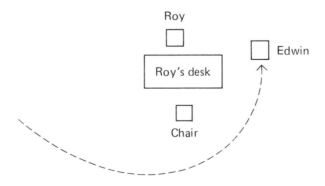

Edwin: "Roy, I'll come right to the point. I'm upset about something that I'd like to straighten out. I feel embarrassed when you criticize me loudly in front of others. I don't know if you're aware you do this, but you know Wally's and Max's offices are right next to mine."

Roy (nods his head knowlingly as if he's been criticized before for speaking loudly): "Sorry, I didn't really intend to criticize you. I was just, you know, giving you some feedback."

Edwin: "OK. I can accept that. It's just that I'm concerned about what my boss thinks when he hears you. Is there some way you can give me feedback in a normal voice and just for *my* ears?"

Roy: "I could save my feedback for when we go over our agenda for the day. We could do that here in my office—that is, if you don't mind meeting here."

Edwin: "OK, that's a good idea. And if I have any negative feedback for you, I'll save it for then, too. All right? While we're talking, I would like you to know that you really contributed a lot to the success of that last project."

Roy (blushing): "Well, er, gee, thanks. I'm glad to know that you . . . er . . . appreciate my work."

Edwin (smiling): "I certainly do, and that's why I'm really glad we were able to reach an agreement. As I understand what we've decided, we'll both save any negative feedback we have for when we go over our agenda and we'll do it here in this office. Is that how you understand it?"

Roy: "Right."

Edwin (rises, smiles, and extends his hand to shake with Roy): "Good!"

Roy (smiles, stands up, and shakes Edwin's hand): "Thanks for leveling with me about this."

Leveling often brings about a change in the quadrants of the Johari awareness model. For example, Edwin decided not to hide his feelings but to express them to Roy. His feedback touched Roy's Blind Self and he became aware of a behavior that had not been clear to him before. Since the problem was open between Edwin and Roy, they were able to come to a mutually satisfying agreement.

The rewards of skillful leveling can be great. Here are excerpts from a letter Dorothy received from a participant who had practiced leveling in a training session and then tried it out:

Dear Dorothy:
  . . . The jobs of the people who work for me demand unusual technical ability, close attention to detail, and a special insight into logical processes. One of my employees seemed to be quite intelligent and possessed admirable personal traits, but just did not possess the peculiar aptitude necessary for the work. His immediate supervisor shared my perception and had tried to discuss the matter with the employee. Their discussions had not been productive and, in fact, had resulted in the immediate supervisor becoming very upset about the situation.

  I had avoided having conversations with the employee myself, principally because I didn't feel I'd be any more successful than the immediate supervisor. Your description of the "leveling" interview gave me new insight, so I decided to give it a try. I began by describing to the employee the problems that I have in comparing the performance of employees working for me, in making appropriate job assignments, and in administering a fair promotion policy.

As I went on, I described the kinds of perceptions and measurements that I use as a manager. After a few minutes of providing background of that kind, I described the particular difficulty that I was having in relating his performance favorably to that of his peers, then asked him how things looked from his viewpoint.

The employee's response rather startled me: he had been going through a similar comparative process and had concluded that he does not possess as strong an aptitude for his job as he perceived in his co-workers. He had even made some inquiries about programs in oceanography, a subject in which he had great interest. At the conclusion of our meeting he mentioned that he was going to pursue his interest in oceanography more actively.

Had I approached the subject differently, I think I would have aroused the same kind of defensive reactions which the employee expressed in his interview with his immediate supervisor. He might well have felt that he had to continue with the organization to defend his self-dignity. I feel that both the organization and the employee gained from the interview as it actually developed.

The employee's performance was not poor enough to warrant his being discharged. Were he to continue his employment, he would continue requiring a great deal of direct supervision with only marginal productivity. The organization can now use his salary to hire someone else with the required aptitude who will be more productive. The employee was assisted in his objective evaluation of his present situation and reached a conclusion which will get him into a more satisfying career in a short time.

I was pleased as a manager for _____ at the favorable outcome of the interview. I was even happier as a human being to feel that I had acted as a catalyst for another human being to make a rational evaluation of a subject which has a great deal of emotional content . . . .

Best regards,

T.C.

Assistant Chief Analyst[5]

You can also apply the ten leveling guidelines we've just described to a situation where another person comes to talk to you. For example, rather than putting the other person off, you can choose to deal with the problem as soon as possible. If a person enters your office, you can arrange the setting for maximum openness by offering that person a seat in a nearby chair so you can transact face to face at eye level, and so on.

APPLICATION ────────────────────────────────────

1 What might you do if a person comes to your work area while you are seated and declines your invitation to sit down?

2 If another person comes to you in a deep feeling state (feeling angry, resentful, depressed, and so on), what is probably the most important guideline to observe?

~ • ~ • ~ • ~ • ~ • ~ • ~ • ~ • ~ • ~ • ~ • ~ • ~ • ~ • ~ • ~

1 If the other person declines your offer to sit down, then you can stand up to ensure a face-to-face transaction.
2 If another person comes to you in a deep emotional state, the most important thing to do is to listen. Active-listening responses such as, "You seem to be saying . . . ." and "You're feeling . . . ." will serve to stroke the other person's activated ego state and at the same time help you to keep your Adult in gear. (See "Active Listening," Chapter 15, page 297.)

SOLICITING FEEDBACK

We can avoid the problem of dealing with negative feedback if we occasionally go to others and ask for feedback before they *need* to come to us. To solicit feedback, go to another worker and say something like:

"Juan, I'd like to talk to you for a few moments about the Broselle project. Do you have a few minutes to talk?" Then, when you find time to get together, say, "Is there any way you think our working together can be improved? Do you need anything else from me?"

In soliciting feedback, remember that your purpose is not to take on some-one else's responsibilities but to open communication lines.

When you first approach a person to ask for feedback, be sure to phrase your question carefully, observing these points:

— Ask about a specific task, activity, or project. (This will limit the per-son's comments to a specific area and you won't be overwhelmed with a barrage of suggestions.)
— Ask about your behavior: behavior that would help your working together, and behavior that the other would like from you.

APPLICATION ————————————————————————

Which of these ways of phrasing a request for feedback follows our guidelines?

___ (a) "Wanda, I'd like you to tell me how you feel about my work on Project X. Is there anything I can do to improve?"

___ (b) "Wanda, is there anything I'm doing that you'd like me to do differently?"

___ (c) "Wanda, about my work on Project X, is there anything I'm doing that could be improved and if so, what would you like me to do instead?"

~ • ~ • ~ • ~ • ~ • ~ • ~ • ~ • ~ • ~ • ~ • ~ • ~ • ~ • ~ • ~

Choice (a) is good in that it focuses on Project X. It's too risky, however, for a first attempt at an authentic transaction because it invites the other person to pour out feelings. Choice (b) covers too broad an area. Choice (c) follows our guidelines: it focuses on a specific project, asks for feedback on behavior, and invites positive suggestions.

The first time you try asking for feedback like this, don't be surprised if the other person is a bit puzzled, if not shocked! So he or she may not be able to respond to your question at first. You may wish to rephrase the question, for example:

"Is there anything I'm doing that's slowing you down or getting in your way? If so, what would you like me to do so that this won't happen?"

The other person may answer, "Gee, I don't know, I'll have to think about that one for awhile and get back to you." When this person *does* start naming specific behaviors that he or she would like you to change, be sure to use your Adult. Use everything you know about active listening, fogging, stroking activated ego states, and negative inquiry to keep the transaction open.

Sometimes a person may get so caught up in giving negative feedback that he or she forgets to give positive suggestions. If this happens, prompt the person by asking again:

"What would you like me to do?"

Once you are able to accept specific feedback without getting unduly upset (it's not that easy when you're getting negative feedback), you may wish to go further and ask for more general comments about your behavior. For example, instead of asking about how you're doing on a specific task or project, you might say, "Is there anything that I'm doing that would help you more if I did it differently?"

When you can do that easily, you may choose to expand your feedback sessions even more. You could do this by asking the other person to tell you how they *feel* about what you're doing. For example, you might ask, "Is there anything that I do or say that you react to with bad feelings?"

Notice that this is a much deeper kind of question because you are asking the other person to express feeling rather than to describe desirable and undesirable behavior. This is best done only with people whose opinions you respect and whom you believe are not out to cash in on you. But think, how many times have you been brought up short by someone saying, "I didn't have any idea you felt that way"? Many times we do not ask people how they feel because we are afraid to. We are afraid that if we allow ourselves to become vulnerable, we will be rejected, put down, abandoned, hurt. The more not-OK feelings we learned as children, the more fearful we are of something terrible happening to us if we open ourselves to others. If this is a particularly painful problem for you, you may find it helpful to ask yourself:

"What's the worst possible thing that can happen to me if I ask for more feedback?"
"Is there some way that I can protect myself so I won't be hurt when I invite people to be candid with me?"

Whenever you ask for feelings, also ask what specific bits of behavior are proving troublesome or irritating. If the other person talks only in abstract terms, using words such as "attitude," "common sense," "laziness," "attentiveness," or "awareness," persist in asking that person (using your Adult, of course) to name specific actions. Remember, you can take steps to change specific behaviors, but it's much more difficult to deal with abstractions. (See "Negative Inquiry," Chapter 15, page 307.)

Timing your requests can be important. You might consider asking for feedback:

— after you're about one-fourth of the way through a project (the other person will have enough basis to answer, while you have time to make changes in your behavior);
— at the end of some meaningful period—for example, at the end of a transaction, a day's work, a week's work, a project, and so on.

EXPRESSING POSITIVE FEELINGS

Remember, what you give often is what you get. A rather delightful development may happen when you start asking for feedback in this way. Some people may come to *you* and say:

"You know, what you were asking for the other day is a two-way street. Is there anything that I'm doing that would be more helpful if I did it differently?"

In addition, they may just give you more *positive* feedback, too—especially if they appreciate your efforts.

We've talked a lot about expressing feelings of resentment and asking for and receiving negative feedback. If you just stop there, however, you would be missing what is perhaps the most enjoyable part of transacting authentically: the expression of positive feelings. Responding honestly and openly doesn't always mean negatively. You are also more true to yourself when you share your appreciations.

For example, if you ask for feedback and the other person reciprocates, you will probably be pleased about that. It's all right to say so—to express your appreciation. This will get a positive energy flow going between you. Similarly, if you've had a successful leveling session, you probably feel pretty good about it. You might express this at closing with something like:

"I'm really glad that we're able to talk to each other like this."
"Dan, I feel much better about what happened now that we've straightened out this problem."

In addition to words, *doing* something to express positive feelings is important. You might share yourself by giving:

— a warm smile,
— a squeeze of an arm,
— a warm, firm handshake.

When these positive strokes are really authentic, they rejuvenate and energize us.

SUGGESTED SELF-CARE PROJECTS

— If you'd like to transact authentically with more people, you may wish to make a list of people (on and off the job) that you are able to carry on authentic relations with. Make a contract with yourself to increase the number of such people in your life. Begin to visualize what this looks like when it starts to happen.
— Keep track of the number of times you approach people and ask for negative and positive feedback. If appropriate, contract with yourself to increase the frequency of such feedback sessions.
— After having a leveling session with someone, critique yourself. How many of the ten leveling guidelines did you follow? Make a record of your performance. Next time, see if you can beat your record. If you are not improving satisfactorily, refer to Chapter 14 for some trouble-shooting guidelines.
— After a leveling session, explore what you have learned. You might ask yourself, "Do I know more about my behavior, feelings, and motivations that I was *blind* to before?" "Do I hide my thoughts and feelings any *less* frequently now?"

APPLICATION —————————————————————

Having read this far in the book, you have probably changed your levels of awareness. To get a visual picture of these changes, you may wish to draw a new Johari window shaped like a circle and then compare it with the one you drew on page 7. Show your Open, Blind, Hidden, and Unknown Selves as you're seeing them now.

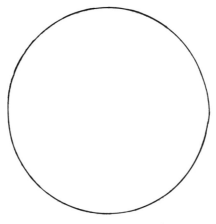

My Levels of Awareness　　　　Date: _____

If you've enlarged your Open Self and cut the size of your Blind, Hidden, or Unknown Selves, you've met one of the important goals of TA and this book. Congratulations!

　　If you find your Open Self hasn't changed much and you'd like to enlarge it,
you may wish to make that a special goal for yourself and review the self-CARE
program (Chapters 9–14).

SUMMARY

Authentic transactions are those that are open, honest, and can stir in us
feelings of tenderness, empathy, and affection. To transact more authentically, try leveling with other people. When leveling, it's important to:

　　— deal with the problem as soon as possible.
　　— arrange the setting for maximum openness.
　　— get right to the problem.
　　— send "I" messages; avoid accusative "you" statements.
　　— stress the positive.
　　— avoid discounting.
　　— listen.
　　— avoid talking about past mistakes.
　　— arrive at a mutual agreement.
　　— confirm the final decision.

　　Another way to transact authentically more often is to approach others
and ask for feedback. The best part of transacting authentically involves
expression of warmth, tenderness, caring, and appreciation. A good time to
express such positive feelings is after you have successfully leveled with
another person.

　　Most of us spend a good share of our lifetimes on the job. We can use
this time to collect bad feelings, to play phony roles, to put on a front that
later crumbles into broken relationships and unfulfilled dreams—or we can

use this time to more fully be and express ourselves. You now have many tools for both awareness and action. As you put these tools to work for you, your energy will thrust toward fulfilling positive goals. Each time you opt for being authentically yourself, you are choosing the success you deserve. You have our best wishes!

SOURCE NOTES

[1] Muriel James and Dorothy Jongeward, *Born to Win: Transactional Analysis with Gestalt Experiments* (Reading, Mass.: Addison-Wesley, 1971), p. 62.

[2] *Ibid.*

[3] Otto Altorfer, *Emotional Job Fitness* (Cupertino, Calif.: Courtney Davis, 1977), p. 84. *Note:* Although this book follows traditional definitions, some finer distinctions regarding "negative strokes" and "discounting" are being drawn by Otto Altorfer and we recommend his book to you.

[4] See Dorothy Jongeward, *Everybody Wins: Transactional Analysis Applied to Organizations* (Reading, Mass.: Addison-Wesley, 1976), pp. 76–78.

[5] *Ibid.*, pp. 97–98. Reprinted by permission of Addison-Wesley Publishing Company.

Appendix A

LIST OF ADJECTIVES

Absent-minded	daring	intolerant	resentful
active	defensive	irresponsible	reserved
adaptable	deliberate	irritable	resourceful
adventurous	demanding	kind	responsible
affectionate	dependable	lazy	restless
aggressive	dependent	loud	rude
alert	destructive	loyal	sarcastic
ambitious	determined	mature	self-centered
anxious	disobedient	meek	self-confident
appreciative	disorderly	methodical	self-denying
argumentative	dissatisfied	mild	self-pitying
arrogant	distrustful	mischievous	selfish
ashamed	dominant	moderate	sensitive
assertive	easy-going	modest	sensuous
attractive	efficient	nagging	serious
authoritarian	egotistical	natural	sexy
awkward	energetic	nurturing	shallow
bitter	enterprising	obedient	shy
boastful	enthusiastic	obliging	sincere
bossy	expressive	opinionated	slipshod
calculating	fearful	opportunistic	spineless
calm	fickle	optimistic	spontaneous
capable	forceful	organized	stable
caring	forgetful	outgoing	strong
cautious	forgiving	outspoken	stubborn
changeable	friendly	patient	submissive
cheerful	frivolous	persevering	suggestible
clear-thinking	fussy	pessimistic	supportive
cold	generous	playful	sympathetic
compliant	gentle	pleasant	tactful
conceited	greedy	poised	tactless
confident	guilty	polite	talkative
confused	hateful	precise	thorough
conscientious	helpful	productive	thoughtful
conservative	honest	protective	tolerant
considerate	hostile	quarrelsome	trusting
contented	impatient	quiet	unassuming
cool	impulsive	rational	undependable
cooperative	inconsiderate	rattlebrained	understanding
courageous	indecisive	realistic	unemotional
coy	independent	reasonable	uninhibited
creative	individualistic	rebellious	unstable
critical	industrious	reckless	uptight
cruel	inhibited	reflective	vindictive
curious	insightful	relaxed	versatile
cynical	intelligent	reliable	warm

Appendix B

RECOMMENDED SOURCES

The following sources are recommended for expanding and releasing the Natural power in your Child.

For prerecorded cassette tapes on such things as deep relaxation, centering, self-hypnosis, systematic desensitization, and meditation, write to:

> Success Dynamics
> 1840 Lambeth Lane
> Concord, CA 94518

Miscellaneous books useful for energizing the Natural Child and Little Professor are:

Benson, Herbert, with Miriam Z. Klipper, *The Relaxation Response* (New York: Avon, 1975).

Carrington, Patricia, *Freedom in Meditation: Getting the Most Out of Meditating* (Garden City, N.Y.: Doubleday, 1977).

Hendricks, Gay, and Russell Wills, *The Centering Book* (Englewood Cliffs, N.J.: Prentice-Hall, 1975).

Huxley, Laura Archera, *You Are Not the Target* (New York: Avon, 1963).

McCarroll, Tolbert, *Exploring the Inner World* (New York: Julian Press, 1974).

Rozman, Deborah, *Meditation for Children* (New York: Pocket Books, 1976).

Sparks, Laurance, *Self Hypnosis* (North Hollywood, Calif.: Wilshire, 1962).

Wilson, Donald L., *Total Mind Power* (Los Angeles: Camaro, 1976).

For further information on meditation, visualization, and health, also see:

Bloomfield, Harold H., et al., *TM: Discovering Inner Energy and Overcoming Stress* (New York: Delacorte Press, 1975).

Carrington, Patricia, *Freedom in Meditation: Getting the Most Out of Meditating* (Garden City, N.Y.: Doubleday, 1977).

Eastcott, Michael J., *The Silent Path* (New York: Samuel Weiser, 1970).

LeShan, Lawrence, *How to Meditate, A Guide to Self Discovery* (Boston: Little, Brown, 1974).

Pelletier, Kenneth R., *Mind as Healer, Mind as Slayer* (New York: Delacorte Press, 1977).

Samuels, Mike, and Nancy Samuels, *Seeing with the Mind's Eye* (New York: Random House, 1975).

Selye, Hans, *Stress Without Distress* (Philadelphia: Lippincott, 1974).

Index